GROC's COMPANION TO

THE GREEK ISLANDS

For the package & villa holiday-maker,
backpacker & independent traveller,
whether journeying by air, car, coach, ferry-boat
or train

by
Geoffrey O'Connell

Published by

Ashford, Buchan
& Enright
1 Church Road
Shedfield
Hampshire
SO2 2HW

CONTENTS

ILLUSTRATIONS

The cover picture of the Monastery of Ag Georgio Krimnou, Zakynthos, is produced by kind permission of GREEK ISLAND PHOTOS, Willowbridge Enterprises, Bletchley, Milton Keynes Bucks.

The Candid Guides
unique
'GROC's Greek Island Hotline'

Available to readers of the guides, this service enables a respondent to receive a bang up-to-the-minute update, to supplement the extensive information contained in a particular Candid Guide.

To obtain this paraphrased computer print-out, covering the Introductory Chapters, Athens, Piraeus & Mainland Ports, as well as any named islands, up to twenty five in number, all that is necessary is to:-

Complete the form, enclosing a payment of £1.50, and send to:-

Willowbridge Publishing, Bridge House, Southwick Village,
Nr Fareham, Hants. PO17 6DZ

Note: The information will be of no use to anyone who does not possess the relevant, most up to date GROC's Candid Greek Island Guide.   We are unable to dispatch the Hotline without details of the guide AND which edition.   This information is on the Inside Front Cover.

Planned departure dates...................................
....
Mr/Mrs/Miss...
of..
....

I possess:		I require:
GROC's Greek Island Guides	Edition	GROC's Greek Island Hotline
to:............................	....	....
....	....	....
....	....	....
....	....	....
....	....	....
....	....	....

and enclose a fee of £1.50.
Signature.......................... Date................
I appreciate that the 'Hotline' may not be dispatched for up to 7-10 days from receipt of this application. Please also enclose a large SAE.

GROC's Candid Guides
introduce to readers

Suretravel '90

A comprehensive holiday insurance plan that 'gives cover that many other policies do not reach', to travellers anywhere in the world. In addition to the more usual cover offered, the

SURETRAVEL HOLIDAY PLAN

includes (where medically necessary):
24 hour World Wide Medical Emergency Service including, where appropriate, repatriation by air ambulance.

Additionally, personal accident, medical and emergency expenses EVEN while hiring a bicycle, scooter or car.

An example premium, in 1990, for a 10-17 day holiday in Greece is £13.50 per person.

Note: all offers & terms are subject to the Insurance Certificate Cover

For an application form please complete the cut-out below and send to:
Willowbridge Publishing, Bridge House, Southwick Village Nr Fareham, Hants. PO17 6DZ

Mr/Mrs/Miss...Age.............

of...

....

I request a **SURETRAVEL** application form

Date of commencement of holiday....................Duration.............

Signature...Date.............

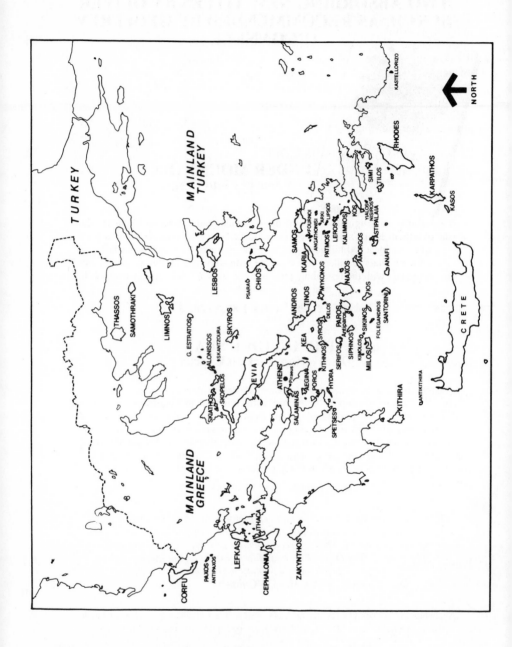

Illustration 1 The Greek Islands

INTRODUCTION

The Companion Guide to the Greek Islands allows a reader to make a value judgement in respect of almost each and every one of the eighty to ninety, inhabited Greek islands. As the Companion Guide is four-square based on the now universally acclaimed *GROC's Candid Guides,* the contents pull no punches. There are no extravagant claims, no erudite, highly imaginative hyperbole, no grandiose prose - this guide is a 'warts and all' island by island synopsis.

The main aim of the Guide is to encourage as many readers as possible to embark upon the magical adventure of Greek island travel, as independent travellers; to help them experience the unparalleled freedom and joy of swanning about the Aegean and Ionian seas, from island to island, as the spirit and whim dictates; to enjoy the indolence of the Greek (lack of) pace of life and the usually warm-hearted hospitality.

Some subscribers may simply wish to armchair travel and the Companion Guide will surely help fulfil these day-dreams. To them the contents will be 'sufficient unto the day thereof'. Others, once having chosen an island, or group of islands, may wish to delve into more detail, than the essential 'bare bones' contained herein, with the use of the appropriate *Candid Guide.* One undoubted plus is the ability to make use of the incomparable *GROC's Greek Island Hotline* service which gives 'by return of post' access to the up-to-the-minute updates.

I have eschewed the temptation to 'rate' islands, as such a system is so subjective. On the other hand, the use of symbols will, at a glance, allow a reader to sum up a particular island's facilities, public offices and services. To this end the following key explains those used throughout the Companion Guide.

Symbols
Available Transport,
to & from the island:

    Ferries   Hydrofoils   Airport

An Island's:
Attractions   **Transport**

    Beaches   Scooter hire

    Water sports   Car hire

Public Offices

(Pc) Town/City police   Taxis

(Pp) Port police   Bus service

(Pt) Tourist police

Facilities

- Banks
- Exchange
- OTE (telephone)
- Post Office
- Information office Government (NTOG) or Municipal sponsored
- Launderettes
- Petrol stations

Services

- Bakers
- Chemist
- Doctor
- Hospital
- Public toilets

Accommodation & Dining

- Rooms in private houses
- Guest House/Pensions
- Hotels
- Youth Hostels
- Camping
- Restaurants & Tavernas

ACKNOWLEDGEMENTS

Apart from those numerous friends and confidants we meet on passage, there are the many correspondents who are kind enough to contact me with useful information, all of who, in the main, remain unnamed.

Rosemary who accompanies me, adding her often unwanted, uninformed comments and asides, requires especial thanks for unrelieved, unstinting (well, almost unstinting) support.

Although receiving reward, other than in heaven, some of those who assisted me in the production of this book require specific acknowledgement, for effort far beyond the siren call of vulgar remuneration! These worthies include Graham Bishop, who drew the maps and plans; Ted Spittles who does clever things with the process camera and other bits and pieces; and Viv Hitie, who now not only controls the word processor, but the laser printer. Soon she will write the wretched things! During the endless months while the year's books are in preparation, Viv's 'playmate' must wonder why she doesn't pick up her bed and move into Bridge House!

I would, this year, like to include a general apology to chums, and more especially my Mother & Father, for the endless times I have had to forego an invitation or a visit... due to the all time consuming demands of authorship. Lastly, and as always, I must admonish Richard Joseph for ever encouraging and cajoling me to take up the pen, surely the sword is more fun?

PART ONE
Chapter 1   Travelling to and from Greece

An initial word of warning is that rules and regulations change from year to year, so specific details herein are worth checking. An example would be the latest information in respect of Charter Flights vis-a-vis accommodation vouchers. Before proceeding to the various methods of travel, any passport with a stamp indicating a visit to the northern Turkish sector of Cyprus could result in a traveller being turned around and refused entry.

Of all the possible modes of travel to and from Greece, it is rather a let down to have to admit that the most comfortable, economical and speediest method is a Charter Flight. On the other hand it would be churlish to dismiss the alternative possibilities, without some discourse.

BUS/COACH In strict monetary terms, the coach is the cheapest method of travel but the journey takes some 3½ to 4 days. Additionally there are 'companies and companies', and those who choose one of the least expensive choices may experience one of the horror journeys so often heard about. Even the 'luxury' firms can inflict a number of indignities on their clients. These may include a shortage of 'comfort' stops and unannounced changes of vehicle, with long delays.

The scheme of things is that the coach proceeds non-stop to Athens, via Yugoslavia and Thessaloniki (Greece), with some three changes of driver, a meal break every 12 hours, at a major stop-over point, and a brief, usually too brief, toilet respite at convenient fuel stations. The problem with the latter 'draining down of the system' is that, even when a halt is declared, there are usually only a limited number of lavatories to go round. As not only the passengers of one's own coach, but probably a number of other coaches are desperate, leg-crossing queues result. It is often best to wander off into the 'bundy', if the matter is very urgent.

Cases and backpacks are crammed away in the baggage stowage space, thus a shoulder or hand bag is essential. Items to put to one side might include: toilet paper; personal toiletry requirements; several paperbacks; the Walkman; emergency rations; and a pack of cards.

CAR This option must be considered where, say, 'three or more are gathered together', and mobility is a necessity. The journey can take anything between 3 to 5 days, depending on the route chosen, the number of co-drivers, and if overnight stops are planned.

The overland choice is about 1900-2000 miles each way, whilst the sea route (*See* **Ferry-boats**), via Italy, is some 1400-1500 miles (plus the sea voyage distance). The selection of a particular route depends upon: the starting point; if travellers wish to include a number of European cities in the itinerary (and which cities); if there is a favourite or particularly disliked European country; and how much money is available. Drivers who opt for the Yugoslavian 'experience' must bear in mind that this alternative has a number of serious disadvantages. Inflation has resulted in an unhappy, expensive country, with exorbitantly expensive toll fees for the short motorway stretches of the main 'through' route, which is, by and

large, a narrow, two-lane highway. The overwhelming number of lorries on
this Belgrade road are propelled at frightening speeds and, if this were not
enough, it is disconcerting to find out that many of the self-employed
drivers are on 'uppers', in order to stop falling asleep at the wheel! The
Adriatic coastal road is a picturesque, if winding and slow alternative, with
the advantage of avoiding the worst of the manic driving.

Those who plump for Italy should realise that they will probably have to
use the motorways, as the alternative roads are slow going. The drawbacks
include the (reasonable) cost of the tolls, whilst the benefits embody the
high average speeds that can be attained and the choice of relatively inexpensive, service station restaurants. Incidentally, almost all Italians, be it
night or day, drive everywhere and anywhere as if on a Grand Prix circuit,
and with almost as much skill. It has to be admitted that it is difficult to
accept being overtaken on both sides of a vehicle, at the same time!
Italian filling stations appear to be run by a 'brotherhood', as there is very
little self-service and the attendants expect to be tipped. Interestingly they
are 'equipped' to clean windscreens and change air filters. Rarely can
payment be made with a credit card (as distinct from France where they are
accepted, almost everywhere), although *Diners* cards are 'creeping in',
here and there. In contrast to motorway facilities, which stay open all day
and night, most other garages close for an afternoon siesta, usually between
1300-1500hrs.

Both United Kingdom motoring organisations (the AA and RAC) prepare
route plans and itineraries, on request, and advise in respect of the current
regulations. An International Driving Licence (IDL) is not required, but the
Italian authorities expect a translation of the UK licence; a Green card
insurance certificate certainly smooths cross-frontier travel (although
strictly speaking, one should not be necessary), and must be 'packed' along
with the original insurance certificate as well as a copy of the vehicle's
Registration document.

FERRY-BOATS International ferry-boats can 'take the strain', for part of
the journey, where, for instance, voyagers select the Italian leg. There are
ferries from Yugoslavia, but they tend to operate only for the height of
season months.

Popular Italian ports include Ancona, Bari and Brindisi, whilst Western
Greek mainland ports embody Igoumenitsa and Patras, with Corfu island
being another entry possibility. Certainly ferry-boat trips present a pleasant
alternative to trudging around Yugoslavia, and there is little difference in
the basic costs, but... There always has to be a caveat, doesn't there? In the
main, the on-board cost of living, on the international ferries, is pricey,
with drinks and meals being very expensive. The duration of the sea voy-
ages varies from between 12-34 hours, depending on the ports of departure
and arrival.

FLYING
Scheduled flights From, for instance, London to Athens, Corfu or Thessa-
loniki are unnecessarily expensive in comparison to:-
Charter flights These offer a wide variety of United Kingdom departure

airports and Greek island destinations, but there are some restrictions placed upon purchasers of charter flight tickets. The important points to bear in mind are that: they must be accompanied by a 'not-to-be-used' accommodation voucher; any overnight visit to Turkey may well invalidate the return part of the ticket; and that a maximum number of six weeks can be spent in Greece. Those able to obtain a student charter flight can stay for longer than this latter stipulation.

Some explanation of these conditions might be of assistance. The accommodation voucher scheme is the usual 'turn-a-blind-eye' comprise necessary to get around the Greek regulation that Charter flight passengers must have accommodation - thus the vouchers. No holder of one of these slips of paper is expected to turn-up at the address - there won't be any room! In the last couple of years the Greek authorities have made 'autumnal noises' that they intend to strictly apply the law, and plug this rule-bending... only to back down in the spring. Should an independent traveller be concerned about these rumblings, or if they were to become particularly strident, it is easy enough to contact an owner of accommodation, at a planned port of call, and make and have confirmed at least a one-night stay. Day visits to Turkey from various Greek islands are grudgingly permitted, under strictly applied, 'nuisance value' regulations imposed, by the Greek authorities. On the other hand, an overnight stop in Turkey, recorded in a traveller's passport, can result in the Greek airport staff tearing up a travellers return Charter flight ticket, thus forcing the 'miscreant' to book a scheduled flight to return home. This may well involve a journey to Athens, which, if holiday-making on a distant island, can prove to be distinctly vexatious. Islands from which Turkish day-trips are available include Chios (for Cesme), Lesbos (for Ayvalic), Rhodes (for Marmaris) and Samos (for Kusadasi & Ephesus). Another little pin-prick or 'hassle factor' is that, for the moment, the authorities do not allow excursions from Kos (for Bodrum).

Travellers choosing Athens as a destination can take advantage of Olympic Airways ever expanding network of island flights, as an alternative to the ubiquitous ferry-boat.

HITCH-HIKING An extremely chancy method of getting to and from Greece unless a 'participant' is lucky enough to get a 'one-hit' lift with a lorry-driver. To keep costs down the Italian/ferry-boat option must be counted out, leaving the Yugoslavian route as the only realistic alternative - but Yugoslavia is not a country in which to be set down, to have to pick up another lift!

PACKAGE HOLIDAYS For those who doubt their ability to cope with, or enjoy the independent traveller's role, a package holiday, with the minimum of accommodation included, is the soft option. It is necessary to abandon the reserved room, taking on the cost of ferry-boats and alternative night-time accommodation, but this allows a fail-safe method of 'dipping the toes' into the delights of Greek island-hopping, whilst maintaining the fall-back ability to retreat to the safety of the 'package womb', without losing face, or fouling up the whole holiday. Not only is this the easy choice, but possibly the cheapest, as most holiday tour companies manage to parcel together a fortnight's flight and accommodation for less than that achieved by the free-wheeling rover.

TRAINS The train takes 3½/4 days and is probably the most expensive and uncomfortable of all the detailed possibilities. It is an attractive prospect for those travellers wishing to stop off in Europe and or for those under 26, who can secure a significant student price reduction. But passengers interrupting their journey must bear in mind that, despite it being listed as an option, a couchette berth is mandatory! Oh yes it is! Thus passengers reboarding a train, *en route*, must ensure there is a couchette available.

As station stops are of a minimal duration, it is absolutely necessary to ensure that reading material, loo rolls, toiletries, change of clothes, as well as food and drink are easily to hand.

At the main Italian railway stations the carriages are besieged by attendants pushing trolleys laden with expensive snack foods and drinks. In addition the major stations have showers as well as victualling facilities.

If the wholly mainland route is selected, on the outward leg, the carriages/train may well be exchanged for a Greek or Yugoslavian set, at Venice. These are often even more uncomfortable and dirty. In Yugoslavia the train is 'accosted' at Belgrade by vendors of food and drinks, but the offerings are of a dubious nature and the operators certainly don't want to be paid in Yugoslavian dinar - marks or dollars will do very nicely, thank you! A cautionary tale involves a Swiss couple of our aquaintance who wanted to look round Belgrade for a day or two, that is until £80 a night was requested at the cheapest hotel available. To add insult to injury they could not get back on the through train, for a few days, as no couchette berths were available. The Yugoslavian stretch of the 'day of the train' is usually very slow going - on some single track sections it is not unusual for gently trotting cows to overhaul the carriages.

The alternative route via Italy, and an international ferry to Greece, costs that much more, due to the extra ferry-boat fares. Added to this, the charges for services on the ferries are usually jolly expensive (*See* **Ferry-boats**).

USEFUL NAMES & ADDRESSES
The Automobile Association, Fanum House, Basingstoke, Hants. RG21 2EA.
Tel (0256) 20123
AA Routes   Tel (0256) 20123
The Greek National Tourist Organisation (EOT or NTOG), 4 Conduit St, London
W1R 0DJ.   Tel (071) 734 5997
The Italian State Tourist Office, 1 Princess St, London W1R 8AY.
Tel (071) 408 1254
The Yugoslavian National Tourist Office, 143 Regent St, London W1R 8AE.
Tel (071) 734 5243
British Rail International, PO Box 303, London SW1 1JY.
Tel (01) 834 2345 - *Author's note - keep ringing*
The Hellenic State Railways (OSE), 1-3 Karolou St, Athens, Greece.
Tel (010301) 5222 491
Thomas Cook Ltd, Publications Dept, PO Box 36, Thorpewood, Peterborough,
PE3 6SB.   Tel (0733) 63200

Other useful names & addresses include:-
Time Out Magazine, Southampton St, London WC2E 7HD.
(For names & addresses of travel opportunities)   Tel (071) 836 4411
Owners Abroad Ltd, 4th Floor, Valentines House, Ilford Hill, Ilford, Essex IG1 2DG
Tel (081) 514 4000
Olympic Airways, 164 Piccadilly, London W1V 9DE.   Tel (081) 846 9080

HolidayCompanies include:-
The Best of Greece (Travel) Ltd, 100 Week St, Maidstone, Kent ME17 4LY.
Tel (0622) 692278
Cricketers Holidays, 4 The White House, Beacon Rd, Crowborough, East Sussex
TN6 1AB   Tel (08926) 64242
Greek Islands Club, 66 High St, Walton-on-Thames, Surrey KT12 1BU.
Tel (0932) 220416
Greek Sun Holidays, 1 Bank St, Sevenoaks, Kent TN13 1UW
Tel (0732) 740317
Laskarina Holidays, St Mary's Gate, Wirksworth, Derbyshire, DE4 4DQ.
Tel (062 982) 2203/4
Martyn Holidays, West Leigh House, 390 London Rd, Isleworth, Middx.
TW7 5AD   Tel (081) 847 5955
Ramblers Holidays Ltd, PO Box 43, Welwyn Garden Cityu, Herts AL8 6PQ
Tel (07073) 31133
Simply Simon Holidays, 1/45 Nevern Sq, London SW5 9PF
Tel (071) 373 1933
Something Special Travel Ltd, 10 Bull Plain, Hertford, Herts SG14 1DT
Tel (0992) 552231
Twelve Islands, Angel way, Romford, Essex RM1 1AB   Tel (0708) 752653

More useful names and addresses include:
STA Travel, 38 Store St, London WC1E 7BZ.   Tel (071) 580 7733
London Student Travel & Eurotrain, both at 52 Grosvenor Gdns, London SW1N 0AG
Tel (071) 730 3402
Euroways Supabus, c/o Euroline, Grosvenor Gdns, London, SW1.
Tel (071) 730 8325
The Greek address is: 1 Karolou St, Athens.   Tel (010301) 5240 519
Eurolines Intercars (Uniroute), 102 Cours de Vincennes, 75012 Paris
(Metro Porte Vincennes)
National Express Co, Westwood Garage, Margate Rd, Ramsgate CT12 6SL.
Tel (0843) 581333
or Victoria Coach Station, 164 Buckingham Palace Road, London, SW1
Tel (071) 730 0202
Consolas Travel, Above Central Post Office, 100 Eolou St, Athens.
Tel (010301) 3219 228

Olympic Airways overseas office addresses are as follows:
America: 647 Fifth Ave, New York, NY 10022.   Tel (0101 212)
(Reservations) 838 3600 (Ticket Office) 735 0290
Canada: 1200 McGill College Ave, Suite 1250, Montreal, Quebec H3B 4G7.
Tel (0101 418) 878 9691
80 Bloor St West, Suite 502 Toronto ONT M5S 2VI.
Tel (0101 416) 920 2452
Australia: 44 Pitt St, 1st Floor, Sydney, NSW 2000.
Tel (01061 2) 251 2044
South Africa: Bank of Athens Buildings, 116 Marshall St, Johannesburg.
Tel (010127 11) 836 5951
Denmark: 4 Jernbanegade DK 1608, Copenhagen.   Tel (010451) 126-100
Sweden: 44 Birger Jarlsgatan, 11429 Stockholm.   Tel (010468) 113-800

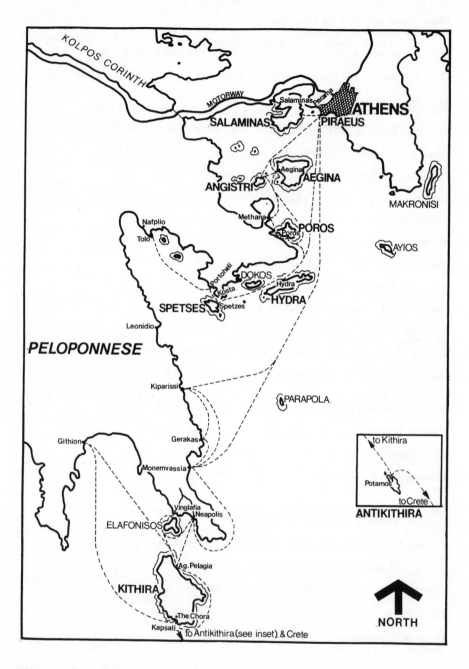

Illustration 2 The Argo-Saronic islands

PART TWO   THE ARGO-SARONIC ISLANDS

The islands that make up the Argo-Saronic group are very widely spaced out, in and around the Saronic Gulf and the Peloponnese coastline. Of the traditionally accepted islands included in the chain, Aegina is one of the most attractive, retaining those quintessential Greek qualities and character. Possibly this is because the port and main town are not the centre of the tourist thrust, an 'honour' reserved for Ag Marina, on the east coast.

The island of Angistri, off the coast of Aegina, possess many of the attributes sought by those casting about for the Greece of old. The inclusion of the island in some package tour brochures must destroy these characteristics, despite which winnowing and cottage looms are still to be seen.

Antikithira island is a little visited, twice weekly ferry-boat port of call on the Peloponnese to Crete schedule. The very small population hangs on, with the balance of the island's fate dependent on continuing government hand-outs.

Elafonisos island once relied solely on fishing but now also 'trawls' Greek mainlanders, whom drop in over the weekends to enjoy the taverna meals. Despite, or perhaps because of, its proximity to the Peloponnese, Elafonisos is not an easy island hopping destination.

Hydra could probably be accepted in the Guinness Book of Records as the single most crowded island location in the Aegean. Daily, a glut of hydrofoils, ferries, trip boats and cruise ships decant innumerable people on the quayside of this stunningly attractive, 'film-set' port, only to scoop them up again as the night hours approach. The problem is that there simply is nowhere for them all to go, once they have filled the town. That is, apart from the very steep mountains that tower behind the port or the short east and west tracks branching out along the coast.

Kithira, once administratively linked to the Ionian islands, is only connected by sea with the other Saronic islands and the Peloponnese. Its far-flung position has ensured that the island still remains a pleasant, relatively isolated location, but the presence of an airfield will, eventually, alter that. Despite its comparative isolation, the island is a convenient stepping stone to reach both Elafonisos and Antikithira

The town and port of Poros is extremely attractively located, overlooking the pretty sound separating the island from the mainland. The waterfront tavernas of the Poros waterfront are, for some obscure reason, a magnetic attraction for day-tripping Greeks, but there is not much easily accessible coastline to absorb the large numbers of visitors.

Few, if any guides describe the island of Salaminas - and I am not surprised! Despite my misgivings I have resisted the temptation to merely consider Salaminas as a suburb of Piraeus.

Spetses is a very popular tourist location, and rightly so. The port town is interesting and the people friendly. Moreover the countryside is extremely attractive, more especially the forests of pine trees edging the track that circumscribes the island. This mainly unsurfaced route dips down, here and there, to the most attractive beach locations.

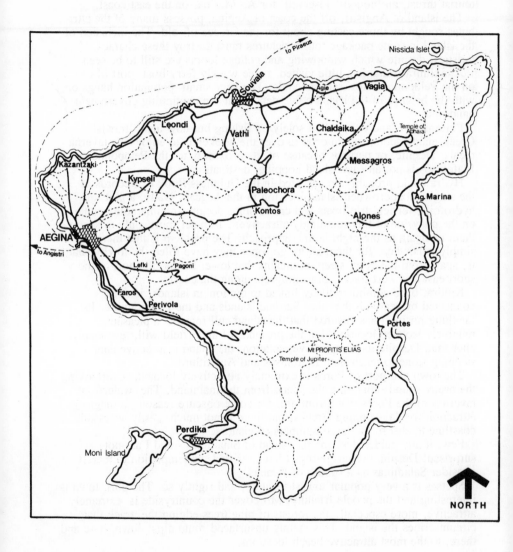

Illustration 3 Aegina island

CHAPTER 2 AEGINA

FACT FILE	TRANSPORT LINKS There are some nine ferries and six hydrofoils each and every day.

FACT FILE

ALTERNATIVE NAMES Egina

IMPRESSIONS Busy port; boats; unattractive countryside; the Temple; a few sandy beaches.

SPECIALITIES Pistachio nuts; ravani - a sponge made with semolina, soused with cognac & orange syrup.

STATISTICS Tel prefix 0297. The island is some 11km from top to bottom, & up to 14km from side to side, with a total area of about 86sq km. Of the total population of circa 10,000, at least 5,000 live in the main town & port.

TRANSPORT LINKS There are some nine ferries and six hydrofoils each and every day.

Ferry Boats link with Methana (M), Poros and Piraeus(M) daily, as well as Hydra and Spetses two days a week. The ferry-boat quay is a very large, exposed sheet of concrete with an extensive pier. Here, as on a number of other islands in the group, visitors are not met by owners of Rooms.

Hydrofoil Hydrofoils, or Flying Dolphins, connect daily with Piraeus(M), as well as six days a week with Methana(M), Poros, Hydra, Ermioni(M), Spetses and Portoheli(M). Hydrofoils conveniently dock inside the harbour.

The island has at least three archaeological sites of repute: Kolona, alongside the present town and port; the Temple of Aphaia, built in 480 BC, and close by Ag Marina; and the Sanctuary of Zeus, located on Mt Profitis Elias (or Mt Oros). Aegina became extremely powerful and prosperous during the 7th and 6th centuries BC, a pre-eminence reflected in the establishment of a mint famous for silver tortoise coins. The island sculptors of this period achieved considerable fame.

In 455 BC, Aegina lost the final battle for supremacy between Aegina and Athens, after which, the island was sacked and the inhabitants driven out. The Romans were given the place in 133 BC.

Due to constant piratical plunderings, the inland capital of Paleochora was founded, sometime in AD 800/900.

Various overlords were followed by the Venetians, rulers between the middle 1450s and 1715, after which the Turks established supremacy. Following the War of Independence, the island achieved modern-day fame when, briefly, it was made the capital for the first Greek Government.

Aegina hosts any number of ferries, express craft, excursion boats and Flying Dolphins. The island is a weekend resort for many Athenians and a holiday destination for European tourists. Overseas tourism plays a significant role in the well-being of the

For greater detail acquire GROC's Candid Guide to The Mainland Islands

island, but its popularity with mainland Greeks ensures continuing prosperity. This fact is reflected in the friendly, relaxed style of the inhabitants and the ambience of quiet affluence.

Of all the islands in the Argo-Saronic group, the main town and port is blessed with the only adjacent, quality beaches of any consequence. Despite the promise of these small but sandy beaches, there is only one other, that at Ag Marina. Consequently the latter location has become an over-developed, 'Kosta'd' resort, the sandy beach of which is swamped by sun-seeking holiday-makers. The island is not very pretty with an unattractive coastline.

Despite accommodation being in short supply, as many owners allocate part of their pensions to tour companies, most supplies and services are less expensive than elsewhere else in this group.

MAIN PORTS & RESORTS

AEGINA (Egina). The capital town and main port is probably the most typically Greek of all the Argo-Saronic locations. Despite this, the waterfront is rather spread out and can be confusing to first time visitors, especially as the outline is more of a bulge than the usual 'U' shaped inlet.

There are a few Monipos and a number of large, retail vegetable and greengrocers' caiques that moor to the harbour quayside. There are not one but two beaches, one at each end of the Esplanade. The beach to the west of the harbour is bordered by a small park and edged by a patch of shore. This spot is probably the site of the ancient city's 'Hidden Port'. The tiny, sandy beach becomes crowded and the sea-bed

gently shelves. At the other end of the Esplanade is a sandy beach with a pebbly shoreline and a slowly shelving, sandy sea-bed.

Lodgings are difficult to locate due to the presence of mainland Greeks and the number of accommodation owners who cater for package tourists. The harbour Esplanade is lined with cafe-bars, tavernas and restaurants but outstanding kafeneions and eateries are not so easy to find.

Places of interest include the:-
Cathedral Behind a park, close by the Museum and built in 1806.
Colona A single column and all that is easily visible of the remains of the ancient Temple of Apollo. Further north, occupying a pleasant headland, are remnants of the rest of the ancient city.
Museum Close by the Cathedral and containing some island finds.

SOUVALA (Suvala) (8km from Aegina Town) A second port and resort, to which there is a pretty centre. The main road borders a comparatively small bay, which has an almost disproportionately large ferry-boat quay. On the left-hand side of the cove is a tiny, pebbly bathing beach. Souvala has a 1960s, 'Costa' milieu, with a surprising quantity of package tourists and the necessary infrastructure of hotels, tavernas, as well as a supermarket. There are a scattering of Rooms and a couple of hotels catering for the independent traveller.

VAGIA (13½km from Aegina Town) A small, straggly, unattractive and older hamlet than Souvala, with a modest sized cove. Unfortunately, the shingly, sandy beach gets more than its fair share of kelp, but is cleaner on the left-hand side. To the right, is a little harbour inlet and mole for small fishing boats. Most of the development is new with a few, older buildings spread about.

AG MARINA (23km from Aegina Town, along the coastal road - 14 ½km via Paleochora) Chips and sun-tan oil with everything, and everybody. The *raison d'etre* for this high street full of burger, cocktail and pub bars, is a small bay with a sandy beach which, by midday, is blanketed by sun-beds, umbrellas and people. There is a small amount of pebble in the first metre or so of the sea-bed, but the beach is a natural for children as it gently shelves beneath the surface of the sea.

There is an abundance of Rooms and hotels.

PORTES (circa 28km from Aegina Town) This small settlement 'clutches' the edge of the bay straddled by a large, grey pebble foreshore to the nearside and, on the far side, beyond a jumble of rocks, another stretch of pebble shore. The clean looking sea-bed is also pebbly. The hamlet, which is experiencing a modest development programme, is backed by an agricultural plain edged by sparsely vegetated, substantial hills. A small, rocky mole encircles the tiny fishing boat harbour.

PERDIKA (9km from Aegina Town) A fishing boat port, set in low, level land bordered by shallow hills. A fair amount of development is taking place on the outskirts but the older part of the village parallels the surprisingly long quay of the port.

To the far left of the bay is a tree lined 'slice' of sandy shore. A waterfront path to the right, towards the looming, offshore island of **Moni**, is edged by a boulderous shoreline on which the locals have created concrete patios for swimmers and sunbathers.

There are some Rooms and a Pension hidden away.

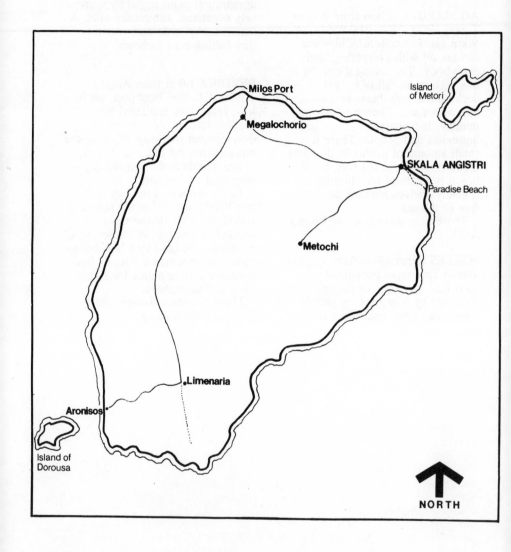

Illustration 4 Angistri island

FACT FILE

ALTERNATIVE NAMES Agistri, Aghistri

IMPRESSIONS A sandy beach; clear seas; comparative inexpensiveness; new buildings; package tourists - despite which the island is still a 'way station'.

SPECIALITIES A local wine is vaunted - when available. Women wear a traditional, rather South American headgear - a black square of material placed over the head, on which is perched a hat.

RELIGIOUS FESTIVALS include: First Friday after Easter - Zoodochos Pighi; 30th June - Ag Anargyroi Church; 7th July - Ag Kiriaki Church.

STATISTICS Tel prefix 0297. The island is approximately 5km from north to south & 3¼km from east to west, with an area of 14 sq km.

TRANSPORT LINKS
Ferry A regular, scheduled daily service connects Angistri directly to Piraeus, There are also at least three return journeys daily, to Aegina, by large cabin caique.

The island's name, in ancient times, was Cecryphalea and, as such, it was mentioned as being close to where an Athenian fleet defeated a Peloponnese navy. It was also referred to by Homer.

The date when tourism commenced was 1957. A Piraeus ferry-boat connection was inaugurated in 1960 whilst water and electricity were installed in 1971.

It would be understandable if those contemplating a visit were to develop the distinct impression that Angistri was one of the 'off-the-beaten- track' islands. Any such ideas will disappear at the sight of the large sign facing disembarking passengers, some metres walk from the small ferry-boat quay. This proclaims "Agistri Tours welcomes you. Call at the office for details of excursions, tours, BBQ's... et al".

Despite the presence of a few package holiday companies, an almost continuous flow of excursion craft, low-key motorbike hire, a bus service and an almost immeasurable number of Rooms to rent, Angistri is still an attractively 'doo-hickey' destination. Naturally the tour operators have spawned a smart hotel or three, one or two discos, and the occasional cocktail bar - attributes unquestionably out of character and well balanced by the rustic charms of the island. Remember not to call at the weekends when visiting mainlanders almost outnumber the flies - a difficult task, believe me!

MAIN PORTS & RESORTS
SKALA ANGISTRI The main settlement and port is a rather spread out, straggling but a strangely attractive location. It has

For greater detail acquire GROC's Candid Guide to The Mainland Islands

to be admitted that old Greece and modern-day package tourism uneasily rub shoulders with each other. For instance the 'way-station' ambience has to compete with a couple of signboards advertising just about every tourist temptation imaginable.

The port must possess one of the most attractive stretches of sandy beach in the Argo-Saronic. The location is littered with Rooms and some hotels, a couple of which are of the 1960s variety, built in the inimitable Greek style of that period. Eating facilities in Skala Angistri are rather limited, and the only alternative is to walk to Megalochorio.

Paradise Beach (about 15mins walk) It is a pity that there is no sand on either the beach or the sea-bed, which is also almost entirely made up of pebbles. The sea is very clear and clean.

MEGALOCHORIO (Milos Port) (About ¾ hr walk from Skala Angistri) The core of Megalochorio is centred on the old, shabby village, whilst the package tour industry has caused a certain amount of development in the area of the port. This harbour is open-ended with a large rocky mole closing in the seaward side. The main beach isn't very good, in fact it is a series of very, very

small inlets set in a largish bay with biscuit rock, weed and very little sand.

There are several hotels and some restaurants/tavernas.

From Megalochorio the road climbs through a pine tree forest to funnel through a narrow, but short, cutting, prior to emerging above and to one side of:-

Limenari (about 2 ½hrs walk from Skala Angistri) To the left of the village is a large, paved, winnowing circle which is still in use. It has to be admitted that this, old-world, 'hillbilly' little settlement is rather fly-blown but has not yet been ravaged by the package tourists. There are a couple of tavernas, a delightful rustic one close to where the bus stops.

A sign indicates the way to a beach, but do not get too excited. Those who venture down the path end up on a concrete platform set in the rocks of a plunging cliff edged bay. To get into the inviting seawater it is necessary to either jump or scramble over the edge.

Aronisos (about 3¼ hours walk) This small harbour is set in the nearside of a rocky bay. A tree crowned islet divides the shoreline, beyond which is the offshore island of **Dorousa**.

FACT FILE
IMPRESSIONS A volcanic, barren location.

STATISTICS Tel prefix 0735. The island is shaped like an elongated ball, being about 10km from top to bottom & 5km wide. The population number circa 110.

TRANSPORT LINKS

Ferry The island is a port of call for the twice weekly, scheduled ferry that plies between Piraeus and Kastelli (Crete), via various East Peloponnese ports and Kithira.

POTAMOS The port and main village is set in a north facing, narrow inlet towards the top end of the island.

There are a few Rooms in private houses, a cafe-bar/taverna, a general store and a telephone. Close to the port is a beach.

Inland and to the south of the port is **Galaniana** village.

FACT FILE

ALTERNATIVE NAMES
Elafonisi, Elaphonisos

IMPRESSIONS The beach.

STATISTICS Tel prefix 0732.
The island is some 5km from top
to bottom & 4km from side to
side, with a population of 500.

TRANSPORT LINKS Being
tucked up into the huge 'U' shaped
Peloponnese inlet of the Gulf of
Lakonikos, the main link is with
the adjacent mainland shore,
about ½km distant.

Caique There is a regular
summer- time caique connection
with mainland **Vinglafia**. The
caique motors backwards and
forth eight or nine times a day.

Ferry In the height of summer
months, a scheduled ferry-boat
calls in. This craft runs up and
down the Peloponnese coastline,
connecting Piraeus with Kastelli
(Crete), via Kithira and Antikithira, calling in at Elafonisos
twice a week. For the same period, a local ferry-boat daily links
mainland **Neapolis**, Elafonisos
and Ag Pelagia (Kithira), in
addition to a Neapolis to
Elafonisos connection.

In antiquity the island was named
Onugnathos - 'jaw of an ass'.

ELAFONISOS The island port and
village, the quayside waterfront of
which contains the few houses that
offer accommodation, as well as a
row of tavernas, at least one of
which possesses a metered telephone. The eating places are
popular at weekends with mainlanders who pop over for a languid
lunchtime meal. There are no
official offices or services, apart
from a couple of general stores
and a baker
  The island's outstanding feature
is a marvellous, unheralded
lagoon-like sweep of beach, as
well as yet another beach that
ordinarily would be highly rated.

FACT FILE

ALTERNATIVE NAMES Idra, Idhra, Ydra

IMPRESSIONS Tourists; yachts; donkey trains; gold shops; lack of beaches; shiny marble streets & pavements; beauty of the port & photogenic quarters of the town.

SPECIALITIES Amigdalota - Turkish delight in which is mixed chopped almonds.

RELIGIOUS FESTIVALS include: 30th January - Festival of the Three Hierarchs, Hydra; 2nd February - Purification of the Virgin Mary, Papandi Chapel, Hydra; 10th February - Festival of Ag Charalambos, Monastery of Panaghia, Hydra; 25th March - The Annunciation, Greek Independence Day; 30th June - Festival of the Holy Apostles, Holy Apostles Chapel, Dokos Island; late June - Miaoulia Feast & Festival over two days to celebrate War of Independence; 8th September - The Birth of the Virgin Mary, Monastery of Panaghia, Zourvas; 14th September - Bell ringing to the Exaltation of the Holy Cross; 13-14th November - Ag Konstan-

tinos, Patron Saint of Hydra; 6th December - Festival Ag Nikolaos,Monastery of Panaghia, Hydra & throughout the island; 12th December - Festival Ag Spyridon, Monastery of Panaghia.

STATISTICS Tel prefix 0298. The island is up to 6km in width & 23km long, with an area of about 52sq km & a population of some 2000.

TRANSPORT LINKS At least one ferry-boat and 'oodles' of hydrofoils dock at the inner harbour. Passengers disembarking are not accosted by waves of room offering Mamas.

Ferry Ferry-boats connect to Spetses, Poros, Methana(M), Aegina and Piraeus(M) daily, whilst one boat a week links with Ermioni(M).

Hydrofoil Every day the service calls at Spetses, Portoheli(M), Ermioni(M), Poros, Aegina and Piraeus (M); two days a week at Leonidio(M), Kiparissi(M), Gerakas(M), Monemvassia(M), Kithira and Neapolis(M).

Mentioned by Homer (Hydrea), the island was sold once or twice, passing from one mainland town to another. But not a lot happened until the 16th century AD. Then this dry, arid island was settled by Albanian refugees, by habit farmers, but who slowly took to

the sea for a living. Due to the location, smallness of overall size and lack of population, the inhabitants were very much left to their own devices, so much so that taxes were not extracted until the mid-1700s.

By the time of the Russo-Turkish

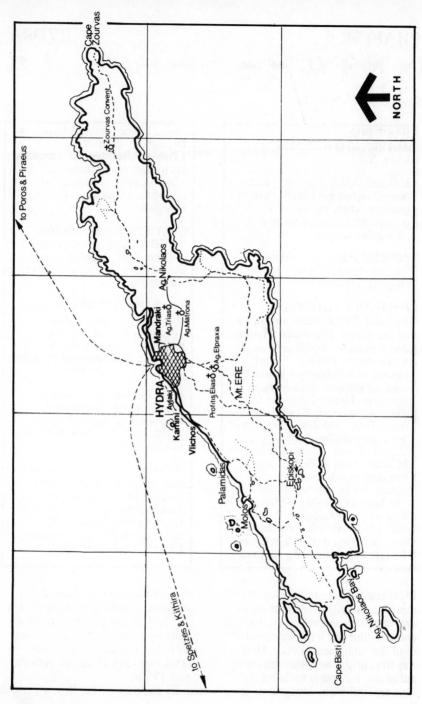

Illustration 5 Hydra island

conflict, Hydriot ships and crews were sailing with the Turkish navy. Running the English blockade of the Napoleonic garrisons enabled the Hydriot skippers to accumulate much wealth.

Unfortunately the outpouring of money and effort, expended to help fight the Greek War of Independence devastated the islands' resources and riches.

It was not until the tourist boom started in the 1970s, that Hydra was able to commence rebuilding its resources and fortunes.

The port and town are scenically most attractive, if not beautiful. Cars and scooters are not allowed, there being only one rubbish truck and one small van. Apart from the exorbitant cost of services and supplies,there are only two or three other, easily accessible settlements and the same number of stony coves. In spite of this, seemingly as many day trippers ebb and flow into Hydra, as do into St Marks Square, Venice.

MAIN PORTS & RESORTS
HYDRA The capital (& only) town and port. Due to the lack of vehicles, all goods are transported by donkeys, strings of which marshal daily on the Esplanade. It makes for a rather strange sight to behold this timeless Greek method of hauling merchandise, tied up amongst all the glitterati'.

As most of the accommodation is booked, especially in the height of season months, it is best not to arrive over a weekend, and it is worth noting that generally little English is spoken. Bedrooms are very expensive, whether staying at one of the smart, provincial hotels, pensions or the numerous Rooms. The number of establishments at

which to eat is only equalled by their overall blandness - and cost. The serried ranks of Esplanade restaurants are not very much more pricey than those dining places situated in the backstreets.

Places of interest include the :-
Monastery of the Panaghia Prominent due to the tall bell and clock tower, which borders the central section of the Esplanade.
Monastery Profitis Elias Located above and looking down on the port, but a 1½-2hr walk.
The Church of St John the Baptist Restored in 1738, the interior is covered with Byzantine style murals illustrating Biblical events.
Mansions (Archontika) There are any number of outstanding family houses ranged around the harbour settlement, mainly dating from the Napoleonic blockade-running years (1789-1815).
Museum A large, modern construction, replacing the original building, pulled down because it was unstable.

Mandraki Beach (about 2km from Hydra Town) The pebble beach is kept quite clean, and is set in bare hillsides at the bottom of a 'U' shaped bay. Water taxis shuttle visitors back and forth to the port.

KAMINI (about 1km from Hydra Town) The small, rocky mole protected harbour is set in a pleasant little cove. Apart from pensions and Rooms, there are a taverna or two.

VLICHOS (about 2km from Hydra Town) The scattered settlement is flyblown but does have a taverna. The messy shore is dirty with tar.

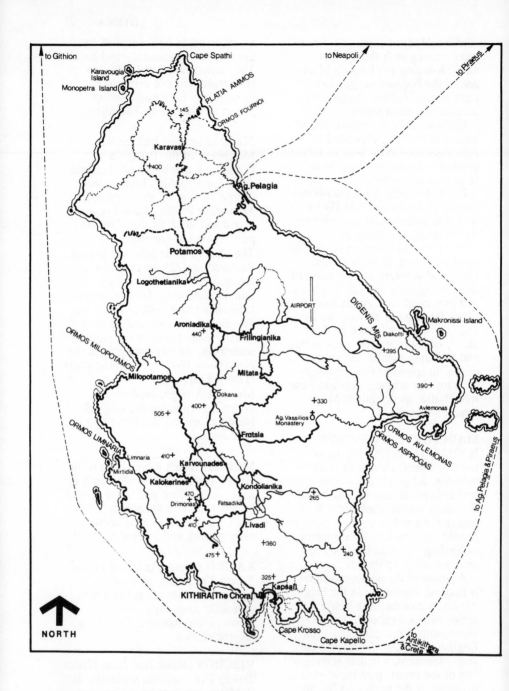

Illustration 6 Kithira island

FACT FILE

ALTERNATIVE NAMES
Kythira, Kythera, Cythera

IMPRESSIONS Lovely countryside; wild flowers & birds; friendly people; wind; lack of kafeneions; tractors (but in the countryside, donkeys); churches, some
with barrel roofs and a few with
wide, tiled roofs; a unique Sunday
market; lack of public transport.

RELIGIOUS FESTIVALS include:
29-30th May - Festival Ag Trias
Church, Mitata; 24th September -
Festivals throughout the island.

STATISTICS Tel prefix 0733. The
island is about 25km from top to
bottom & up to 16km in width,
with an area of 280sq km. The
population is 'rumoured' to be
about 3500.

TRANSPORT LINKS Kithira is
accessible from Piraeus, as well as
a number of the Peloponnese
mainland ports that the ferries and
hydrofoils call in at during the
journey from Piraeus to Kithira.

Arrivals are not generally met
with offers of accommodation.

Air The airfield is situated out in
the wilds of the low hills to the
east of the island. Taxis are the
only form of public transport.
There is one flight a day to and
from Athens.

Ferry The ferry-boat quay at Ag
Pelagia is truly very large. The
other island port is Kapsali (the
Chora's port), at the south end of
the island. The sea's around
Kithira can become very rough,
which state causes ferry-boats to
dock at Kapsali, rather than Ag
Pelagia. Ferry-boats link two
days a week with Antikithira,
Kastelli(Crete), Githion(M), Mon-
emvassia(M) and Piraeus(M), and
one day a week to Neapolis(M).

Hydrofoil These only dock at the
port of Ag Pelagia. Two days a
week hydrofoils dock at
Neapolis(M), Monemvassia(M),
Kiparissi(M), Leonidio(M),
Portoheli(M) and Piraeus(M); and
one day a week to Gerakas(M)
and Spetses.

Apart from Cretan Minoan asso-
ciations, and being involved in the
Athenian-Spartan wars, between
the 6th and 4th centuries BC, the
island had an undistinguished
history. After the withdrawal of
the Romans, the island became the
possession of various Byzantine
and Venetian overlords. Unfortunately for the natives, the island
was also a target for piratical raids,

including visitations from the
infamous Barbarossa. Ownership
became almost frenetic from 1715
onwards, when the Turks took
over from the Venetians, who recaptured it three years later.
Pirates took over in the 1750s,
after which the French, in 1797,
imprinted their authority. Only a
year later a Russo-Turkish force
arrived, to be followed by the

For greater detail acquire GROC's Candid Guide to The Mainland Islands

French (again) in 1807. They were followed, in 1809, by the British who descended on most of the other Ionian islands. The United Kingdom finally had to cede dominion in 1864.

Being at the end of a series of tempting and more sophisticated islands en route, Kithira has remained remote and comparatively unfashionable, even with 'Independent' travellers. The building of the airport has enabled the more adventurous package tour companies to exploit Kithira's advantages. Now, with little infrastructure of suitable accommodation, the tour operators have taken up most of that available, leaving very little for unheralded visitors. Generally, accommodation and tavernas may be few and far between but, even more unusually, so are the traditional kafeneions.

Even more annoying and inconveniently unusual, is the lack of any bus service, so travel is in the hands of the taxi drivers.

The island's countryside is immensely attractive with any number of delightful farming villages dotted about the landscape. There are no dramatic mountain elevations, there is plentiful wildlife and flora, but few donkeys.

MAIN PORTS & RESORTS
AG PELAGIA The main island port, considering which, it is really rather shabby, 'doo-hickey', scrubbly and one-eyed. The settlement spreads along the sea-shore from the bottom of the ferry-boat quay. The central beach is sandy, the backshore of which is edged by heavily pollarded arethemusa trees. Further to the south-east leads to a narrow beach which appears to be white shingle. Actually the back-

shore is made up of gritty sand, the middle is pebbles and kelp, and the foreshore fine pebbles, with a pebbly sea bottom.

THE CHORA (Kithira) (some 25km from Ag Pelagia) The island capital is a most attractive development ranged either side of the hill climbing, winding High Street. It is very similar to an archetypal Cycladean town, even down to the detail of being overlooked by a ruined, Venetian castle.

Attractive as the town may be there is very little accommodation, there is a distinct lack of kafeneions and there are not many eating places either.

Places of interest include the:-
Castle Imposing from a distance, this Venetian fort is rather uninteresting once inside the walls. There are masses of summer flowers and a cluster of English made cannons scattered about.
Museum. A few metres up the Livadi road from the Chora, and on the right.

KAPSALI (2km from the Chora) The island's second port and might be considered the best of the three island alternatives at which to make a base. The location is attractive, the beaches good and there is more accommodation and eating place options than in the Chora, but not a lot more.

The large Gulf of Kapsali is split into two by a rather large headland. The settlement lies across the neck linking the larger, nearside bay and the further, almost circular, fishing boat cove. The Esplanade of the nearside bay, is dramatically overlooked by the Castle topped Chora. The beach is narrow and stony but widens out in a sweep of stony backshore and sandy foreshore. The rest of the central side of the headland is an extensive concrete quayside that includes the ferry-boat quay. There are some Rooms, a campsite and a few tavernas.

AVLEMONAS (32km from the Chora) An almost obsessively neat, whitewashed fishing village built around the rocky, volcanic inlets that indent the coastline.

DIAKOFTI (some 33km from the Chora) This sparse hamlet is set on the edge of the sea, backed by a rather barren, wide plain, flanked by the foothills of the Digenis Mountain. Offshore is the elongated islet of **Makronissi** that almost connects to the shoreline. To the right of the quay is a lovely, sandy beach cove and clear sea, unfortunately set in fairly squalid surrounds and spotted with tar. There are several tavernas but accommodation is a problem as the comparatively few Rooms are more often than not fully booked.

PLATIA AMMOS (36km from the Chora) A pleasant fishing port/hamlet with a sweeping bay bordered by a broad beach made up of small shingle. The backshore is almost wholly sand in composition and here there are a couple of tavernas.

For greater detail acquire GROC's Candid Guide to The Mainland Islands

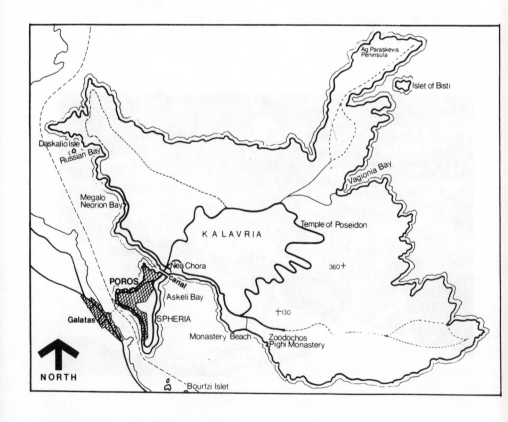

Illustration 7 Poros island

FACT FILE
IMPRESSIONS Friendly people; pretty countryside; 'imported' beach; flotilla yachts.

RELIGIOUS FESTIVALS include: 23rd April - Festival, Cathedral of Ag Giorgios, Poros Town; 3-4th June - Flower Festival, Galatas (M); 8th June - Panaghia; Last week of June - Navy Week, Poros Town.

STATISTICS Tel prefix 0298. Poros island is made up of Kalavria, the large, main island, & Spheria (Sferia), the main town and port islet. The two are separated by a very narrow ditch. The overall island area is some 31sq km, with an east to west length of 6km & a maximum top to bottom distance of 3km (excluding the Ag Paraskevis peninsula). The channel between the mainland and Poros Town is only 370m wide & up to

2km in length. The population numbers some 4000 plus.

TRANSPORT LINKS
It is almost like 'Clapham Junction', with boats, ferries and hydrofoils docking and departing all day long. A central section of quayside, adjacent to the main square, caters for all the passenger craft. The citizens proposition disembarking passengers with offers of accommodation.

Ferry Boats daily continue on to Methana(M), Aegina, Piraeus (M), Hydra and Spetses.

Hydrofoil Craft daily proceed to Methana (M), Aegina, Piraeus (M), Hydra, Ermioni(M), Spetses and Portoheli(M); four days a week to Leonidio(M), Kiparissi (M), Monemvassia(M); and two days a week to Gerakas(M), Kithira and Neapolis(M).

The island's early history was dominated by its association with the ancient mainland city of Trizina. The mythological character Theseus, who slayed the Cretan Minotaur with the aid of Ariadne, is linked with the island by his mother Aethra. The Temple of Poseidon, established about 500 BC, is the island's most famous link with early history. The Temple was well known as a sanctuary for fugitives, one of the most famous of whom was the renowned Athenian orator, Demosthenes. Hounded by his enemies, he is

supposed to have committed suicide in 322 BC with poison he carried in a quill pen.
From about the middle of the first century BC the island was laid waste, on a fairly regular basis, by the incursions of various invaders and pirates.
The Venetians established a castle on Bourtzi islet, to the south-west of Poros Town. The island probably reached its zenith of modern-day historical fame during the Greek War of Independence when the favourable anchorages hosted various allied

For greater detail acquire GROC's Candid Guide to The Mainland Islands

naval fleets and other vessels.

The setting is lovely, with the mountains of the Peloponnese forming an attractive backdrop to the sea passageway that beguilingly separates Poros from the mainland. Scenically the island is attractive; the town port is very interesting, with enough of a hill to allow an upper village; the people are most friendly and there are adequate Rooms and tavernas. So where's the catch? Simply put, there aren't any satisfactory beaches.

One day's hire of transport suffices to allow all the island's attractions to be visited, still allowing time to catch a ferry across to the mainland and take in at least one of the sights.

MAIN PORTS & RESORTS

POROS The capital town and port Esplanade borders the town's waterfront and requires every metre to cater for the extensive use to which it is put. These demands include: the local fisherman, the flotilla sailing fleets, hydrofoils, Piraeus ferries, excursion craft, 'so-many-islands-in-a-day' boats, large inter-island Ro-Ro's and mini car ferries (that connect Poros to mainland Galatas).

The quayside and its development is a semicircle, radiating out from a conical hill-side. The latter is capped by a quiet 'upper village'. The closest stretch of sand is across the canal separating the port islet from the main body of the island. Unfortunately, it is a dirty shingle, scrubbly shore of pebble with a round stone sea-bed.

There are plenty of Hotels and Rooms whilst the main square and Esplanade is edged by cafe-bars, tavernas and restaurants, as well as fast food breakfast places.

Places of interest include:-
Museum To the rear of an Esplanade square.

Megalo Neorion Bay (approx 1 ¼ km from Poros Town) The road rims the backshore of this pleasant and pretty location. The gentle, tree planted hillsides to the right fringe the long bay and the Peloponnese mountains continue to form a beautiful backdrop. Surprise, surprise, the sea-bed to the nearside is sand.

Russian Bay (approx 2km from Poros Town) A large inlet with small coves spread round the periphery. The setting is lovely, even if the beaches of the coves are nothing more than shingle and pebble. The surrounding hillsides are sparsely vegetated.

Temple of Poseidon (approx 5km from Poros Town) A rather pathetic, fenced off pile of rubble is all that remains of the once mighty and sacred edifice.

Monastery Beach (approx 3km from Poros Town) The beach cove is semicircular and clean with a pebble beach and sea-bed. Three beach tavernas compete for the trade and water sports include pedaloes and wind surfers.

Askell Beach (approx 1km from Poros Town) Askell is the major package tourist centre. On either side of the very narrow, curved beach is a stretch of foreshore the whole, rather shadeless sweep, being edged by a large number of hotels and some Rooms. The sea-bed is pebble and the beach has been overlaid with an unpleasantly coarse, gritty sand.

FACT FILE
ALTERNATIVE NAMES
Salamina, Salalaminos, Salamis

IMPRESSIONS Ramshackle, shanty town development; filthy beaches & dirty seas; messy countryside; swarms of cars & people.

SPECIALITIES An island bread.

RELIGIOUS FESTIVALS include: 4th September - Festival at Faneromeni (Phaneromeni) Monastery.

STATISTICS Tel prefix 01 - as for Athens. Up to 15km from side to side & 15km from top to bottom, with an area of some 93sq km. The population numbers about 22,000, with 17,500 living in the main town of Salamina.

TRANSPORT LINKS
Ferry The Piraeus passenger ferries are large, decrepit river boats which dock at Selinia. There is no formal ticket office, the fares being paid on board and the voyage duration is ½hr.
There is a Ro-Ro landing craft ferry-boat service between Paloukia and Perama on the mainland that operates hour in, hour out, day in, day out.

It comes as a surprise, bearing in mind the general unattractiveness of the island, to realise how pivotal Salaminas was in historical times. It was here that the Greeks sprung the trap that allowed their Triremes to smash the overwhelming, all-conquering Persian Navy of Xerxes, in 480 BC. It is adjudged that this victory saved the Western European nations from the until then, unstopable advance of the Persians. It is written that the Persian King sat on his silver and gold throne, high on Mt Aegalus to watch the battle. Little did he expect to observe his fleet being destroyed.
Over the next two or three hundred years, the island slid into the cloak of obscurity, which it was to wear with consummate ease up to modern times.

Salaminas is a suburb, for all intents and purposes, of Athens and Piraeus. Over the years the worthy citizens of the Athens, desperate to escape the smog, human, car and garbage polluted capital, have escaped to the 'attractions' of Salaminas, not only for *Le Weekend* but even a night out. In so doing they have created a home from home - that is a human, car and garbage polluted holiday environment. The sight of the massed ranks of main-landers disporting themselves on and in the thoroughly polluted surrounds of the filthy, narrow, pebbly foreshores and the very dirty seas, never ceases to amaze me. Tourist office inspired litera-ture referring to golden beaches must have be ignored.
To add to the drawback of the

For greater detail acquire GROC's Candid Guide to The Mainland Islands

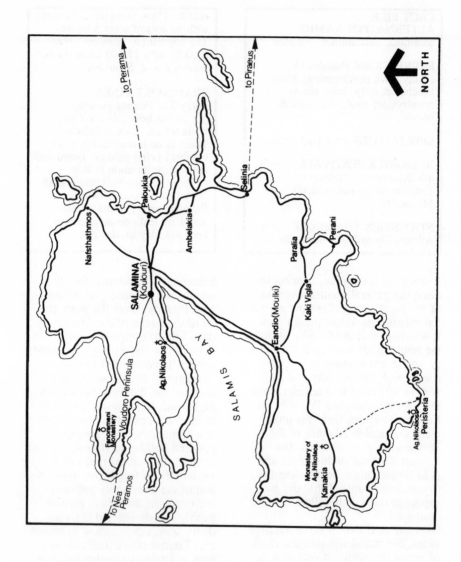

Illustration 8 Salaminas island

massive weekend invasion, and a chronic lack of suitable bathing, there are only a few hotels. There are none at the main port of Paloukia, two at the passenger ferry port of Selinia, and supposedly two in Salamina Town, where no ferries dock, and which should be avoided like the plague!

MAIN PORTS & RESORTS

SELINIA (7km from Salamina) A passenger ferry-boat port. A neat place, especially when considering the rest of the island, and possessing two hotels.

SALAMINA The capital is a rather squalid town and not a place in which to be stranded. Despite being at the end of the large Bay of Salamis, there are no ferry-boats.

EANDIO (Eantio, Eantion, Moulki, Mouliki) (5km from Salamina Town) Facilities include probably the friendliest hotel on the island and several tavernas, one being in the 'top ten' of the Argo-Saronic. There is some pebbly beach but the sea is disgusting.

Perhaps the loveliest area of the island is covered by the route from Eandio to Kanakia. It may be nothing remarkable where other, 'normal' islands are concerned but

here on Salaminas...! This is a 2½ hour walk up and over the mountain, or a taxi ride, as the buses do not operate a service.

KANAKIA (Karakiani) (13km from Salamina Town) It really is a most awful place, a parody of a Greek seaside settlement. The shanty hamlet, laid out on a grid basis, is set some way back from the pebble foreshore that circles the bay, in which is set down a rather bare, granite surface islet. The indescribable filth and litter that was the narrow shore, is unbelievable. It would be a help if the sea was clean and clear but even that is unattractive, due to the weed covered nature of the pebble sea-bed. To the right is a large, ugly, single storey taverna with an extensive, covered patio in front.

PALOUKIA (3km from Salamina Town) The ferry-boat port. This truly is an amazing 'way-station' of a place with a Naval Base blocking off the northern end of the port, and the island. The main road widens out to motorway proportions, alongside the quay, to cater for the enormous number of cars that zip on and off the island. There is a fifteen minute ferry-boat link to the appalling, ship-building port of mainland Perama.

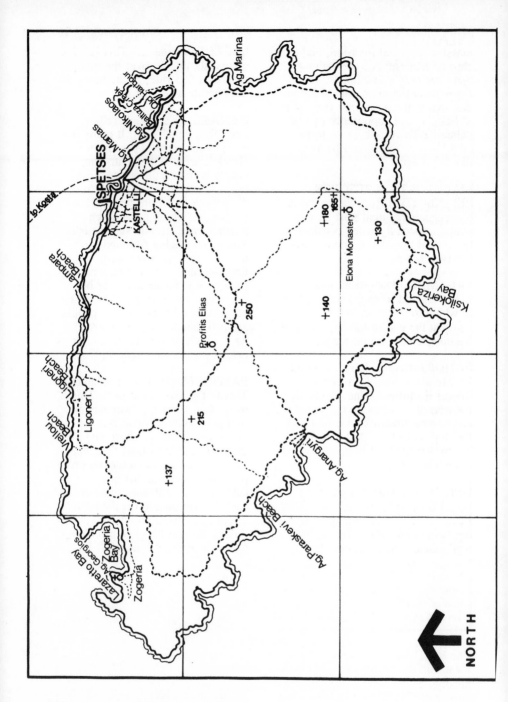

Illustration 9 Spetses island

CHAPTER 10   SPETSES

FACT FILE

ALTERNATIVE NAMES Spetsai, Spetsae

IMPRESSIONS Horse drawn carriages; beautiful flowers & gardens; pine forests; tourists; rocky inlets & clear seas; baroque buildings; some rubbish.

SPECIALITIES Amygdalota - a cone shaped, almond cake covered in sugar & flavoured with rosewater; Ergolavos - a macaroon like almond cake.

RELIGIOUS FESTIVALS include: Epiphany, 6th January - Tis Vaftisios, Ag. Nikolaos, celebrating Christ's baptism; 3rd February - Service for the Three Spetsiot Martyrs at the church alongside the Monastery of Ag Nikolaos, Spetses Town; 23rd April - Festival of Ag Georgios, Zogeria; Friday after Easter - Festival of Zoodochos Pighis, Monastery of Elona; 1st July - Festival, Ag Anargyri Church; 17th July - Festival, Ag Marina Church; 20th July - Profitis Elias Church; 26th July - Ag Paraskevi Church; 15th August - tis Theotokou (The Assumption of the Virgin Mary), Panaghia Church, Kastelli, Spetses Town; weekend closest to 8th September - Celebration of The Battle of the Straits of Spetses (1822), Spetses Town; 8th

September - Birth of the Virgin Mary, Panaghia Armata Church, Lighthouse headland, Old Harbour, Spetses Town; 1st November - Festival of the Penniless Saints Cosmas & Damian, Ag Anargyri Church; 6th December - Service for sailors & fishermen, Monastery Ag Nikolaos.

STATISTICS Tel prefix 0298. Spetses, an oval island, has an area of some 22sq km, is about 10km from side to side & 7km from top to bottom. The population is circa 3,500.

TRANSPORT LINKS
Ferry Seven days a week a ferry-boat goes on to Hydra, Poros, Methana(M), Aegina, and Piraeus(M); and two days a week to Ermioni(M). Owners of Rooms generally do not meet ferry-boat arrivals.

Hydrofoil Craft connect daily to Ermioni(M), Hydra, Poros, Methana(M), Aegina, Piraeus(M) and Portoheli(M); four days a week Leionidio(M), Kiparissi (M), Monemvassia(M), and two days a week to Gerakas(M), Kithira and Neapolis(M).

Water Taxis Fast passenger boats allow a daily shuttle service to the adjacent Peloponnese port of Kosta.

The island was not a star performer in the annals of early Greek history. Albanian refugees arrived during the 16/17th centuries, as did

Peloponnese Greeks, in the 18th century. It was from their numbers that some of the prominent Spetses families originated.

For greater detail acquire GROC's Candid Guide to The Mainland Islands

Support by the islanders for the Russians, during their war with the Ottoman Empire (1768-1774), resulted in the Turks exacting retribution, killing many inhabitants and setting fire to Kastelli the original settlement above the port.

The home-grown boat and ship-building industry, which established itself in the 17th century, expanded hand-in-hand with the increasing prosperity of the merchants. In company with other Aegean island opportunists, the running of the British blockade, during the Napoleonic Wars, resulted in ever increasing wealth and numbers of ships. The enlarged fleet worried the island's Turkish overlords, rightly so as it turned out, for, at the outset of the War of Independence (1821), the Spetsiots were able to supply some fifty-four fighting ships, as well as other support craft. After the glories of the War of Independence, the island's fortunes declined.

Strangely enough, Spetses is no newcomer to tourism for the island became fashionable, and enjoyed a resurgence of prosperity, between the First and Second World Wars. There was a casino, as well as a massive hotel.

A spacious, sunny, old and new world port/town presages well for the visitor. It has to be admitted that the constant ebb and flow of package holiday-makers has resulted in the eateries being rather mediocre and expensive.

Apart from the rather bare slopes of the south-east, the island is extensively forested and the journey affords wonderful glimpses of the beautiful coastline. Here and there a track branches off, or the main, unmade 'highway' dips down to sea-level, to this or that bay or cove. The beaches will be a disappointment to sand lovers, but quite a few are acceptable fine shingle and the sea is almost entirely clear, clean and inviting.

Cars are banned, the Monipo reigns, and there is only one taxi. As one observer put it "As cars are not allowed, Spetses only has three problems - scooters, water and rubbish."

MAIN PORTS & RESORTS

SPETSES (Dapia) The capital town and main port has the added attraction of the nearby and equally engaging Old Harbour. The small town beach is supplemented by a number of strips of foreshore beside the very long seafront. It has to be said that these beaches become rather crowded. There is no doubt that some of the town's buildings are impressive, especially the Hotel Posidonion.

Many of the older businesses have colourful ceramic tiles lettered with the original name of the firm, and sections of the old streets are still pebble mosaics.

There are a number of hotels close by the waterfront, some of which rather mar the skyline. The Pensions and Rooms are almost entirely under the control of a few travel agents, but there are one or two owners of accommodation who remain independent. The predominance of English package tourists has ensured a plethora of 'English Breakfast' and cocktail bar locations with the resultant demise of traditional kafeneions.

Places of interest include the:-
The Monastery of Ag Nikolaos Conspicuous for its Ionian style campanile and large pebble mosaic courtyard, the building was erected in the 17th century. It was

at the Monastery that the islanders raised their flag of Independence, on 3rd April 1821.

Mansions More commonly called Archontika, these were the homes of the wealthy, 18th & 19th century families, usually shipowners.

Vrellou Beach (4½km from Spetses Town). A small, pebble cove. The backshore is messy and the coastline is rather gravelly.

Zogeria Bay (6km from Spetses Town) A truly beautiful and picturesque area made up of rocky inlets set in low, pine tree covered slopes. It is unfortunate that there are no sandy beaches, but some of the pebble shores sally forth to a sandy sea-bed.

Ag Paraskevi (10km from Spetses Town) A lovely little bay. The backshore is made up of larger pebbles but the seashore is finer, more comfortable pebbles.

Ag Anargyri (11km from Spetses Town). Rather more developed than the other bays and coves. The beach backshore is medium sized pebbles, the foreshore fine pebbles and the sea-bed pebble, but the sea is clean and pleasant. Even out of the height of the season, the location becomes crowded. There is a hotel and taverna.

Ksilokeriza Bay (14km from Spetses Town) A lovely, 'U' shaped cove with a shingle beach. Due to the lack of any tourist facilities, and the difficulties of reaching the spot, it remains fairly deserted when other beaches are absolutely jam-packed.

For greater detail acquire GROC's Candid Guide to The Mainland Islands

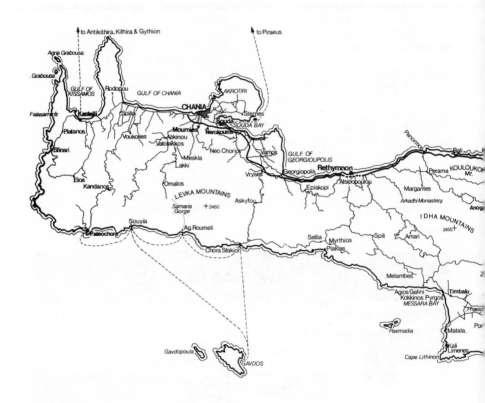

Illustration 10 Crete

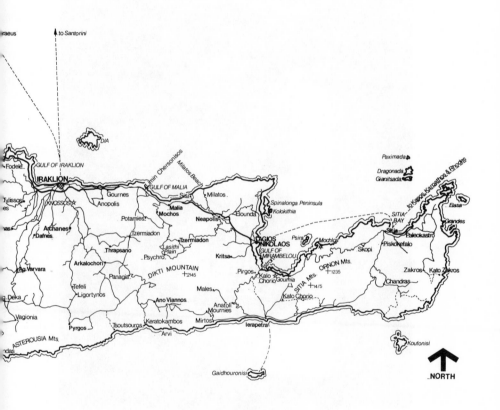

PART THREE
CHAPTER 11

CRETE

FACT FILE
ALTERNATIVE NAMES Kriti

SPECIALITIES Yoghurt; tighan-
ites - pancakes covered with honey
& sesame seeds; Cretan wine,
including *Minos, Gortinos &
Kissamos*; *Mandareeni* - a tanger-
ine liqueur; raki - a stronger ouzo;
herbal tea; embroidery.

RELIGIOUS FESTIVALS include:
(in addition to the Greek national
celebrations) two weeks before
Lent, a carnival celebrated
throughout the island; 24th June -
island-wide bonfires - birthday of
St John the Baptist; 2nd-10th July,
Kornaria - cultural & artistic
festivities; 28th July-10th August,
Vamos - cultural & artistic events;
15th August, religious fairs in
many villages - Assumption of
Virgin Mary.

STATISTICS The island is approximately 264 km long, & averages some 55km in width, with
an area estimated at 8,200 sq km.
The population is about 500,000.

TRANSPORT LINKS
Air There are airports at Iraklion,
Chania and Sitia.

Bus Most of the buses that connect to Crete, do so via the
Iraklion ferry-boat link.

Ferry There are scheduled inter-
island ferry-boat ports at Ag
Nikolaos, Chania, Iraklion,
Kastelli and Sitia.

Hydrofoil Iraklion is the island's
hydrofoil port.

The individual centres list the
frequency of the connections.

Crete is almost a land in its own
right and offers offers almost
every type of scenery and terrain.

Due to the clement weather,
Crete enjoys a long tourist season,
stretching from the beginning of
April to the end of October.

The island's complicated and
convolted past is reflected in the
almost embarrassing wealth of archaeological remains and numerous historical sites.

Most travellers arrive on Crete
at the airports or harbours of the
north coast cities of Iraklion or
Chania. Some more intrepid voyagers may dock at the ports of Kastelli, in the north-west, Agios Nikolaos, or Sitia, in the north-east.
The geographical spread and spac-

ing of the major towns and the
mountain ranges that form east to
west barriers, make it more com-
prehensible to split this chapter
into regions based on the north
coast settlements.

Crete has sufficient accommodation to cope with all but the height
of season influx.

Once extensively forested, the
island is now only lightly wooded.

There is an abundance of flora,
some of which are indigenous to
Crete. Wild life includes the very
interesting 'Kri-Kri' (the Agrimi -
a mountain goat) but no other
creature of note. Crete is an orni-
thologist's delight, the most impressive of the species surely being
the majestic birds of prey.

For greater detail acquire GROC's Candid Guide to Crete

FACT FILE

ALTERNATIVE NAMES
Heraklion, Iraklio, Heracleion

IMPRESSIONS A dusty, bustling, cosmopolitan city port; one-way traffic systems, traffic police, traffic lights and parking meters.

RELIGIOUS FESTIVALS include: 25th March at the Church of Prasas - Announciation of Our Lady; First Sunday after Easter at the Monasteries of Vrondisi & Zaros - St Thomas; 23rd April at the Monastery of Ag Georgios Epanosifi - a religious feast & celebratory mass; 1st-15th July, Dafnes - wine festival, folk art exhibition; 15th-17th July, Voni (Nr Thrapsano) - religious fair; 29th-31st July, Archanes - painting & handicraft exhibition; 13th-15th August, Archanes - Festival 27th August, Vrondisi Monastery - religious fair, St Fanourios; 11th November, Iraklion - religious procession for patron saint of the town, St Menas; 4th December, Ag Varvara; 6th December, Agios Nikolaos (Lasithi) - St. Nicholas.

STATISTICS Tel. prefix 081. Population about 85,000.

TRANSPORT LINKS
Air There are 5 flights a day to Athens; 1 a day to Rhodes; flights 6 days a week to Mykonos; 3 days a week to Paros & Santorini; and 2 days a week to Thessaloniki(M). The airport is fairly close to the City centre, and can be reached by taxi, a 4km walk or a 10 minute bus ride. The city bus stops at the junction of the airport access road and the main north coast road.

Bus Buses arrive by ferry-boat.

Ferry Boats connect daily to Santorini, Ios, Paros, Piraeus(M); six days a week to Naxos; five days a week to Mykonos; 3 days a week to Serifos and Siphnos; 2 days a week to Skiathos, Thessaloniki(M) and Tinos; and 1 day a week to Rhodes, Sikinos, Folegandros and Siros.

Hydrofoil Catamarans link five days a week to Santorini, Ios, Paros; and two days a week to Naxos & Mykonos.

The settlement was known as Herakleium in Roman times. In 1210 the Venetians made the city their capital and named it, and the island Candia. They fortified the city over the next 400 years but the Turks wore down the inhabitants, after a 22 year seige, in 1669.

Iraklion has all the features that should ensure a satisfactory location, including a Venetian harbour

and other fine buildings, a walled city, a lively street market and a cosmopolitan fountain square, as well as a convenient commercial port and airport. Despite these attractions, Iraklion is a rather messy, dusty capital, lacking a beach. Additionally the Venetian harbour is not sited in such a way as to act as an attractive focal point. Buildings are coming down

and going up all over the place.
Many will find Iraklion to be full
of interest and fascination: the
unexpected and narrow side-streets
rambling almost drunkenly from
one part of the City to another; the
sheer excitement of Plateia Venizelos, (the fountain square), thron-
ged with a cosmopolitan society;
the throbbing street market that
fills Odhos 1866, and its associated side lanes; the Archaeological
Museum and its outstanding
collection of exhibits; the Venetian
Arsenal; the Byzantine and Venetian churches; and the night-time
bustle of the pedestrian street of
Dhedhalou, with rows of restaurant chairs and tables lining one
side of the wide passageway. To
enjoy a beach it is necessary to
travel at least 5km to the west or
east of the City.

Iraklion is no exception to the
rule and bursts with quarters of
every class and type. There are
sufficient eating establishments on
offer, which may be the reason why
few are pre-eminent.

Places of interest include the:-
The Basilica of St Mark The oft-
restored church houses frescoes
from the 13th-15th century.
The Cathedral of Ag Minas Built
in the late 1850s and beautifully
decorated inside.
The Cathedral dominates the
Plateia Ekaterini and towers above
both the Church of Ag Ekaterini
and the Church of Ag Minas.
Ag Titos Church Originally a
Turkish mosque, the building re-
verted to the Orthodox faith, in the
late 19th century.
Koules Castle The Castle was constructed in the early 1500s, by the
busy Venetians.
Festival This takes place between
July and September.

Morosini Fountain The squat,
circular fountain dominates the
untidy Plateia Venizelos.
The Archaeological Museum The
museum is an impressive display.
On the first floor are exhibited the
Minoan frescoes from Knossos.
The Historical Museum Contains
exhibits from the early Christian
period, up to and including the
Battle of Crete.
Venetian Arsenals Built in the 16th
century, those still standing are of
a very large size.
Venetian Loggia The building, has
been totally reconstructed and is
now the City Hall.
Venetian Walls These are in an
impressive state of preservation
and were built in the 15th century.

MAIN PORTS & RESORTS
To the west of Iraklion, along the
north coast are:-

AG PELAGIA (21km from Iraklion) The eastern end of the very
pleasant beach consists of large
pebbles, followed by the slabs of
concrete or rock bedded into the
surrounding sand, and then by
sand and very fine shingle. The
backshore is bordered by the high
concrete patios of restaurants, tavernas, bars and shops and accommodation, here and there pierced by access steps. To the west,
the sandy beach is wide but a bit of
an assault course, due to the massed sun-beds, umbrellas and people.

A large luxury complex straddles
the headland. There are Rooms
and other hotels. The taverna and
restaurant prices are slightly higher
than the average, as the resort is
good quality holiday territory.

BALI (50km from Iraklion) The
heart of this once-upon-a-time
fishing boat hamlet is gathered

around and up a headland. To the right is the beach, a short stretch of grey sand, pebble and shingle. The backshore is edged by some five tavernas. Amongst the buildings that scale the left-hand hillside, are a few shops and Rooms.

PANORMOS (59km from Iraklion) Tel prefix 0834. The road into the attractive village leads past a hotel, and there are quite a few Rooms spaced about. To the west of the taverna edged village square is a short, sandy stretch of beach, bounded, on the far side by a harbour quay wall.

Lasithi Plain The almost kingdom-like, inland plain is remarkable for its hundreds of skeletal water windmills with their reefing sails, even if most are now in ruins. The fertile land is highly cultivated and amongst the massed fruit trees and apple orchards, graze many cows and donkeys. In and around the villages, spaced out around the plain, are plenty of Rooms, hotels pensions, restaurants and tavernas.

To the east of Iraklion, along the north coast are:
Amnisos Beach (about 5km from Iraklion) This is an excellent, 1km long, broad sweep of gently shelving sand and sea-bed, with a tiny inshore islet. A short corniche along the rocky coast is yet another wide, long sandy beach. Between the pair are a number of Rooms, hotels, and beach tavernas.

LIMIN CHERSONISOS (28km from Iraklion) Tel prefix 0897. A small, Cycladean style chapel is built into the side of a headland which unequally divides the sweep of the large bay into two. To the west of the promontory there is a crescent-shaped, sandy beach.
Proceeding eastwards for the next two kilometres or so, the rocky waterfront is bordered by an Esplanade and edged by literally dozens of hotels, pensions, restaurants and tavernas, and their awning covered patios. Both beaches are clean and the sea clear, with a gently shelving sea-bed.

MALIA (36km from Iraklion) Tel prefix 0897. A sweeping bay, sandy beach, pleasant vistas, agricultural activity and proximity to Iraklion airport, combined to popularise the once open-spaces of Malia and its environs.

SISI (43km from Iraklion) Tel prefix 0841. Development has almost completely swamped both Sisi and its environs. The majority of the beach is grey shingle and pebble. There is no shortage of accommodation and dining establishments.

Milatos Beach The hamlet's small, sea-bordering, irregular square, is edged by a few tavernas, one or two Rooms and a small, grey, large pebble, wall contained beach.

KNOSSOS (5km from Iraklion) The great palace of this extensively restored site was built around a central court from which spread a succession of buildings, rooms, small courtyards and cellars connected by stair-cases, small courtyards, corridors and magazines for storage jars and urns.

RETHYMNON

FACT FILE
ALTERNATIVE NAMES
Rethymno

IMPRESSIONS Harbour city;
seaside tourist resort; Old Quarter.

RELIGIOUS FESTIVALS include,
15th-30th July, Rethymnon - wine
festival; 16th-31st July, Rethymnon - handicraft exhibition; 28th
July-10th August, Vamos - cultural & artistic events; 12th-15th
August, Anogia (Rethymnon
County) - cultural & artistic festivities; 13th-20th August, Perama

(Rethymnon County) - raisin
festival; 25th August, Amari
(Rethymnon County) - religious
fairs, St Titus day; 8th November, Arkadhi Monastery (Rethymnon County) - anniversary of
the 1866 holocaust, folklore
dancing in Rethymnon town.

STATISTICS Tel prefix 0831.
Population about 15,000.

TRANSPORT LINKS
Bus Most travellers turn up at the
dusty, disorganised chaos of the
main Bus Square, located to the
south of the Main Road.

Rethymnon has some late Minoan
traces; the Venetians were responsible for much of the town's development and the construction of
the walls and fort. Despite the
fortifications, in common with the
rest of the island, the City was
overwhelmed by the all conquer-
ing Turks, in 1645.

Rethymnon is possibly the most
complete and rounded of all the
major Cretan towns. In addition to
the Venetian fortress, City walls,
harbour, churches, Turkish Old
Quarter, mosques, minarets and
fountains, there is a splendid,
sandy beach.

To the east along the seafront
Esplanade, is a seemingly endless
stretch of modern development.
This borders an acceptable beach
and backshore planted with young
trees. To the west is the original
town Esplanade, attractively lined
with mature palm trees, which

edge a very generous swathe of
sandy beach, and bordered by a
variety of old buildings. At the far
end of the avenue is the tiny and
pretty inner Venetian Harbour,
lined by restaurants that circle the
quay wall.

Almost hidden away from the
attractions of the seafront, is an
extensive and attractive Old Quarter. Both accommodation and
eating places are very plentiful.

Places of interest include the:-
Arimondi Fountain Only three
heads and a part of the back wall
of the pretty fountain survive.
The Venetian Castle The outer
walls and one main town gate are
in a good state of restoration.
Archaeological Museum A new
facility, high up on a hill, close to
the east walls of the Castle.
Historical & Folk Art Museum
The Old Quarter This area is ex-

For greater detail acquire GROC's Candid Guide to Crete

tensive and most interesting. Many of the narrow, winding streets and lanes are overhung by Turkish, wooden, first storey balconies.
Public Gardens The formally arranged gardens were originally a Turkish cemetery. Every year a summer wine festival is held in the large grounds.
Religious Buildings These include the Mosque of Kara Pasha; the Minaret of Nerantzes; the newly constructed Church of Tessaron Martyron, which possesses splendid and vast interior murals; and, an extensively restored Mosque and Minaret.

MAIN RESORTS & PORTS
GEORGIOUPOLIS (32km from Rethymnon) This charming north coast location is now a very popular, package holiday resort, with accommodation a height of season problem. The roads are most attractively lined with massive eucalyptus trees. The similarly tree shaded, very large Main Square is not very distant from a bridge over the unexpectedly wide, summer-full River Almyros. Around to the right of the river is the delightfully sandy, long beach.

PLAKIAS (38km from Rethymnon) The waterfront is a strip of holiday businesses, which edge a mainly pebble beach. The majority of the community lies to the west, whilst the sea-shore spreads out to the east, the very long frontage edging the large Plaka Bay. The majority of the smart hotels are package holiday booked.

SPILI (30km from Rethymnon) (Tel prefix 0832) A lovely, clean, bustling, inland 'alpine' village, almost smothered in flowers and set in a green, fertile, cultivated plain snuggling at the foot of the mountain. It is a base for mountain walkers and organised ramblers.

Arkadhi Monastery (About 24km) Inland and to the south-east of Rethymnon. Apart from the symbolic importance, the buildings are baroquely attractive and still house a working community. The fame of the cloistered Monastery is soundly and dramatically based on the events of 1866. In that year Cretan patriots and villagers were besieged by an numerically overwhelming force of Turks.

FACT FILE

ALTERNATIVE NAMES Hania, Xania, Khania

IMPRESSIONS Venetian quarter & harbour; sophisticated, cosmopolitan activity; friendly people.

RELIGIOUS FESTIVALS include: 25th March, Apokorona Church (Chania County - Annunciation of Our Lady; First Sunday after Easter at the Monasteries of Neo Chorio & Apokorona (Chania County) - St Thomas; 20th-27th May, Chania City - anniversary of the Battle of Crete; 13th-18th July, Voukolies (Chania County) - cultural & artistic events; 27th August, Vryses (Chania County) - religious fair, St Fanourios; 29th August, Kournas & Ghionna site (both in Chania County) - religious fair, St John the Baptist; 1st-10th September, Gavalochori (Chania County) - folklore manifestations; 14th September, Alikianos, Varypetro (Chania County) & villages around Mt Idha - religious fairs, Raising the Holy Cross; 7th October, Monastery of Gouverneto (Chania County) - St John the Hermit.

STATISTICS Tel prefix 0821. Population about 55,000.

TRANSPORT LINKS
Air There are at least three flights a day to Athens and one flight a week to Thessaloniki(M). The airport, some 18km distant at Sternes, is now quite well-organised. Arrivals have the choice of the Olympic bus or taxis to get into town.

Ferry There is a once a day ferry-boat link with Piraeus(M). The port of Chania is 6½km across the neck of the Akrotiri peninsula, at Souda, a Naval base. An excellent bus service connects the two.

Neolithic and Minoan remains have been found in an old quarter. The Venetians named the city *La Canea,* lost it to the Genoese for a few years, between 1267 and 1290, and then retook the place. The Venetians built many fine buildings and fortified the city but relinquished control in 1645. In that year the Turks overwhelmed the whole island, only to be expelled themselves, in 1898.

The Harbour is magnificent, as are the Castle walls; the Venetian Arsenals are noteworthy; the quayside activity is fascinating; the Topanas, Kastelli, Chiones and Splantzia Old Quarters are aesthetically pleasing; and the Market is incomparable. Certainly Chania is a city that richly rewards exploration and the areas encompassed by the old walls are particularly interesting. The hub of the city is a Square bordering the Outer Harbour, a view from which encompasses the square, the rather lovely, domed roofs of the old Turkish mosque, the lighthouse and the sweep of the quayside Esplanade.

For greater detail acquire GROC's Candid Guide to Crete

The main beach is a few kilometres to the west. The beach backshore is edged by a Esplanade, which is bordered by a row of three to five storey buildings accommodating a few hotels, pensions, restaurants, tavernas and various businesses. Almost all the accommodation and dining facilities are within the old City Walls.

Places of interest include:-
The Minoan Palace
The Church of San Salvatore A 13/14th Century church, at one time converted to a mosque.
The Church of Ag Anargyri
The Church of St Nicholas Once a Monastery, then a Mosque, before being re-dedicated to the Orthodox faith. This alternation of religions has resulted in a remarkable coupling of minaret and campanile.
Archaeological Museum Once San Francesco Church and a mosque.
Historical Museum The exhibits are considered to be outstanding.
Naval Museum

Venetian Arsenals & Walls The crumbling Arsenals are still inspiring, as is St Marks Arcade.

MAIN PORTS & RESORTS
To the west of Chania are:-
AG MARINA (about 5km from Chania) The once lovely strip of beach is now submerged in a welter of tourist shops and hotels.

PLATANIAS (some 8km from Chania) The original village has spread down off its small, flat-topped hill into a sprawl. The beach here is low, flat and sandy.

Frangokastello Castle (some 76km from Chania) The impressive, if squat Venetian fortress still dominates the unattractive, large, level, south coast plateau. The restored fort was built in the 14th century. It overlooks a marvellous, large spit of sandy beach, and a line of houses, mostly offering Rooms, which sweep down to a lone Martello tower, standing sentinel on a low promontory.

CHORA SFAKION

FACT FILE

ALTERNATIVE NAMES Chora Sphakion, Khora Sfakion, Hora Sfakion, Sfakia

RELIGIOUS FESTIVALS include: 26-27th May, Chora Sfakion - anniversary of the Declaration of the 1821 Revolution;

STATISTICS Tel prefix 0825.

A south coast harbour village, which has developed as the main exit point for Ag Roumeli, the settlement at the bottom of the Samaria Gorge.

MAIN PORTS & RESORTS LOUTRO (Lutron, Loutron) (about 16km from Chora Sfakion) Originally a fishing boat port, Loutro lies inset at the far end of a mountain enclosed bay. The homes, lodging houses and tavernas are linked by a series of concrete paths and terraces. About a third of the way round, to the east, is a narrow, stony beach, which occupies the middle ground. The backshore is now dominated by a smart, low-rise hotel.

SAMARIA GORGE The extremely beautiful Gorge is possibly the longest and largest in Europe. At the bottom, sea end of the Gorge is:-

AG ROUMELI (60km from Chania) Resembles a hot, Alaskan shanty town. To cater for the thousands of walkers who descend the Gorge every day there are some fairly low-key hotels and tavernas. The surprisingly large, very wide, fine pebble, black beach extends away to the west.

FACT FILE

ALTERNATIVE NAMES
Palaiokhora, Kastelli Selinou

IMPRESSIONS The large, sweeping, magnificent beach.

STATISTICS Tel prefix 0823.

TRANSPORT LINKS

Bus The buses pull up on the High St, towards the south of town.

Ferry Small, south coast ferries, link daily with Souyia, Ag Roumeli, Loutro and Chora Sfakion, as well as a Gavdos island connection.

Paleochora was once a fishing village, as evidenced by the disproportionately large harbour installation, at the lighthouse end of the peninsula. The eastern Esplanade borders a neat, but initially rocky sea's edge, at the north end of which is an extremely pebbly beach. The western Esplanade edges probably one of the finest beaches on Crete, with a huge, gently curving, large, tree fringed, sandy shore, set in an impressive, distantly cliff edged bay.

Dining places abound. There is a plethora of Rooms and hotels, even if most of the latter are 'dedicated' to the package tourists.

MAIN PORTS & RESORTS
SOUYIA (Sougia, Soughia) Tel prefix 0823. The spaced out, scattered dwellings of Souyia border a rather lifeless, great sweep of pebble beach. A tamarisk tree lined, metalled track edges the backshore to the west. There are Rooms, tavernas with accommodation, and some dining establishments.

KASTELLI

FACT FILE	STATISTICS Tel prefix 0822.
ALTERNATIVE NAMES Kastellio, Kisamos, Kissamos, Kisamou	**TRANSPORT LINKS** **Bus** These park on an elongated square, alongside the Main road.
IMPRESSIONS An (English) market town & ferry-boat port	**Ferry** Two boats a week link Kastelli to Piraeus(M), via Antikithira, Kithira, and the east
RELIGIOUS FESTIVALS Falasarna (Nr Kastelli) - a moveable tomato fiesta.	Peloponnese ports of Neapoli and Monemvassia. The large harbour quay is 2km west of the town.

A rapidly expanding and thriving 'country' town. The mainly pebble beach backshore is rapidly infilling with rather disjointed, package holiday development. To the east, the dirt Esplanade edges the long seafront which faces up the huge Gulf of Kissamos.

There has been a marked increase in the number of Rooms, pensions, hotels, and dining establishments.

MAIN RESORTS & PORTS
Falasarna Beach (18km) To the west of Kastelli, the narrow plain edges a gentle bay, rimmed by a glorious sweep of sand. Close to

the bluff at the north end are a few pension-cum-tavernas.

To the south of Kastelli, along the west coast are:-
Sfinari Beach The shoreline is an unprepossessing stretch of grey pebble, in which is some similarly coloured sand.
Elafonisi Beach (60km from Kastelli) On the very south-western corner of Crete and a beautiful, idyllic, gorgeous sweep of sandy lagoon. Not far offshore is the stunning:-
Elafonisi Islet A paradise of beaches reached by wading across the waters of the lagoon.

For greater detail acquire GROC's Candid Guide to Crete

FACT FILE **ALTERNATIVE NAMES** Ayia Galini **IMPRESSIONS** Look-alike for a Cornish fishing village; masses of villa tourists.	**STATISTICS** Tel prefix 0832. **TRANSPORT LINKS** **Bus** The Bus square is on the outskirts of the 'core of the village'.

The village is sandwiched in a narrow defile, but very little of the original, old-world, fishing village charm has been retained. The shingly beach is around to the east of a prominent headland.

Apartments, hotels, pensions and Rooms line the Main road, whilst the majority of tavernas and restaurants are spread throughout the old village, which overlooks the harbour.

MAIN RESORTS & PORTS
MATALA (31km from Ag Galini) The comparatively small, shadeless, sand, fine shingle and pebble beach is set at the bottom of an indented bay. The high cliffs, forming the north horn of the inlet, contain caves used by Christians, in the 5th century AD. Nowadays Matala is a package tourist resort, with plenty of accommodation, tavernas, restaurants and people.

FACT FILE

ALTERNATIVE NAMES Aghios, Ayios Nikolaos

IMPRESSIONS Still attractive harbour town & package holiday resort; strident discos & glitzy cocktail bars.

STATISTICS Tel prefix 0841. Population 6500.

TRANSPORT LINKS

Bus The Bus square is to the south of the town.

Ferry Ferry-boats connect five days a week with Sitia(Crete); four days a week with Kasos and Piraeus(M); three days a week with Milos, Karpathos, Chalki and Rhodes; two days a week to Anafi and Santorini; and once a week to Sikinos, Folegandros, Simi, Tilos, Nisiros, Astipalaia, Amorgos and Paros.

Ag Nikolaos has little history of note, the modern town being a comparatively recent 19th century development. The clean, lovely, tree lined avenues, pretty lake and harbour compensate for the lack of the usual historical prerequisites. Ag Nikolaos is probably the most tourist developed of all the Cretan holiday resorts. The main square crowns the hill dominating the town. From the far side, the High St plunges down to the Harbour where a bridge spans the Lake Voulismeni sea inlet. For a town with this number of tourists, there isn't very much beach. To the east is a fairly small, grey sand, stony beach. The other beach is a very narrow strip of fine pebble bordering an Esplanade that runs away south of Ag Nikolaos.

Unsurprisingly, there is any amount of accommodation of all sorts, shapes and sizes, whilst eating places range from fast food snackbars to luxury restaurants.

MAIN PORTS & RESORTS
KRITSA (11km from Ag Nikolaos) An attractive, inland mountain village, famed for local handicrafts. There are several pensions, some Rooms, and a sprinkling of tavernas spread along the lanes.

To the east of Ag Nikolaos, along the north coast are:-
ISTRON (13km from Ag Nikolaos) A spaced out resort, the beach of which is a lovely sandy sweep, with a pebbly middleshore.

MOCHLOS (47km from Ag Nikolaos) The heart of this nicely off-beat hamlet edges a steeply shelving, pebble shoreline. The 'Esplanade', which is pleasantly shaded by mature, pollarded arethemusa trees, advances past a number of small, provincial hotels and rustic tavernas.

Two hundred metres from the foreshore is the small, barren islet named after the settlement.

For greater detail acquire GROC's Candid Guide to Crete

On the south coast are:-

MIRTOS (52km from Ag Nikolaos) Tel prefix 0842. The settlement stretches out along a fairly lengthy, not very wide, grey sand, pebble beach. There are a couple of hotels, Rooms and tavernas are spaced out through Mirtos.

ARVI (81km from Ag Nikolaos) Tel prefix 0895. A pleasant, long village paralleling the narrow strip of pebble shore, with some grey sand, bordering the clean sea. There isn't an Esplanade, more a string of inter-connected patios and terraces of the various tavernas and accommodation establishments that line the sea wall.

KERATOKAMBOS (90km from Ag Nikolaos) The tiny, seaside hamlet edges a long, tree lined back-shore of the narrow, mainly pebble beach, that extends away to left and right. There are a few pensions and tavernas.

North along the coast from Ag Nikolaos are:-

ELOUNDA (11km from Ag Nikolaos) Tel prefix 0841. A smart, international holiday resort with an air of quiet dignity. A few of the old buildings have survived. The shadeless beach is agreeably sandy, if small.

PLAKA (16km from Ag Nikolaos) The lovely, quiet hamlet and tiny fishing boat port is draped over a headland projecting into the sea. Close by where the Spinalonga islet boats dock, is accommodation and a couple of tavernas. At the north end is a large pebble beach.

SPINALONGA ISLET Once known as 'the island of the living dead', whilst used as a leper colony. The fortress was built by the Venetians, in 1579. They managed to hold out against the all-conquering Turks, until 1715. The Ottomans, in their turn, stayed in occupation of this remarkable outpost for some years after they had departed 'mainland' Crete. Some time in 1904 it became a leper colony, which finally closed its doors in 1957.

SITIA

FACT FILE
ALTERNATIVE NAME Siteia

IMPRESSIONS An island like town & port; a lack of Venetian or Turkish remains.

RELIGIOUS FESTIVALS include, 2nd-10th July, Sitia - cultural & artistic festivities; 19th-22nd July, Sitia - raisin festival;

STATISTICS Tel prefix 0843. The population is about 6500.

TRANSPORT LINKS
Air The town has a 'small' island airport, with flights on four days a week to Karpathos and Rhodes; and two days a week to nearby Kasos.

Bus The Bus terminus is close to the waterfront.

Ferry Scheduled ferry-boats connect four days a week to Kasos, Karpathos, Rhodes and Piraeus (M); three days a week to Chalki, Ag Nikolaos(Crete) and Milos; and one day a week to Tilos, Nisiros, Astipalaia, Amorgos and Paros.

The Venetians built a fortified wall and castle. Otherwise history bypassed Sitia. The town to the north of the main square is 'pure' island harbour charm. The terraces of square, white houses are interspaced with steep, broad steps climbing seemingly ever upwards. The 'Chora' hillside is topped, to one side, by the fort and chapel cemetery. Sitia might well be considered an ideal seaside resort as it possesses a splendid, long, sandy beach; an interesting old town; a fishing boat, cargo ship and ferry-boat port; and a picturesque waterfront packed with lively tavernas.

There is a surprisingly wide choice and variety of accommodation, as well as a plethora of waterside restaurants and tavernas.

MAIN PORTS & RESORTS
To the east of Sitia are:-

Toplou Monastery (17km from Sitia) The fortified Venetian monastery is built on a sparse, bare and isolated location.

Erimoupolis Beach (24km from Sitia) Also known as Itanos, after a Minoan settlement. A gritty sand cove, with a few boulders scattered about and some angled biscuit rock. Over the headland to the north is a much larger but shadeless cove, with a lovely sandy sea's edge and a fine, gritty sand beach. To the right is yet another, small, sandy beach cove.

The general setting is magnificent, with **Elasa** islet to the east and the **Cape of Sideros** curving away in the distance.

Vai Beach (some 24km from Sitia) This renowned seaside beauty spot has a gritty sand beach, the backshore of which is edged by groves of palm trees, giving the appearance of a tropical location.

KATO ZAKROS (58km from Sitia) A sparse attractive, sleepy, fishing boat hamlet, edging a clean, pebbly beach. The waterfront tavernas offer sustenance, and limited accommodation.

Palace of Zakros Excavations of this marvelleous site were started at the turn of the century.

Across the island, on the south coast, is one of the most despoiled, widely spaced out holiday resort stretches of any Cretan coastline.

ANALIPSI (32km from Sitia) The resort has a pleasant, if small bay, with a tamarisk tree shaded, big pebble backshore, a 2-3 m wide swathe of grey, sharp sand beach, and a fine pebble foreshore.

MAKRI GIALOS This settlement is based on an older, dusty core.

The bay is quite large and pleasant, with a rather shadeless beach of sharp, grey sand and a very fine pebble sea's edge.

KOUTSOURAS (37km from Sitia) A once rural site which is now nothing more than a messy sprawl of development. In the boulderous and sloping flat rock foreshore are little coves of grey sharp sand, and along the length of which stretches the ribbon development.

AG FOTIA (46km from Sitia) A little bay edges a grey, gritty sand, beach. The tiny agricultural plain is being taken over by the building of Rooms and restaurants.

FERMA Notable for several, massive hotel developments, but lacking any infrastructure.

KOUTSOUNARI (52km from Sitia) Hard by a little cove of pebble beach is a resort development and its suburbs.

FACT FILE	STATISTICS Tel prefix 0842.
IMPRESSIONS	The population now totals some 12500 inhabitants.
A scattered, messy, industrious, seaside town, lacking charm and a centre; very small old quarter and fort.	**TRANSPORT LINKS**
	Bus The buses terminus on the outskirts of the town.

The modern town is based on the ancient seaport of Ierapetra. The Venetians and Turks occupied the site, as evidenced by the Venetian fort and the Turkish minaret.

The outer suburbs and immediate surrounds of Ierapetra are appallingly squalid.

Most of the hotel development stretches along the eastern beach backshore. At the western end of the town is the tiny Old Quarter and a small cargo ship harbour. Ierapetra has a wealth of beaches, mainly made up of grey coloured sand and pebble.

There are any number of hotels and Rooms, as well as sufficient, if not outstanding, restaurants and tavernas lining the waterfront.

Places of interest include the: Venetian Castle; Mosque and Minaret; a Turkish fountain; and 'Napoleon's' House. The latter is where Bonaparte is rumoured to have stayed for a night, on his way to campaign in Egypt, in 1798. **Archaeological Museum** A single storey, Turkish building.

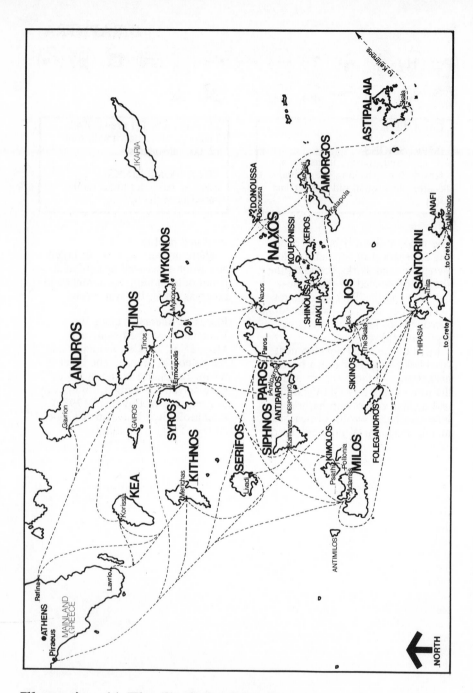

Illustration 11 The Cyclades islands

PART FOUR   THE CYCLADES ISLANDS
(Kiklades, Kikladhes, Kykladen)

A loosely knit scattering of some twenty six inhabited islands, set in the Aegean, stretching south towards Crete, west beneath the island of Evia and east towards the island groupings that edge the Turkish mainland.

The Cyclades range from tiny to large; arid to verdant; gentle hills to mountains; plain-featured to beautiful; and thoroughly rural to garish, Western sophistication. They alone offer almost every possible hue, shade, type and variety of Greek island. Certainly there is a magic quality to the islands: whether steaming past the rocky fastness of their shores or urgently bustling into port; whether it is a cool, clear morning, a hot, windy afternoon or, perchance, a deep purple night, with the lights of other steamers and scattered island settlements winking in the distant darkness.

No two islands are the same, but rarely are they so entirely different that each port of call will not recall both the similarities and dissimilarities to others in the chain. A couple of impressions, amongst all the others, will surely prevail - the wind and the granite mountainsides. Generally, during the summer, the gusts come and go, but, from the middle of July to the middle of September, the *Meltemi* blows continuously from the north.

There certainly is an almost impossible choice of islands on offer. Final selection can only depend on a traveller's own sensibilities. Whatever his or her fancy, the Cyclades will surely fulfil most, if not all of them.

It would be a travesty not to sound a warning note. The simple, naive, primitive Greece of only thirty years or so ago has all but disappeared. Mass tourism is not entirely to blame, for once the decision had been made that the Greeks should be pitchforked into the 20th century, then the curtain was slowly but surely rung down on the past. But all is not lost as the Greek people, in the main, retain their exuberance and simple charm, in addition to which centuries old customs, ways and manners have not changed or disappeared altogether - 'Plus ca change, plus non ca change'.

Astipalaia is included in the Cyclades for reasons of practicality. Undoubtedly the island is infinitely easier to reach from certain of the Cyclades islands, than from the Dodecanese, with which it is usually bracketed. Additionally its geography and Chora are distinctly Cycladean, bearing little similarity to any of the Dodecanese islands. I accept that Patmos (alone of the Dodecanese) has a Chora, but very much a 'fortified monastery Chora', rather than the typical, Cycladean, hilltop capital.

The history of the islands grouped together under the loose geographical ties of the Cyclades is, as elsewhere in Greece, confusing, to say the least. Even the nomenclature and number of islands in the group has been the subject of much change and alteration over the years. By about 1000 BC, the Ionians from the west coast of Greece had imposed the worship of Letos on Delos, as well as imbued that island with various myths honouring Apollo. Thus, for a time, tiny Delos became the most important island in the whole Aegean. At about this time the Cyclades (or Kyklos), referred to the twelve or fifteen islands circled around Delos. Nowadays it refers to an administrative area encompassing some thirty or so islands.

Settlement of the group can be traced as far back as 7000 BC but the earliest, easily identifiable period of occupation was between 3000-2600 BC. An early attraction, to outsiders, was the volcanic mineral obsidian, centred on Milos island. By about 2000 BC the Minoans of Crete were in command and had established large settlements on the islands of Milos and Santorini. They were followed by the Mycenaeans, a Dark Age and then the Ionians. In their turn these invaders were routed by the Persians, in 490 BC, who were on their way to a naval battle with the City-State of Athens, at Salamis. The Persians lost, after which the Athenians created an Empire, although they had the cunning to call it a League or Confederation. The Cycladian islands baulked against this regime, but were brought back into line by Athens, under the guise of a Second Confederation. From then on times were turbulent, with the Egyptian Ptolemies. and others, variously, emerging winners, until the Romans cropped up in 197 BC. The latter allowed the patriarchs of Rhodes island to run 'the show', taking the reins of power back again, until their own empire fragmented in AD 395. The Cycladians were then left to the ravages of various invading hordes.

The Byzantine Empire, which remotely involved itself in the Cyclades, took a beating, in the early 1200s, from Crusaders who, instead of sorting out the Arabs and Jerusalem, found an easier target in Constantinople, which they laid waste. The Venetians, who had been keeping a close eye on events, took over the Cyclades, as well as other bits of Greece, which included Crete, Rhodes, some of the Dodecanese, as well as the Ionian islands. The Venetians parcelled up their various holdings and handed them out to the cities' ruling families. One of these patriarchs, having taken the title of Duke of Naxos, sided with the Franks and managed to hang on to that particular island until the 1560s, by which time most of the others had been lost to the Turks. Not a nation to give in easily, the Venetians pursued a running battle with the Turks, taking back this or that island until they irrevocably lost Crete in 1669. However, one outpost, Tinos, remained in Venetian hands until the early 1700s. With the Turks firmly at the helm in the Aegean, a hundred years of peace ensued until the Russians and Turks pitched into each other, in 1770. The Russians annexed numerous of the islands, for the next five years, after which the Turks took over again, until 1821. In this year the Greeks kicked over the traces, once and for all, and painfully and slowly drove out their erstwhile overlords, with the resultant formation of the independent Greek State.

The principle religion is Greek Orthodox, with Catholic enclaves left over from the Venetian occupation.

FACT FILE

IMPRESSIONS Splendid sea cliff vistas; parched, mountainous countryside; older women's white, triangular headscarves.

SPECIALITIES Herbs; pastelli (sweetbread).

RELIGIOUS FESTIVALS include: 15th August - Festival Panaghia Ag Epanochori; 26th July - Ag Paraskevi, Kolophana; 14th September, Stavros; 21st November - Festival Hozviotizza Monastery; 8th December Ag Nikolaos, Aegiali.

STATISTICS Tel prefix 0285. The elongated island lies obliquely north-east to south-west. It is approximately 32km in length & up to 11km in width, with an area of about 130sq km. The population numbers some 1,800.

TRANSPORT LINKS

Ferry The boats dock at either the west coast, northern port of Aegiali or the central island port of Katapola. At Aegiali it is a long walk down the massive quay to the outset of the settlement, whilst at Katapola the ferries dock a pace or two from the main square. Ferries connect daily with Naxos; six days a week with Paros; five days a week with Donoussa, Koufonissi and Iraklia; four days a week with Shinoussa, Astipalaia, Syros and Piraeus(M); three days a week with Rhodes and Mykonos; two days a week with Kalimnos, Kos, Nisiros, Tilos, Simi and Rafina(M); and once a week with Ios and Santorini.

At both locations passengers are met by Room owners.

It seems unlikely now, but in days of antiquity the island sported three city states: 'Minoa' on a hill to the south of and close by Katapola Port; 'Arkesini' to the north of the modern-day hamlet of the same name; and 'Aegiali' situated on the site of Aegiali Port. Excavations at Aegiali, in 1888, revealed a Gymnasium, Stadium and a Temple dedicated to Apollo, not a lot of which is now discernible.

The Romans used the island for the incarceration of exiles, which rather set the tone for the future. The usual bunch of savage marauders mauled Amorgos and its inhabitants over the years. The Duke of Naxos took the place under his wing, in 1209, and a castle was built alongside the Chora. During the Turkish occupation, the island women are supposed to have contributed significantly to the wealth of Amorgos by dint of their embroidery output, the fame of which spread throughout Europe.

The far-flung position of Amorgos, coupled with the lack of numerous daily ferry-boat connections, results in the island receiving less visitors than its more popular and accessible western neighbours. The Amorgots seem reluctant to go the whole hog, best exemplified by

---

For greater detail acquire GROC's Candid Guide to The Cyclades Islands

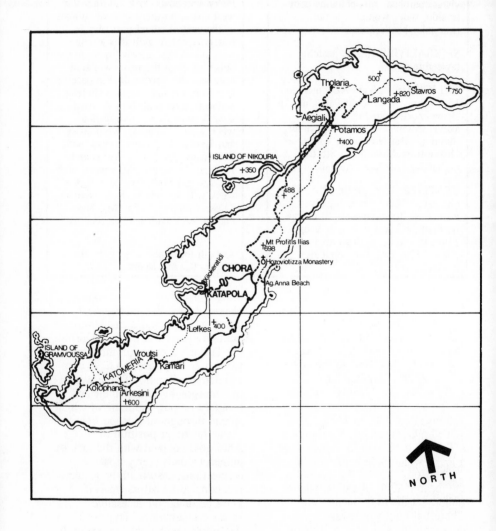

Illustration 12 Amorgos island

their reluctance to advertise accommodation, at all.

The island is rugged and the
barrier of its mountainous spine
creates the impression that the two
ends of Amorgos have evolved as
distinct islands. Access to the
south is via the main port of Katapola and to the north via the port
of Aegiali. Caiques and ferries are
still the easiest means of travel
between the two, even though a
rough road, wrested from the unyielding terrain, runs between the
two locations.

In the north, unsurfaced roads
link the villages of **Tholaria** and
Langada to Aegiali, and they enjoy
a regular bus service, as does
Katapola to the Chora.

Unfortunately a fire, in 1835,
destroyed the forests which once
clad the land, thus the arid hills
and mountains.

MAIN PORTS & RESORTS
KATAPOLA This is the main port
made up of three village/hamlets.
Katapola, the ferry-boat port, is to
the south of the bay; Rachidi, the
rather drab, central settlement, is
set back from the centre of the bay
and dominated by a twin tower
church; and Xilokeratidi, is a small
fishing boat hamlet to the north of
the bay, with some lovely, aged,
flower bestrewn buildings and
remnants of an Old Quarter.

The bottom of the bay, between
the Katapola side and Xilokeratidi,
has two narrow strips of dirty
grey, coarse sand and pebble
beach. On the Xilokeratidi side, a
track progresses to a shingly sand
beach with a scrubbly, scruffy
backshore, and no shade.

The phenomenon of unadver-
tised, unproclaimed Rooms is pre-
valent and accommodation tends to
be overpriced. There is a definite

move towards up-market eating
houses and cocktail bars, despite
which a couple of traditional tavernas are still present.

THE CHORA (Amorgos) (Some
5km from Katapola) The inland,
mountain-top capital, the 'High' St
of which wanders through the
charming settlement. Spread along
its length are are several Rooms
and a taverna or two.

Hozoviotizza Monastery About an
hours walk east from the Chora,
the nine hundred year old, white,
cliff-hugging religious house hangs
limpet-like to a drab brown, grey
and orange rock-face.

Ag Anna Beach From the outskirts
of the Chora, the track zig-zags
down the hillside goat path, or
catch the bus for the one hour
journey to the east coast.

A clean, grey pebble beach with
clear, brilliantly blue waters.

AEGIALI (Aigiali, Agiali, Egiali)
The northern port has a few distinct advantages over Katapola,
the most important being the
splendid beach in addition to eating out costing less.

The port is located on the right-
hand corner of the broad 'U' of an
extremely large and dramatic bay,
bordering the bottom of which is a
long, tree edged beach.

The immediate shoreline, beyond a rubbly quay area, is a
small, sandy stretch. Although the
shore is a bit pebbly, to begin
with, it soon becomes sandy, getting better the further round one
proceeds, with a fine sandy bottom
to the shallow shelving sea-bed.

The boats are met by the owners
of the few hotels and owners of
private house accommodation.

For greater detail acquire GROC's Candid Guide to The Cyclades Islands

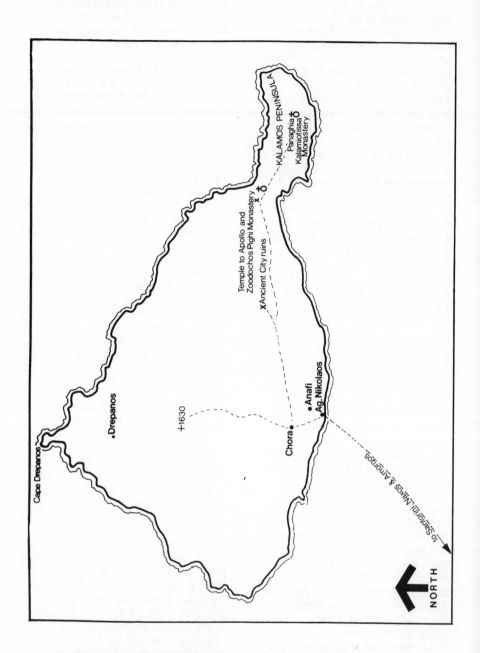

Illustration 13 Anafi island

FACT FILE

ALTERNATIVE NAMES Anaphi, Anaphe

IMPRESSIONS Wind; barren landscape.

SPECIALITIES Saligari (snails) - eaten only in September; Mizithra cheese; Brusko wine.

RELIGIOUS FESTIVALS include: 15th August - Festival, Panaghia Kalamiotissa Monastery; 8th September - Panaghia Kalamiotissa Monastery. An image of the Virgin Mary was found on a bamboo plant or 'kalami', hence the island's saint being Ag Kalamiotissa.

STATISTICS Tel prefix 0286. The island is squarish in shape, with the Kalamos headland at the eastern end. The population fluctuates, according to the time of year, but averages about 200, most of whom live in the Chora.

TRANSPORT LINKS

Ferry During the summer months there is, on average, a boat a day to and from various destinations. Three days a week ferries link with Santorini, Piraeus(M); two days a week with Ios, Naxos, Paros, Crete, Kasos, Karpathos and Rhodes; and once a week to Sikinos, Folegandros, Milos, Syros and Rafina(M).

At no time do the owners of accommodation meet the boats.

Fable has it that the island emerged from the sea at the command of Apollo, in order to shelter Jason and the Argonauts, who were beset by a storm. Quite possibly this legend relates to the Santorini 'big bang'. Whatever, Apollo was worshipped, and a temple dedicated to him, located close to the nearest of the two monasteries, Zoodochos Pighi.

The word 'anaphi' actually comes from the ancient Greek, and literally translated, indicates 'no snakes.' According to local legend, snakes cannot survive here, whilst the neighbouring islands are, or were, covered in them.

The Russians ruled briefly, in the sixteenth century, and more recently, during the Second World War, Anafi was under Italian rule. According to the older locals, the Italian soldiers were well liked and the island 'enjoyed' a peaceful war. During the Greek Civil War, Anafi became a place of exile for political prisoners. Here again, it was all rather low-key, with the prisoners billeted in the homes of local families.

Until fairly recently Anafi was an 'undiscovered' island, with no roads, cars, hotels or anything else associated with tourism. However, with the more intrepid tourists searching for 'the original Greek way of life', this is no longer so true. Sadly, a new road is under construction, leading from the port

---

For greater detail acquire GROCs Candid Guide to The Cyclades Islands

to the Chora. On completion, Anafi will probably go the way of other, lesser known islands.

AG NIKOLAOS (or Skala) The tiny port is both dusty and unremarkable, but it fulfils its *raison d'etre* as a way-station.

About ten minutes walk to the right of the port, along the cliff-edge is a quite pleasant, if windy, little sandy beach, with clear water. There are a few Rooms here, at reasonable prices and a lot of people camp on the beach itself, which also boasts a couple of small tavernas, packed day and night. A further thirty minutes along the cliff path to the right is a long, sandy beach, an ideal place for those who want to be quite alone. Be prepared and carry a torch if planning to stay late.

Boatmen 'ferry' passengers to all and any coastal location, but are rather expensive.

A few Rooms are available in the port, but not many, and there is a grand total of two tavernas and one rather small bar.

THE CHORA (about 1km, or 1 hour from Ag Nikolaos) The capital and only (small) village is located on the site of a Venetian fortress, of which little or nothing remains, even if bits of pottery can still be found lying around.

The Chora is, for all intents and purposes, one long passageway with small pathways leading off. A charming place full of nooks and crannies, and little else, with a deserted ambiance to the place. The locals are shy but extremely friendly and helpful. Various paths promisingly make off into the hills, but don't go too far.

Locating Rooms is left totally to the visitor, but almost every house provides accommodation. The dining out possibilities are limited, which is only to be expected in a place of such a small size.

Excursion To The Monasteries
There are two monasteries. About 5km along the path is a branch to the left which leads to the old 'Kastelli' or original settlement (ancient Anaphe), but this has been deserted for the last 800 years. At some 7km, in the Kalamos isthmus, is the **Monastery Zoodochos Pighi**, built in the 1830s. Most of the structure was destroyed in the 1956 earthquake, killing a lot of the monks. There is also a Temple of Apollo close by, the ruins of which are still visible. Still further, along the scenically beautiful Kalamos peninsula is the older **Monastery Panaghia Kalamiotissa**, built around 1710, and repository for the miracle working icon of the island saint.

The path is a total of about 10km. Being a dry island and lacking any villages, walkers must take drinking water despite which the monasteries are worth seeing.

FACT FILE

IMPRESSIONS Verdant island; space & breadth; flowers & wonderful scents; prosperity; Greeks on holiday; red roofs; neat villages; unplastered walls.

SPECIALITIES Mineral water; unique walls; 'frontalia' omelette (includes potatoes, sausage & bacon or pork - scrumptious).

RELIGIOUS FESTIVALS include: 27th July - Feast of Ag Panteleimon, the Monastery of Panachrantos; 6th December - Feast of Ag Nikolaos, the Monastery of Ag Nikolaos.

STATISTICS Tel prefix 0282. The most northerly & second largest of the Cyclades islands (to Naxos). Up to 39 ½km from NW to SE, up to 16km in width, with an area of some 373sq km. The population numbers approximately 10,000, of which about 1,800 live in the capital, Andros Town.

TRANSPORT LINKS
Ferry Rather out of the ordinary, the ferry-boat port of Gavrion is not the capital, a main town or even an important holiday resort. The boats are not met by any owners of accommodation. However, the local buses, any number of taxis and a campsite van all attend a docking. Every day ferries connect to Tinos, Mykonos and Rafina(M), and two days a week boats run to Syros.

The island was subject to the average historical mix, although the Andriots appear to have caused their various overlords rather more difficulties than most other Cycladean islands. This may have been due to the large number of Albanians who settled on the island, during the Middle-Ages.

Andros experienced an Axis troops 'fall-out' (as did, for example, Cephalonia in the Ionian), with the Germans bombing the resident Italian soldiers into submission, in 1943.

Geographically a very large island, but, despite this massive physical presence, Andros somehow gives the impression of being smaller. In part this is not surprising, considering the comparatively puny size of the main centres. The scruffy port of Gavrion would be more suitable for one of the small island, 'off-the-cuff' ferry-boat calls; the villa holiday resort of Vatsi (Batsi) could be swallowed by many other popular locations, and Andros Town lacks a Chora, and is more a seaside resort than the capital. On the other hand, nothing can detract from the island's soft, awesome beauty of the rolling mountains which are divided by large fertile plains. Wealthy Athenians have developed many of the villages into neat, red tile roofed, tidy, bi-annual commuter settlements, nestling in tree-clad mountainsides.

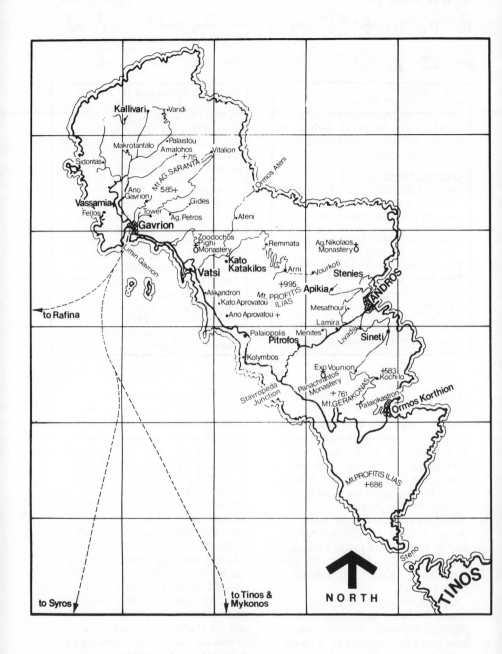

Illustration 14 Andros island

Moreover, the plenteous supply of water supports not only rich agricultural vistas, but cypress tree plantations that 'march' up the hillside amphitheatres.

Although Venetian dovecotes are not so numerous as on Tinos, the Andriots have their own country-side quirk - unique walling in which large, triangulated plates of stone are inserted sideways-on into the wall. If all this were not enough, there are lovely, relatively empty beaches.

MAIN RESORTS & PORTS
GAVRION The main port, where a disembarking traveller has a dilemma - to stay in Gavrion or make for Vatsi (Batsi) or Andros Town. Gavrion is not a very prepossessing location, although it may well grow on a visitor, if allowed the time to weave its spell. The port and village is to the right of the encircling bay, with a small, haphazard, shanty bungalow development on the beach backshore, at the bottom of the bay. Almost the whole settlement borders the 'High St-cum- Esplanade'.

Local benzinas are anchored in the shallow water of the first half of the flat, narrow beach, but it will suffice as a bather's stand-by.

There is not a superabundance of places to stay. Similarly, there are not many eating establishments, despite which Gavrion has at least one excellent taverna.

VATSI (Batsi) (8km from Gavrion Port) An attractive Greek 'St Ives' - part port, part summer resort, with the holiday aspect increasingly dominant. The long main beach is coarse sand and a scatter-ing of large pebbles, with a shingly foreshore and sea-bed.

There are plenty of Rooms, but the package firms have a toe-hold.

ANDROS TOWN (35km from Gavrion Port) The capital, which resembles a Greek Eastbourne or Weymouth. Moreover it doesn't have a Chora, more the vestiges of an Old Quarter.

Many of the official buildings are imposing, 19th century 'municipal', and a notable feature is that the long High street is a marble paved pedestrian way. The town is built on a high headland promontory that juts out into and divides Kastrou Bay, leaving an expansive stretch of sandy beach, way down below, on either side.

The citizens make little or no attempt to accommodate tourists.

ORMOS KORTHION (20km from Andros Town) A messy, 'rustic', 'provincial', scruffy, smelly, spread out village port. The attentions of the wealthy mainlanders appear to have bypassed this more traditional mixture of old and new, neat and dilapidated, surfaced roads and potholed streets. The 'Esplanade', if that is not too smart a word, edges the gently curving bay.

Stretching away to the right is a long, sandy beach curving around the bay. It has some sea-weed, but the water is very clear and the sea-bed slopes gently.

Several hotels and a pension furnish accommodation, whilst a few old world kafeneions and tavernas more than suffice in attending to food and drink requirements of any visitors.

For greater detail acquire GROC's Candid Guide to The Cyclades Islands

FACT FILE	TRANSPORT LINKS
IMPRESSIONS A small, unforgiving island. **STATISTICS** Tel prefix 0284. The island is 12km from north to south, up to 6km wide, with an area of 40 sq km & a population of 650.	Trip-boats run from the Paros island main port of **Paroikias** (Paros) daily and have their schedules fixed to the side of the boat. The journey takes between ¾ and 1 hour. The other Paros departure point is **Pounta**, on Paros, from whence the short sea journey takes about ten minutes.

It is common practice to treat Antiparos as an adjunct of Paros, but it is bigger than, for instance, Folegandros and is a location in its own right.

There is only one settlement of any size, the fortified town of **Antiparos**, or Kastro, separated from the lagoon-like ferry-boat quay, by a few minutes walk. The island's hotels, pensions, rooms, restaurants, tavernas and kafeneions are gathered about the quay, the town and the connecting road.

At the north end of the shallow lagoon is a narrow, hard sand beach, backed by trees.

One kilometre or so of dirt track leads to a rocky coastline, indented with shallow, sandy coves. A small, bushy headland divides this bay from the next, which has a benzina jetty and is backed by a camping site and a beach bar. Incidentally, everything on the island is a walk or a boat trip**,**

including the:-

Cave of Antiparos The track from the Kastro is in good condition but it is a 1½-2hr tramp and on a hot day... The other method of getting there is by trip boat which depart from the port. The cave is sited close to the top of Mt Ag Yianni and the arduous climb from the docking area takes up to ½ hour. During the summer months donkeys ease the slog, at a cost, and a makeshift cafe looks after the 'inner' man or woman.

The cave's attractions are the stalactites and stalagmites, the fame of which has been well known for centuries. Entrance is alongside a small chapel and modern-day descent into the cave is made rather easier by the deployment of some four hundred concrete steps, in place of the hanging ropes that used to be the *modus operandi*.

FACT FILE
ALTERNATIVE NAMES
Astypalaia, Astypalea, Astipalea

IMPRESSIONS Chapel-like water wells; colourful, purposeful fishing fleet; steps & more steps; fair haired Greeks; aridity.

SPECIALITIES No snakes; curiously elaborate females traditional costume; 'Gasosa' lemonade.

RELIGIOUS FESTIVALS include: 2nd February - Candlemas; 21st May - Saints Constantine & Helen; 2nd July - St Panteleimon; 20th July - Prophet Elijah; 15th August - Dormition of the Virgin; 29th-31st August - Festival & feast, Monastery of St John the Beheaded (west of island).

STATISTICS
Tel prefix 0242. The overall length (or width in this case) is 18km, the greatest width (or depth) is 24km, with an area of some 99sq km. The population numbers about 1,100, of whom 700-800 or so live in Skala Port and or the Chora.

TRANSPORT LINKS
Ferry The comparatively infrequent ferries are met any time of day and night by hotel and Room owners, including some from Livadia.
   Ferries dock two days a week, going on to Amorgos, Naxos, Syros and Piraeus(M), as well as Kalimnos, Kos and Rhodes. One day a week a ferry-boat links with Nisiros and Simi.

Possibly the island's most famous historical and mythological citizen was the disgraced Olympian athlete Kleomedes. During a wrestling competition, in the 71st Olympiad, he killed a competitor with a foul blow, for which Kleomedes was disgraced and deprived of his victory. On his return home he gave the supporting columns of the local school a bear-hug, pulling the roof down, and killed sixty or seventy pupils. The incensed parents sought him out to exact revenge, only to be advised by the Delphic Oracle that Kleomedes had been immortalised.
   The Minoan Cretans had an outpost and the island was written about in glowing terms regarding its fertility. The Romans allowed Astipalaia autonomy, in exchange for the right to take advantage of its strategic position. The Venetians ran affairs during the Middle Ages, were followed by the Turks, between about 1540 and 1912, after which the Italians took over. These latter-day Romans used Astipalaia as a launching pad for the assault on Rhodes, and final domination of the Dodecanese.
   This arid island is popularly described as being shaped like a pair of butterfly wings. This is because the two major land areas are linked by a tiny, narrow neck of land, thinning to less than 300m.
   Astipalaia is administratively incorporated in the Dodecanese,

For greater detail acquire GROC's Candid Guide to The Cyclades Islands

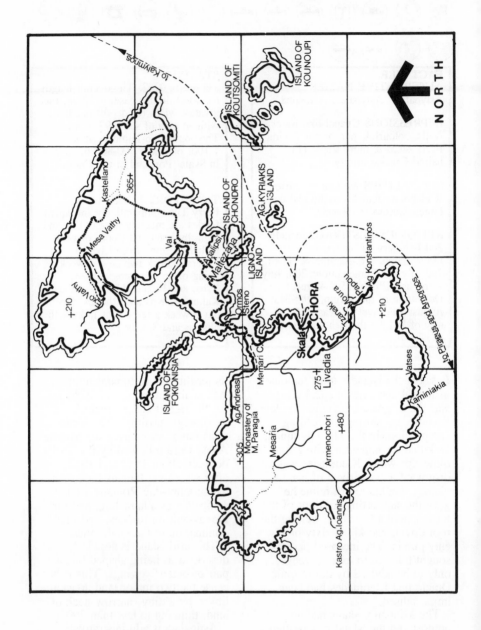

Illustration 15 Astipalaia island

but is almost more Cycladean than many of the other Cyclades islands. Typically the dwellings of the Port corkscrew up to a dramatic Chora, topped off by the remains of a once splendid Venetian castle. Furthermore the ferry-boat connections from the Cycladean outposts are more frequent than those from the Dodecanese islands. Admittedly there is the mandatory Dodecanese style, Italian inspired, colonnaded Municipal building, even if it is rather insignificant.

The few beaches are not golden sand, more grey pebble, a shortcoming more than compensated for by the contented and intrinsically Greek nature of the inhabitants, and their environment.

MAIN PORTS & RESORTS
SKALA The main bustling and noisy port and harbour is dominated by the Kastro topped Chora. The buildings stretch all the way up from the pleasantly scruffy and intimate port, which exhibits few concessions to tourism. Perhaps the most eye-catching sight is the Italian constructed Municipal building. On many islands similar edifices would be tarted up, perhaps even gleaming, but not here.

The port beach is adequate if rather small and scrubbly, consisting of shale and grey pebble. The island's best beaches are generally inaccessible by land.

The port is blessed with acceptable and sufficient hotels, pensions, tavernas and restaurants.

THE CHORA (about 1km from Skala) The capital is a truly Cycladean Chora, divided into the 'Middle' or saddle level, and the Upper Castle level.

The 'Middle' level encompasses the municipal buildings and business life of the Chora, whilst the 'Upper' level is dominated by a heavily restored Venetian Castle. The latter is encircled by a very pretty parade, with an oleander planted walk on the far side. There are masses of churches, higgledy-piggledly, medieval private houses and quite a few discreet bars.

LIVADIA (2km from the Chora) The outset of the road is dominated by eight windmills in fairly good condition and one ruin.

The river-bed 'Highway' is bounded by a wall right up to the beach backshore, the latter forming a tree lined and shaded, grey, rough sand and pebble surfaced 'Esplanade'.

The messy beach is made up of light brown shale and pebbles. The backshore is fringed by a continuous, narrow, but comparatively thick stand of trees. On both sides of the 'Highway', prior to the 'Esplanade', are Rooms, in addition the tavernas.

MALTEZANA (9km from Skala) Upper Maltezana is an untidy sprawl with most of the settlement set in a verdant oasis supporting a widespread farming community. An inordinately large quay juts into a smallish, tree edged bay. There is the semblance of a narrow beach to the left and a stony, grassy sea-bed.

CHAPTER 17

DELOS
(Dhilos, Dilos)

Visitors arrive on a daily excursion trip from Mykonos or Tinos.
The whole island is an immense archaeological site and tourists are not allowed (legally) to stay overnight or camp.
Due to the complexities of the excavations it is probably preferable to join a guided party. The average visitor can only hope, in the short time available, to absorb part of the rarefied atmosphere and wonder at the vast extent of the wild flower and weed bestrewn ruins in which nestle marvellous mosaics, terraces, cisterns and from which sprout rich outcrops of statues, stoas, columns, crepidoma, shrines and altars.

The amazing site includes a sacred harbour and lake; temples to Apollo and the Athenian; houses of the Naxians, Poseidoniasts, Cleopatra, Dionysos, Tritons, Masks and Dolphins; sanctuaries; sacred ways; porticos; the Terrace of Lions; the Theatre, and Mt Kynthos.

CHAPTER 18

DONOUSSA
(The Back Islands)

FACT FILE

ALTERNATIVE NAMES
Dhenoussa, Dhonoussa

IMPRESSION Sandy beaches;
rough donkey tracks; choppy seas.

STATISTICS Tel prefix 0285. The
population is 115 & the island's area
13sq km.

TRANSPORT LINKS
Ferry The larger ferry-boats
dock at the new quay.Smaller
ferries still berth at the old tiny
quay. At least twice weekly, a
local craft links with Amorgos,
Koufonissi, Shinoussa, Iraklia
and Naxos. A ferry connects,
three days a week, to Naxos,
Paros, Syros and Piraeus(M).

The past is tied in with that of
Amorgos and Naxos. In recent history, the island has only been settled for the last couple of hundred
years, when farmers and fishermen
ventured here from Amorgos. Previous to that it was a pirates lair.
Over the past thirty years or so the
population has halved.
 The island finally caught up with
the twentieth century, in the last
decade. Water and electricity were
installed in 1981 and a full-blown
ferry-boat quay, in 1988.
 Donoussa has, to date, remained a relatively little visited,
wild island surrounded by unpre-
dictable seas and currents. It is fre-
quently isolated in the winter
months, sometimes for as long as
15 days at a time, as happened as
recently as 1988. Even in the summer months, the island is prone to
being cut off in adverse weather
conditions. As the modern-day
conveniences were installed, so the
tourists arrived, and enough stop
off nowadays to over-fill the available accommodation, in the peak

season months. Visitors may well
continue to increase as facilities
improve, because the island has
some marvellous, sandy beaches
and, as yet, a delicious flavour
of the Greece of yester-year.

DONOUSSA The main town and
port. The superb, sandy town
beach stretches away around the
bay and there is a sign forbidding
nudism and camping. Those who
want to 'nude', or camp, should
cross the town beach and head up
the concrete path, over the headland, to another excellent, sandy
beach. There are beaches at
Livadia, near the village of **Mersini**, and **Kalotaritissa**. It is a 1½
hour walk to Mersini on the circular donkey path, and a 5 hour
walk to Kalotaritissa.
 . Few of the island's Rooms are
advertised. Neither is there a vast
choice of tavernas or, for that matter, varied menus, but what selection is available is pleasant
enough. The dishes rather depends
on what the boats unload!

For greater detail acquire GROCs Candid Guide to The Cyclades Islands

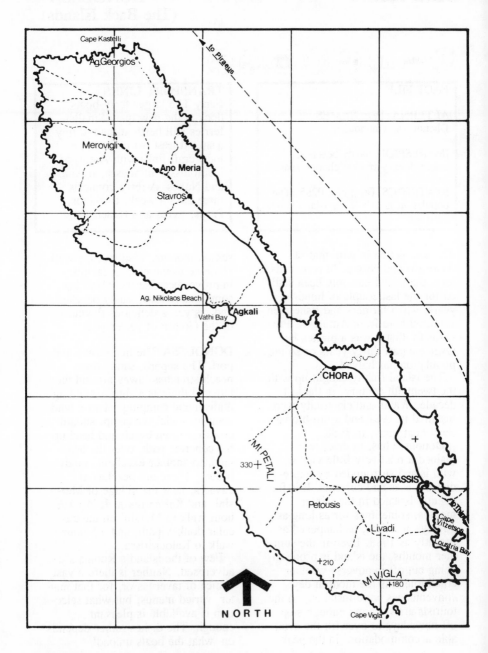

Illustration 16 Folegandros island

CHAPTER 19   FOLEGANDROS

FACT FILE	
ALTERNATIVE NAMES Pholegandros, Polycandros	35sq km. The population numbers some 700, spread between Karavo-stassis' Port, the Chora & the northern settlement of Ano Meria.
IMPRESSIONS Arid, terraced mountain slopes; water short; Danish holiday-makers; no taxis; a 'Santorini' Chora.	**TRANSPORT LINKS** Ferry Ferries connect four days a week with Sikinos and Santorini; three days a week to Ios, Naxos, Paros and Piraeus(M); two days a
SPECIALITIES Koukoulas - distinctive women's hats.	week to Syros; and one day a week to Milos, Siphnos, Serifos, Anafi, Crete, Kasos, Karpathos, Chalki and Rhodes.
STATISTICS Tel prefix 0286. The island is some 12km long, orientated NW/ SE, up to 4km at the widest & under 1km at the narrowest, with an area of about	Some owners of accommodation sidle up to stragglers in the street and buses meet ferry-boat arrivals.

Previous 'owners' were the usual mixture of Cretans, Romans (who used the island as a place of exile), Venetians and Turks.

Folegandros is usually lumped together with Sikinos, at the tail-end of an Ios chapter. This is a travesty. Both islands deserve separate treatment and are almost totally dissimilar. For example, the construction of a 'proper' ferry-boat quay, capable of handling the larger craft, has allowed Folegandros to become a much more sophisticated location than Sikinos, with the to-be-expected increase in the number of tourists. These are supplemented by a series of Danish inspired, teaching holiday-courses, during the months of June, July and August, an influx which has resulted in a comparatively hefty increase in prices.

The 'mains' drinking water is only turned on for a few hours in the morning, a very necessary act of conservation as most of the wells have slimy water.

Despite these irritating short-comings, Folegandros must still rate as one of the more idyllic Cyclades islands. Once away from the simply beautiful and verdant Chora, the remaining countryside and few villages are delightful, agricultural backwoods. The lack of other than generally inferior beaches is more than adequately offset by the island's other attractions. These include the: stunning, 'Santorini-like' scenery to the north of the Chora, the latter being perched precipitously close to the edge of the east coast mountain-sides that plunge steeply into the distant seas; the simple, fishing hamlet of Agkali, nestling at the foot of an almost dry river

---

For greater detail acquire GROC's Candid Guide to The Cyclades Islands

gorge; and **Ano Meria**, the quiet, northern cluster of inland agrarian hamlets, strung along the spine of a mountain range.

A general warning is to note that, outside of the very short summer season (July-September), many of the accommodation and eating places are closed and the bus timetables severely curtailed.

MAIN PORTS & RESORTS
KARAVOSTASSIS The approach to the port, from the direction of Sikinos island, is marked by a number of rocky outcrops. The quay is set in a craggy inlet of a generally untidy bay, with most of the development crammed into a stretch on the right. There is a certain amount of 'creeping infill' round the nearside of the beach. Facilities include a hotel, one taverna, a cafe-bar taverna, a kafeneion, a 'canteen' periptero, but no shops.

The main beach fills the bottom of the small bay, is tree-edged and rather scrubbly with a shore of big pebbles. The first metre of sea-bed is made up of rather slimy stones, beyond which the bottom is sandy and the water very clear.

Karavostassis does not have a surfeit of either accommodation or eating places. The height of summer presence of a disproportionate number of Danes has hardened up prices, especially in the Chora.

Loustria Bay (2km) An unlovely, grey sand and shingle beach alongside a grove of arethemusa bush trees. These groves spread along and shelter the backshore of the beach. The sea bottom is weedy with a tendency to being slimy

and the far end consists of slate stones, pebbles and biscuit rock.

THE CHORA (2½km from Karavostassis) The capital is a Chora of water wells and churches, which may be one of the most beautiful in the Cyclades. There are the inevitable whitewashed buildings and churches but, unusually, the village is spread out. There are two, not one, large squares, both fully shaded by the branches of the numerous trees, which almost form a canopy. The extremely picturesque Old Quarter of the Chora consists essentially of two paved streets that, with the remainder of the Castle wall, form a rectangle enclosing some of the village's oldest houses. These are two storey buildings with external stone staircases to the upper floor front doors.

A number of vantage points on the north side of the Chora allow lovely, 'Santorini-like' views over the terraced slopes that tumble into the sea, way down below.

A fair number of Rooms are available and there are even a hotel or two, as well as a number of excellent kafeneions, cafe-bar restaurants and tavernas.

Agkali Beach (about 2½km from the Chora) The final descent by path from the main road is through massed oleanders, before breaking out on to the scrubbly, coarse sand, pebble littered backshore of the cove. The beach is hemmed in by steep hillsides on either side, edging Vathi Bay, and over which are set a scattering of houses, tavernas and Rooms.

FACT FILE

ALTERNATIVE NAME Nios

IMPRESSIONS Sand, sea, sun, youngsters, fun & discos; wind

SPECIALITIES Homer; chapels; pasteli (sesame cake) & cheese.

RELIGIOUS FESTIVALS include: 22nd June - Festival of St John, Pyrgos; 2nd August - Festival of Ag Theodotis, Psathis Bay; 29th August - Feast & festival of St John (Ag Yiannis), Kalamos Bay; 8th September - Feast & festival of the Virgin, Theodotis Bay.

STATISTICS Tel prefix 0286. The island is 18km in length, up to 10km wide, with an area of about 105sq km. Most of the 1,300 population live in or around the Chora & Gialos Port.

TRANSPORT LINKS

Ferry Not a major Cyclades terminus, but a very important junction, with connections to the most important islands, as well as being a stepping-stone for nearby Sikinos and Folegandros. Ferry-boats link daily with Naxos, Paros, Santorini and Piraeus(M); five days a week to Mykonos; four days a week to Sikinos and Folegandros; three days a week to Syros; two days a week to Tinos, Siphnos and Serifos; and once a week with Milos and Kimolos.

Hydrofoil Five days a week hydrofoils proceed to Paros, Santorini and Crete, and two days a week to Mykonos, and Naxos. The boats are met by more than sufficient owners of accommodation from the Port, Chora and Milopotamos Beach, even late into the night.

The history of Ios followed the pattern of the other, adjacent islands. It was colonised by the Ionians; became a member of the Delian League; endured Egyptian and then Roman rule and, in the Middle Ages, the omnipresent Dukes of Naxos. On the death of one of the Dukes, a son, Marcos, assumed the mantle of suzerainty and built a now long lost castle on 'Chora Hill'. He was an interesting fellow and, to bolster the lack of native muscle, imported a number of Albanians.

In line with general Cycladic history, the Turks took over in

1536/37. In 1558 they razed the island and sold off those inhabitants they could lay their hands on. In 1579 the Turks decided to recolonize the island, once again with Albanians.

For a short time, as elsewhere, the Russians took over, in the 1770s. The islanders joined in the struggle for independence, joining the new Greek state in 1829.

Perhaps the most interesting historical event is the possibility that Homer, shipwrecked on his way from Samos to Athens, died and was buried on the island. A Dutchman landed on Ios in the

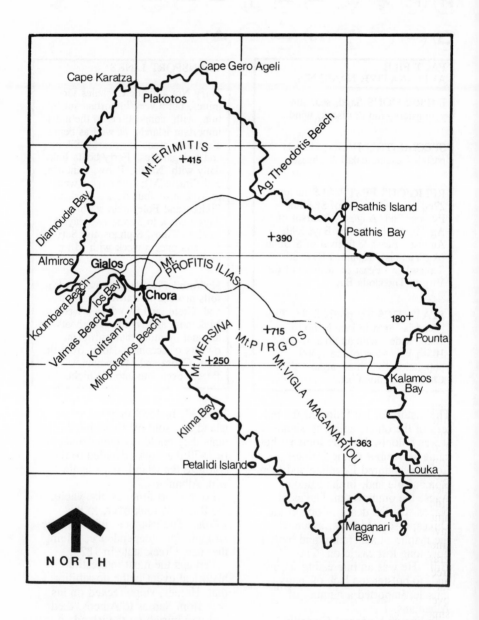

Illustration 17 Ios island

1770s and carried out excavations in the area of **Plakotos**, to the north of the island. He supposedly found Homer's grave, even down to a detailed inscription.

To the present-day visitor it may well seem unbelievable that an earthquake, in 1951, caused Gialos Port to be totally devastated. In fact there was every chance that the island would be deserted. Fortunately the lure of prosperity held the natives rooted to the spot as the 1960s trickle of overseas visitors became a deluge. It is interesting to contemplate that, even in the 1970s, most passengers had to be taken on and off the ferry-boats by caique, and up until 1979/80 only one or two passenger boats docked each week.

MAIN PORTS & RESORTS
GIALOS (Ormos Iou) The island port and harbour, high above which are the white cubes of the Chora, peeping out from around the sides of its hilltop fastness.

On the right of the harbour is a narrow foreshore, cluttered with small boats and benzinas, in various states of decaying repair, and littered with rubbish. A twenty minute, cliff-edge walk away is **Valmas Beach**. The trek ends some way above the nearside of the small, sandy beach, set in the cleft of a cove. On the opposite side is a cluster of buildings amongst which is a small, simple taverna. The narrow Port beach, of fine shingle, backed by scrubbly grass with two separate clumps of trees is round to the left. From the far end, a rough, stony track winds over to **Koumbara Beach**. Here a small chapel edges a rocky bay and beyond a caique mole is a curving cove with a lovely, coarse sand beach. The stony backshore ends in a short isthmus with a low islet seemingly sunbathing in the sparkling sea-water. To the right of the neck of land are a couple of very small, stony and sand coves. The water is clean and crystal clear, the beach is quiet and the needs of the scattered population are catered for by two tavernas.

The ferry-boat quay is conveniently central. Away to the left are a number of Rooms. Straight ahead are a clutch of hotels, travel agents, cafe-bars, tavernas and the Bus turn-round. From the 'Bus' Square, steps and the main road ascends to the Chora, both bordered by a scattering of hotels and Rooms. To the right, round the dock, is a hotel, a couple of pensions and some Rooms, all within 200/300m.

Ag Theodoti Beach The rough, stone path, once only used by the devoted for a particular panayieri, has been engineered sufficiently to accommodate a midsummer, daily 'bus' service. Naturally the promotion of this large bay and valley has ensured that it can now hardly be an isolated find.

Maganari Beach This spot is only accessibly by trip boat, but boasts a hotel, restaurant and disco.

THE CHORA (2km from Gialos Port) Also known as the 'Village' or the 'Jungle'. Even during daylight hours, there is a thinly veiled suggestion of youthful, vibrant energy, a scarcely concealed warning of the frenetic activity that bursts asunder once darkness descends. In the morning hours the majority of visitors sit around at the various cafe-bars. Midday and afternoon, the sun

worshippers tumble down to Milopotamos Beach, to bathe away the
excesses of the night. Even in daylight, almost every other doorway
emits sound and light in varying
degrees of intensity.

Oddly enough, even in this
'jungle' it is only necessary to
climb to the upper reaches of the
village to slip gradually out of the
20th century into the Greece of
old, with donkeys unexpectedly
emerging from picturesque pass-
ageways. The climb up the ever
ascending alleys to the little chapel
that tops the wedding cake of a
town is particularly pleasant.

There are a number of Rooms,
as well as innumerable, if
unmemorable, eating places.

Places of interest include the:-
Ag Gremmiotissa A pleasant,
flagstone yard surrounds the
church, which has an attractive
campanile and a solitary, rather
lean palm tree planted one side of
the whitewash outlined courtyard.

Above Ag Gremmiotissa, on the
way to the topmost chapel, is the
Church of Christ of Castro and on
the very highest, rocky point,
picked out in whitewash, is the:-
Chapel of Ag Elephterios Once
pleasantly decorated by frescoes
but both Elephterios and Castro

have been allowed to fall into disrepair and the interiors are supposed to be ruined. The exteriors
are thick with whitewash.
Windmill Square Once known as
Plateia Plano, or Upper Square,
and originally laid out with circular, paved winnowing ground-
works. The three windmills pres-
ently stand mutely silent on an
unattractive, raised area, now
flanked by two disco bars.

MILOPOTAMOS BAY (3km
from the Chora) The view out over
the bay reveals one of the greatest
sweeps of beach in the Cyclades. It
has to be admitted that the magnificence of the panorama is accentuated by the approach being from
high on the mountainside. The
very wide, long, slow curve of
glorious sand is framed by a
broad, fertile plain, itself bordered
by a large range of mountains and,
on the far side, rocky hillsides
which encircle the bay.

Although, during the height of
summer months, the foreshore
does become almost jam-packed
with sun worshippers, even at its
most crowded, the far end is
usually empty. There are quite a
few hotels and pensions, which
also serve meals, as well as a
taverna or three.

FACT FILE
IMPRESSIONS Tranquillity; remoteness; lack of facilities.

RELIGIOUS FESTIVALS include: 23rd April - Ag Georgios Church, Ag Georgios; 8th November - Taxiarchis Church, Ag Georgios.

STATISTICS Tel. prefix 0285. The area of the island is 17sq km and the population is about 100.

TRANSPORT LINKS
Ferry Fairly well connected, ferry-boats call in five days a week with connections to Amorgos, Naxos, Donoussa, Koufonissi, Shinoussa, as well as Paros, Naxos, Mykonos, Syros and Piraeus(M). Outside of the four week period, between 15th July-15th August, owners of accommodation meet the boats.

Of the four 'Back Islands' of Donoussa, Koufonissi, Shinoussa and Iraklia, this is the least developed, and the quietest. It has two villages, the port Ag Georgios and, inland, the Chora (more generally known as Iraklia or Panaghia). Both have some fifty people each.
A few modern, purpose built Rooms and tavernas provide the only facilities for tourists.

AG GEORGIOS The port, within easy reach of which are two excellent, sandy beaches. One is in the bay and the other is at Livadia, some fifteen minutes walk over the hill.

Livadia Beach is particularly impressive - vast, sandy and practically deserted, with two

tavernas on the backshore.
Between the 15th July and 15th August, the island's thirty rooms are full. There are five tavernas in the port area: three in Ag Georgios and two by Livadia.

THE CHORA (Panaghia/Iraklia) This is a good hour's walk from the Port, up the road which first passes by Livadia beach. The road is paved in parts, not in others. To avoid walking, hitch a lift with one of the tractors/jeeps or take the bread van.
The town stands half-way up the mountain and is a very down-to-earth, whitewashed settlement. The big, white domed church, Panaghia gives the settlement its more usual name. There are two general stores, one kafeneion, but no accommodation or tavernas.

For greater detail acquire GROC's Candid Guide to The Cyclades Islands

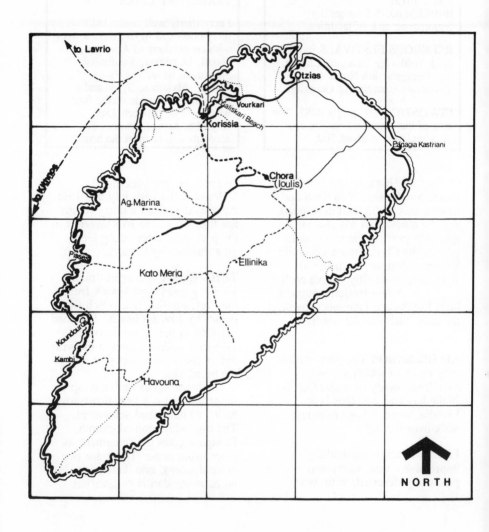

Illustration 18 Kea island

FACT FILE
ALTERNATIVE NAMES Tzia.

IMPRESSIONS Low mountains; buddleia & butterflies; mules & cows; oak trees.

SPECIALITIES Pasteli (bars of sesame seeds & honey).

RELIGIOUS FESTIVALS include: 17th July - Festival, Ag Marina above Pisses; 7th September - Festival, Ag Sostis, Otzias.

STATISTICS
Tel prefix 0288. The pear shaped island is 19km from top to bottom, up to 9 ½km wide, with an area of 121sq km. The population is between 1,600 & 1,700 people.

TRANSPORT LINKS
Ferry There is a daily ferry service to Lavrio(M), and the rumour of a Kithnos link. The boats are rarely, if ever met by Room owners, as most of the proprietors operate through a co-operative.

In vivid contrast to its close neighbour Kithnos, which accrued little history of outstanding note, Kea has a rich and vivid past with a number of ancient city sites. Excavations on the small headland of **Ag Irini**, opposite the fishing port village of Vourkari, have uncovered a Bronze Age settlement and Minoan palace. Apart from poets, a philosopher, a politician and an anatomist of note, the Keans were famous for their athletes. They were also renowned for a simplistic cure for old age when a citizen reached his or her 60th, a dose of hemlock was administered! Korissia yielded up a Kouros which is now in Athens Archaeological Museum and the island's ancient wealth was based on mineral exploitation.

During the War of Independence, a Greek ship's captain wrought havoc against the Turkish Navy. When boxed into the large bay, on which are sited the ports of Korissia and Vourkari, he is supposed to have escaped to the open sea, by dragging his fleet over a shallow neck of land. This rather upset the Turks who promptly burnt Korissia to the ground!

Kea is a lovely island and, in terms of geographical make-up, a smaller version of Andros. In common with Kithnos, Andros and Tinos, lying as it does to one side of the main ferry-boat routes, it has remained remote from the hordes of overseas tourists. In fact, Kea is almost solely the preserve of the Greek holiday-maker. During summer weekends the island is crowded and most of the beds are taken. This pressure is reflected in the islanders' attitudes to visitors, for they are, in the main, disinterested, with a tendency to rudeness. During the week Kea reverts to a sleepy, none-too-busy-location.

The cost of accommodation is high and shopping is expensive.

For greater detail acquire GROC's Candid Guide to The Cyclade Islands

There are a number of far-flung beaches, as well as the most lovely agricultural hillside routes running the length of the island.

MAIN PORTS & RESORTS

KORISSIA The port is a pleasant enough harbour village, even if the beach, at the bottom of the bay, is not very appealing.

Most of the available Rooms are part of a collaborative association and, generally, prices for accommodation and dining out range from the medium to expensive.

Yialiskari Beach (1km from Korissia Port) A very pleasant, popular, small, sandy beach cove backed by verdant groves of gum and tamarisk trees. The foreshore sports some green weed, whilst on the nearside is a beach taverna, a public toilet and tap water. Despite signs forbidding it, a few 'wild' camp at the far end of the beach.

VOURKARI (2½km from Korissia Port) Once a fishing port, but now host to a multitude of motor boats, yachts and a few, very large private caiques, all mooring bow or stern-on to the quay. The right-hand side of the quay is lined by businesses, homes and tavernas.

The busy waterfront forms the through road and the port smart.

Otzias (5½km from Korissia Port) A very pleasant, deeply inset, circular bay with, along the right-hand edge, a narrow, sandy beach, edged by young tamarisk trees. To the left is a wide, coarse sand, rather scrubbly beach with a few rocks dotted about, and some beach shelters.

CHORA (Ioulis) (5km from Korissia Port) The access road decants on to a smart square edged by a Post Office, a pharmacy, a hardware-cum-general-store-cum-drink shop, and a chic restaurant. The covered way from this square, leads to a 'kafeneion cluttered' junction with the Chora 'High' Street. To the left, progresses through the remnants of the old Kastro walls to a hotel. To the right ascends the steeply rising main street, past a large, three storey Museum and an impressive 'comic opera' Town Hall. This latter municipal edifice really is an extraordinary building with a kafeneion in the basement and the roof-top balcony pedestals topped off by rows of small statues. There are a couple of acceptable hotels, some rustic kafeneions and a few restaurant/tavernas.

FACT FILE
The island has an area of 36sq km, a population of about 1,000. The name is the Greek for chalk.

TRANSPORT LINKS
Ferry Weather permitting , a caique daily shuttles back and forth to Pollonia (Milos). During in-different conditions, it is more reliable to catch the inter-island ferry. One day a week scheduled boats link with Siphnos, Serifos, Kithnos, Syros, Folegandros, Sikinos, Ios, Santorini, Rafina(M) and Piraeus(M).

How the beautifully simple, lovely island of Kimolos can have remain-ed unsung for so long is a mystery. Even the local, Milos island guide, which comments on all the neigh-bouring islets, give Kimolos no more than a passing mention.

The island has been the scene of much mining activity in the past, but somehow less intrusively than at Milos. The low, chalky white cliff-faces manifest the occasional evidence of quarrying and shore-to-ship loading gear. Originally chalk was extracted, but a crushed stone used for chemical purposes is still excavated.

At **Palaiokastro,** on the west coast side are the remains of a Venetian castle and an old church; to the north-east is **Klima** hamlet and at **Prassa** (about 6½km), there are a beach and sulphur springs.

PSATHI The port is set in compa-ratively gentle hills, the middle of the range being crowned by the Chora. To the right of centre, the peaks are spotted with windmills.

Ferry-boats dock at the end of the small quay, to the extreme right of the lovely harbour cove. The inter-island caique berths at about the middle of the quayside.

Stretching along the rest of the bay, to the west, is a pebble beach backed by a scattering of trees and buildings. The first section has a narrow concrete track, up against which is a kafeneion-cum-store.

CHORA (Kimolos) (A twenty minute walk from Psathi Port) This mountainside village is a crumbling, twisting, confusing maze of lanes and alleys, which often end above a ruin, or in a backyard animal enclosure. There are a number of lovely old chur-ches, some Rooms, two tavernas and one kafeneion.

Above the Chora are six wind-mills, one of which is still in wor-king order.

OUPA A twenty minute descent from the Chora falls to this stunn-ingly beautiful, if rudimentary hamlet. The bottom of the cove is riven by a narrow band of sand enabling bathers to walk painlessly into the sea. There aren't any Rooms, tavernas or even a kafeneion, but what an absolutely delightful spot to while away all or part of a day.

For greater detail acquire GROC's Candid Guide to The Cyclades Islands

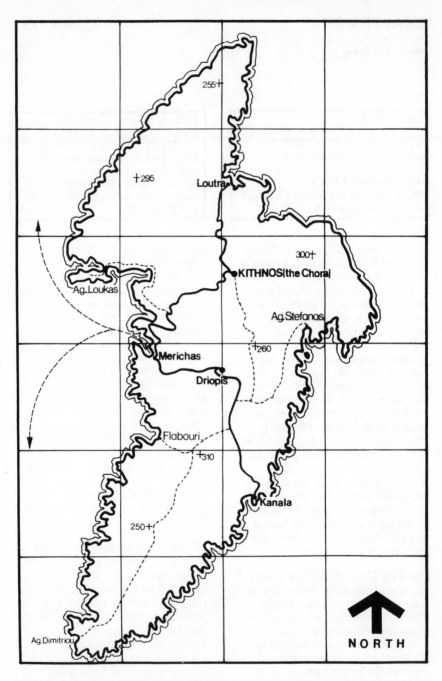

Illustration 19 Kithnos island

FACT FILE

ALTERNATIVE NAMES
Kythnos, Thermia

IMPRESSIONS
A Greek holiday island; friendly inhabitants.

SPECIALITIES
Basket weaving; cheese.

RELIGIOUS FESTIVALS include:
8th September - Festival, Monastery Panaghia, Kanala (SE coast).

STATISTICS Tel prefix 0281. Kithnos is 22½km from top to bottom & at the widest part 11¼km across, with an area of 86sq km. The population is about 1,500.

TRANSPORT LINKS
Ferry Boats link with Serifos, Siphnos, Milos and Lavrio(M) six days a week; Piraeus(M) five days a week; Kimolos four days a week; Syros and Rafina(M) two days a week; and Kea, Tinos and Andros one day a week. The boats are not met by owners of accommodation.

Apart from the usual Cycladean story, the island's history reveals nothing outstanding.

A comparatively small, dry and arid island. Apart from the river-beds and valleys, there are no out-standing features or out-of-the-ordinary beauty. In common with a number of other islands close to the mainland, Kithnos is almost solely the preserve of holiday-making Greeks. The latter presents accommodation problems, for visitors in the peak summer period, and more especially weekends.

The other island villages include the attractive fishing port of Lou-tra, the small residential beach re-sort of Kanala as well as the un-distinguished inland settlements of the Chora (Kithnos) and **Driopis**. Kithnos is sometimes water-short but the listed times and places when the hydrants are turned on do not seem to tie up with any of the island locations!

MERICHAS The port of Merichas was once a small hamlet with a few, old, red-tile roofed buildings scattered along the backshore. Now it is crowded out by small, round edged, cubic dwellings, dominated by a six storey hotel, at the far west side of the bay.

There is a rather frontier town atmosphere, accentuated by the makeshift character of the unsur-faced tracks that spread out around the bay. The 'Esplanade' con-stantly remains in danger of being completed and tidied up, despite being in part, nothing more than a cleared swathe. The narrow, tree edged, dirty, grey coarse sand beach is scrubbly and much of the backshore is piled high with build-ing materials, shale and lumps of concrete. Additionally the sea bottom is made up of slimy pebbles covered with weeds.

A number of fjord-like bays with beaches lie north of the port, to

For greater detail acquire GROC's Candid Guide to The Cyclades Islands

which a small, blue hulled cabin boat runs a water-taxi service. The first of these beaches is a five minute walk along the Chora road, from whence a path and steps angle down to the very pleasant, narrow, coarse sand cove set at the end of a fertile valley. Beside the path are Rooms.The beach is planted with small arethemusa trees, which shade a few tents. The grey, coarse sand beach is in surprisingly good condition, considering the presence of the 'wild' campers. The sea edge is biscuit rock, except at the far side, but the quickly shelving sea-bed is sandy. A taverna has an accessible toilet and serves the usual fare. To the right is the small islet of **Ag Loukas** which is attractively connected to the 'mainland' by a narrow neck of sand and is a worthwhile destination, using the water-taxi.

Even the Greeks are asked to vacate their Rooms over weekends and accommodation is often booked by long standing holidaymakers, from one year to the next. No one establishment redeems the ports lack of any gastronomic excellence.

KITHNOS (The Chora) (5km from Merichas Port) Set on a high, rolling, inland agricultural plain, but lacking the traditional white washed, hill-capping beauty usually associated with the 'standard model' Chora.

There is no accommodation but the village is well resourced with shops, several kafeneions and a smart taverna, all widely spaced out throughout the settlement.

LOUTRA (8km from Merichas Port) This truly natural, 'lovely' fishing village, inhabited by

friendly people, is situated on an attractive bay, at the end of a wide river valley. The site has been a spa since ancient times, hence the name Loutra, derived from the word for bath ('Lutra').

The left-hand horn of the bay has a bluff dominated by a white wall enclosed church, an old mining jetty and the ruins of a castle, beyond which is a small cove. To the right-hand side of the bay is a continually running, warm, brown coloured stream that bubbles over a wide, stony riverbed, edged and contained by a low concrete border. The beach stretches away to the right and the backshore is bordered by a large area of waste ground. The centre section of the foreshore is made up of fine pebbles and the sea bottom is sandy, whilst at the far end, by the stream outfall, the beach is coarse sand and pebbles.

Apart from a spa-hotel, there are Rooms and eating places.

KANALA (8km from Merichas Port) Not at all typical, this neat, verdant, modern holiday resort, with a few Rooms, sits on top of a tongue of headland, flanked by a bay to either side. Flowers, trees and roses bedeck the gardens.

The left-hand, small cove is coarse sand and pebbles, with biscuit rock at the sea's edge, and a sandy sea bottom. To the right-hand is a very small, generally crowded cove with a tiny, rock edged, sandy beach. Beyond this, and a rocky outcrop, is a large spread out bay with a narrow, sandy, fine shingle beach, and some buildings behind the wall edged backshore. The latter include a Pension, cafe-bar and breakfast restaurant.

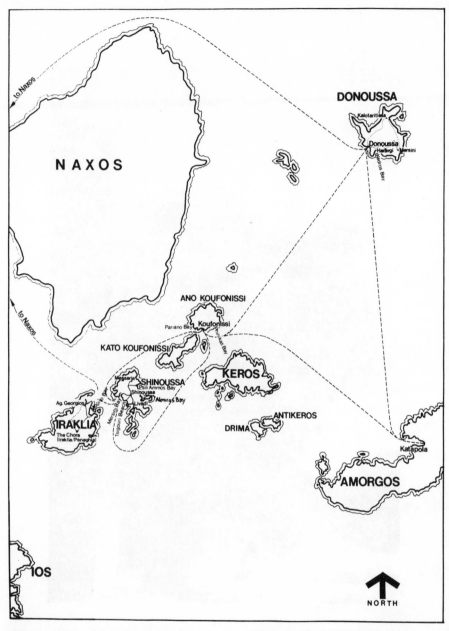

Illustration 20 The Back islands - Koufonissi, Donoussa, Shinoussa Iraklia

FACT FILE	STATISTICS Tel. prefix 0285.

FACT FILE

ALTERNATIVE NAMES
Koufonisia, Koufonisi

IMPRESSIONS Sandy beaches; flat countryside; caiques anchored in the bay, not at the jetty; windy.

RELIGIOUS FESTIVALS include:
23rd April - Panaghia, Ag Giorgios.

STATISTICS Tel. prefix 0285.
Koufonissi has a population of 240, (the adjacent island of Kato Koufonissi 10.) Koufonissi is flat & low lying with an area of 3.8sq km.

TRANSPORT LINKS
Ferry Ferries dock four days a week with links to Amorgos, Shinoussa, Iraklia, Naxos, Paros, Mykonos, Syros and Piraeus(M).

The generic name Koufonissi covers two small islands. Ano (upper) Koufonissi has the majority of the inhabitants, all of them concentrated in the town of Koufonissi, which is close to the ferry-boat quay. Kato (lower) Koufonissi is almost deserted but has three small beaches and lots of fish. Fishing boats cross the narrow channel to Kato Koufonissi.

Ano Koufonissi lacks anything approaching a mountain, even a hill, and its thriving population. These advantages are coupled to a flourishing fishing fleet of some forty caiques.

The island has around two hundred beds, and the number is growing rapidly, despite which, scarcity of rooms, and even food, are not unknown during July and the first two weeks of August.

KOUFONISSI The capital and port. The port beach looks good, being long and sandy, but it is nothing in comparison to the string of three, sandy beaches which stretch along at Phinikas Bay.

There are Rooms beside the main street into the heart of the settlement, as well as pensions behind the port beach. The tavernas are concentrated around the back of the beach and along the main street of the town. Prices are reasonable, as is fish, but the menu depends on the boats. In the peak months some tavernas run out of food, later on in the evening.

Phinikas Beach A rough, unpaved road leads over the low rise from Koufonissi Port to the beaches - about a 20 minute walk. Some scant shade is provided by low trees, and 'wild' campers abound. With the latter in mind, the owner of the first backshore taverna has thoughtfully erected free showers and toilets up against the backshore of the beach.

Accommodation is available in the two large, blue and white arched tavernas.

More sandy beaches can be found at **Poriou,** which are accessible by unpaved road.

For greater detail acquire GROC's Candid Guide to The Cyclades Islands

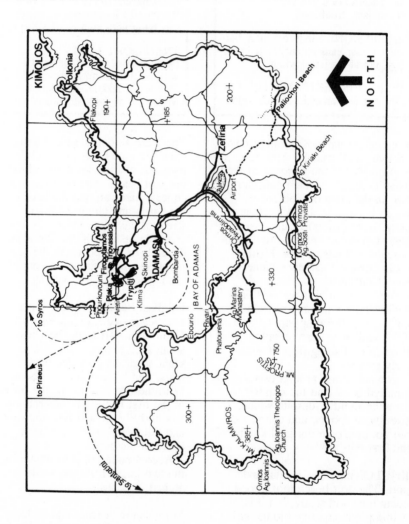

Illustration 21 Milos island

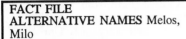

FACT FILE
ALTERNATIVE NAMES Melos, Milo

IMPRESSIONS Attractive sea approach; dramatic coastline; the island appears to be under reconstruction by mining & quarrying; saline water; old men's attire includes a cummerbund.

SPECIALITIES Venus de Milo; mining; hot thermal springs.

RELIGIOUS FESTIVALS include: 7th May - Feast & Festival, Church Ag Ioannis Theologos (south-west of island); 8th September - Feast of Birth of Virgin Mary, Church Panaghia Korfiatissa (Plaka).

STATISTICS Tel prefix 0287. The island has an area of about 160sq km, is roughly 20km wide, 13km deep & would resemble a flattened circle, if it were not for the huge horseshoe bay that almost divides the island in two. The population numbers between 4500 & 5000.

TRANSPORT LINKS
Air The small, dusty airstrip and a collection of 'large garden sheds' lies about 4½km from Adamas. There are at least two flights a day to and from Athens.

Ferry The ferry-boats run down the east shoreline of the very large Adamas Bay. To the right, about 8km offshore, is the comparatively large, uninhabited island of **Antimilos**, a sanctuary for chamois. The boats cut in between the untenanted, inshore islets of **Akradies** and Milos island. They steam past some fascinating geological formations, as well as the colourful, picturesque, 'Venetian' fishing hamlets of **Phourkovouni**, **Areti**, **Klima** and **Skinopi**. The buildings of these settlements cling so low to the waters edge that an onlooker can only marvel that the wash of the larger boats doesn't swamp them. These 'ports' are only inhabited during the summer months, the citizens returning to the Plaka for the winter. Ferries connect to Piraeus (M) six days a week; Siphnos, Serifos and Kithnos four days a week; Kimolos three days a week; Folegandros and Santorini two days a week; and Syros, Rafina (M), Sikinos, Ios, Anafi, Crete, Kasos, Karpathos and Rhodes one day a week.

The ferry-boats dock at a large quay and are met by any number of hotel and Room owners.

The nature of the rocks and the huge Adamas Bay indicates that an ancient volcanic eruption tore the centre out of the island.

Milos served as an important Minoan outpost, and has been mined and quarried throughout the centuries. The obsidian, a glassy, volcanic stone, was used for all manner of implements (including knives as well as spear and arrow heads), prior to perfection of the treatment of metal ore. Apart from the mining activities, the

---

history has tended to follow the Cycladean historical 'norm'.
The association with Venus often misleads visitors into believing that this most southerly island of the Western Cyclades will be 'a jewel in the Aegean Sea'. But Milos is not everyone's dream, having been constantly mined for thousands of years. The main port and town of Adamas lies on the edge of the huge, but not very attractive bay. Advantages are that the islanders are very friendly; much of the countryside not being quarried is fertile; there are some superb beaches, more especially on the south coast; it is very easy to escape the height of season hordes; and accommodation is plentiful, even in August.

MAIN PORTS & RESORTS
ADAMAS The sprawling main town and a rather dusty, unattractive mishmash of a port. Set in a ring of hills and with a southerly aspect, if there is no wind, the settlement becomes hot and sticky.
With so much waterfront it would be nice if there were glorious beaches, but there aren't. To the west of the ferry-boat quay is a small cove, bordered by a plethora of new hotels and a ''Village' complex. The backshore of the coarse sand beach is pleasantly tree shaded but the sea bottom becomes rather weedy. East from Adamas, a narrow shoreline edges the bay.
Accommodation, does not pose a problem, even in the month of August, on the other hand there aren't many decent eating places.

Places of interest include the:-
The Catholic Church The tiny building lies neatly 'snuggled' in and around by surrounding houses. West of Adamas, is a monument to

French sailors killed in the Crimean War.
Round island trip A tour office runs a boat that circumnavigates the island.

TRYPITI (6km from Adamas Port) Here are windmills, an Ancient Theatre and very early Christian catacombs dating back to the 1st century AD.

PLAKA (6km from Adamas Port) The Plaka is an absolute pedestrian maze, with a couple of friendly cafe-bar tavernas, and Rooms.

Paliochori Beach (9km from Adamas Port) Encircled by extensively quarry- scarred countryside which, with the shack-like nature of some of the buildings, imparts a 'frontier feel'. There is a large, central, clean beach of grey sand with a pebble sea's edge and two wing coves. A couple of tavernas and three or more Rooms encircle the surrounds.

Ag Kiriaki Beach (10km from Adamas Port) The beach is wide and sandy and sits between two low-lying hills, with a few houses in the background, one being a taverna and another offering accommodation.

POLLONIA (9 ½km from Adamas Port) A pretty, typical, quiet fishing port set in a small, semi-circular bay, with the hamlet and quay to the right. Centre is a narrow, tree-lined, sandy beach running around to the left of the bay, on the far horn of which are a surprising number of Greek villas and holiday homes.
Pollonia has plenty of Rooms and some dining places.

FACT FILE ALTERNATIVE NAMES Myconos, Mikonos, Miconos

IMPRESSIONS Wind; rubbish; discos; tourists; numerous chapels; stone walls; stony countryside dotted with (ugly) modern 'Mykonos style' buildings; wells; red as well as blue domed churches; wind-swept south coast.

SPECIALITIES Almond sweetmeats; Louza-seasoned & smoked rabbit meat; hand-woven items; manganese ore; *Kopanisti*, a very creamy, pungent cheese.

RELIGIOUS FESTIVALS include: 20th July - to celebrate the Prophet Elias; 15th August - Virgin Mary, Tourliani Monastery, Ano Mera; 29th August - St John the Baptist.

STATISTICS Tel prefix 0289. The island is some 18km from west to east, 12½km north to south, with an area of about 75sq km & a population of 4000.

TRANSPORT LINKS

Air Apart from numerous domestic connections, some daily international flights land. There are at least seven flights a day to Athens; one a day to Rhodes and Santorini; a flight six days a week to Crete; and two days a week to Chios, Lesbos and Samos. Mykonos Town is about 3km distant. The Olympic bus and taxis run into town.

Ferry Boats connect every day with Piraeus(M), Paros, Tinos and Syros; six days a week with Rafina(M) and Andros; and at least once a week with Naxos, Santorini, Anafi and Ag Nikolaos(Crete).

Hydrofoil A service calls two days a week continuing on to Paros, Ios, Santorini and Crete.
Disembarking travellers have to run the gauntlet of throngs of islanders frantically thrusting details of accommodation in their faces.

Possibly due to the proximity of Delos, Mykonos does not receive many early historical mentions. The islanders gained infamy by siding with the Persians, during the wars with the Athenians, between 500 BC and 480 BC. These culminated in famous Greek victories on land, at Marathon, and at sea, in the naval battle of Salamis. Mykonos followed the historical path of a number of Cycladean islands joining, or being 'co-opted', into the Delian League, a set-up organised by Athens.

After the eclipse of the Athenian empire and absorption into the Macedonian Kingdom, Mykonos followed the general drift of the regions. The Romans slowly gained the ascendency from about the last century BC, until the fourth century AD. As a result of the void created by the collapse of the Roman dominion, there was a fair amount of piratical rape and

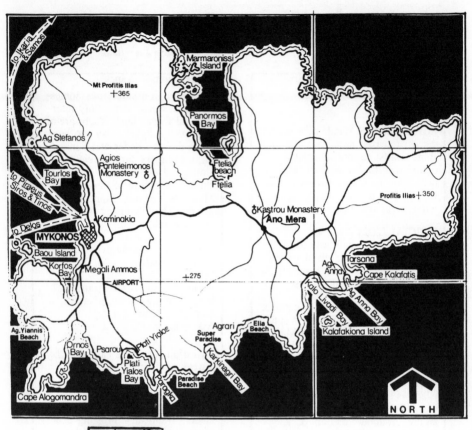

Illustration 22 Mykonos & Rheneia islands

pillage, although the Byzantine Empire was nominally in control.

The Venetians took over in the early 12th century, but power was wrested from them, in 1537, when the Turk Barbarossa invaded. During the Turkish occupation, the islanders expanded their fleets and piracy became an island occupation, even an enterprise. The islanders' skills and wealth were put to good use when the Mykoniots threw their energy into the Greek War of Independence (1821-1828). They contributed some 22 ships armed with a total of 132 cannon. The overall change in emphasis and direction of the shipping world resulted, here as elsewhere in the Aegean, in a general and steady decline of the island's wealth and population. This downward trend reached its nadir by 1950. Then, from being nothing more than a 'stepping stone' to the archaeological riches of adjacent Delos, the naive, simple, white cubist simplicity of Mykonos port and Chora, combined with some relatively far-flung but gloriously sandy beaches, came to the attention of European sophisticates. They were followed by the rich, 'beautiful people' who were, in their turn, succeeded by a train of more mundane vassals.

Visitors should not forget to pack their glad-rags. Evenings in Mykonos Town are spent parading the Esplanade.

MAIN PORTS & RESORTS

MYKONOS The capital and port is one of the few Cycladean island Chora's set in comparatively flat surrounds, not winding up the contours of a steep hillside with the town perched atop. Almost the whole town is a startlingly colourful, dazzlingly white and cubist Chora, with a multitude of whitewashed lanes, steps and houses. The port area/harbour Esplanade is, in stark contrast to the Chora, disappointingly grubby and unattractive.

To the north of the town is a delightful, narrow, small but very sandy beach. At the height of the season it must be very, very crowded but early and late in the year has surprisingly few visitors.

Unless pre-booked, this really is an island to avoid in the months of July, August and September and then the choice is whether to stay in the Chora or head for the country locations, where it is quieter, and cheaper. Equally expensive is eating out, the portions are generally small and restaurants and tavernas fill comparatively early, due to the press of tourists being topped up with cruise-liner passengers. Snackbar prices are reasonable.

Places of interest include the:-
Paraportian Church A most unusual, whitewashed structure cobbled together from four separate chapels, and situated on the Kastro bluff.
Ag Kyriaki Just off the Esplanade and possessed of some old icons.
Eklissoula Ton Ghatlou More colloquially known as the 'Church of the Cat'.

Other religious buildings are the: **Metropolis Cathedral** - Orthodox faith; **Catholic Church** - blue domed and white walled; **The Four Gossiping Churches** - quaintly named, if nothing else; and **Koutsomboles Church** - known as the Four Churches.
Delos island Undeniably top of the excursion hit parade. *See* the Delos island chapter.

For greater detail acquire CROC's Candid Guide to The Cyclades Islands

Archaeological Museums Towards the eastern end of the port. Five small rooms display, amongst other items, an unusual collection of ancient vases and pithoi.

Folklore Museum A square, white-washed, 18th century mansion with contrasting wooden shutters and doors, an external staircase and a low, curved roof building butted on the side.

Naval Museum Adjacent to the Popular Museum, close by the Three Wells fountain.

Popular Art Museum In the Galatis or Venetian Mansion.

Tria Pigadia or Three Wells Three carved fountain heads sited on the right of a picturesque lane.

Harbour Esplanade The wide, curved, paved, pedestrian only waterfront is where the majority of the action takes place.

Attractive spots take in:-
Alefkandra Popularly known as the Venice Quarter, the houses of which unevenly edge the sea with their dissimilar, railed and roofed balconies projecting over the water. Further south and over-looking this beautiful spot is the:-
Plateia Milon A 'Windmill Square' on which four, now disused, round, mill buildings, with their forever still, projecting, circular sail frameworks. I write disused, but they are occasionally turned on for the benefit of summer tourists but only the sails rotate, there being no internal workings.

Another Mykonos sight is:-
Petros The island pelican, but not the original bird.

TOURLOS (2km from Mykonos Town) A broad bay with coarse sand coves, and several hotels.

AG STEFANOS (4km from Mykonos Town) A 'chatty', busy, coarse sand beach, with a plush hillside hotel and three restaurants edging the backshore, at the far end. The foreshore is kelpy and Ag Stefanos is on the aircraft flight path. Other 'attractions' include pedaloes, Rent-A-Bike, Rooms and, on the right, a hotel.

Ftelia Beach (5km from Mykonos Town) The large, indented Bay of Panormos on the north coast, skirted by many chapels, is as attractive as the landward is forgettable. The right-hand side is mucky, but to the left there is a very pleasant, clean, coarse sand beach (often spoiled by the presence of some tar). This sweeps round to a pleasant restaurant.

Along the south coast are:
Elia Beach (8km from Mykonos Town) The lovely, broad, coarse sand beach is surrounded by hillsides. The foreshore is clean, despite some scattered kelp. There are a couple of tavernas to the left of the track that runs out on the backshore of the beach.

Kalo Livadi Beach (10km from Mykonos Town) The beach is very long, pleasant and sandy.

Tarsana Beach (12km from Mykonos Town) A long, clean, coarse sand beach, with some kelp which slowly curves around the clear sea's edge of the bay.
    To the far left is an extremely expensive hotel, constructed in a series of cubes up the foothill of the backing hillside.

Ag Anna Beach (12km from Mykonos Town) Not the Paradise

beach Ag Anna, but a small bay and fine shingle beach, with a line of tar and some kelp bordering the sparkling sea. The location is rather ramshackle.

Psarou Beach (4km from Mykonos Town) The coarse sand beach is scattered with straw sun umbrellas and deck chairs. At the far end of the cove is a beach taverna. Water sports include hang-gliding, wind-surfing and pedaloes. There is a smart milieu to this location which is fairly crowded, even early and late in the year.

Plati Yialos Beach (4km from Mykonos Town) The near end of the beach is 'planted' with beach umbrellas and deck chairs, the whole edged with bar/taverna/restaurants. An expensive feel, no water sports and crowded, even early and late in the summer. To

the right, around a low cliff-edge, is a jetty from which there are 'continuous' daily boat trips to **Paragka, Paradise Beach, Super Paradise Beach, Agrari** and **Elia** beaches. **Paradise Beach** Here nude bathing is allowed. There is a very popular taverna, the acclaim of which is well founded.

Super Paradise Beach The majority of the more unusual, if 'beautiful' young men sunbathe and disport themselves in the nude.

Ornos Beach (3½km from Mykonos Town) The coarse sand beach, is edged by a number of taverna/restaurants and a couple of hotels.

Excursion to: Rheneia Island Some Mykonos (and Tinos) travel agencies run day-trips to Rheneia, a completely uninhabited island to the west of Delos.

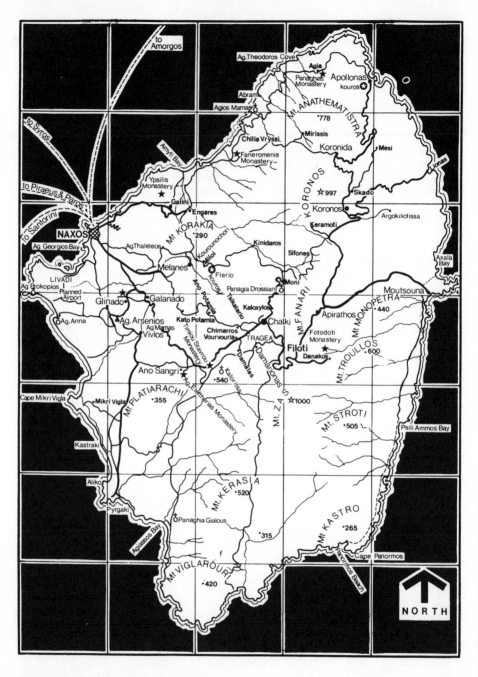

Illustration 23 Naxos island

FACT FILE
IMPRESSIONS Venetian towers; tourist development; river-beds & waterfalls of oleanders cascading down the mountainsides.

SPECIALITIES *Kitron* liqueur (made from lemon tree leaves); white *Promponas* wine; Naxos sausage (tasting like a shish-kebab); emery.

STATISTICS The largest of the Cyclades, the island is 32km long & 24½km wide, with an area of 428 sq km. The population totals about 14,000, of which Naxos Town contains some 3,700.

RELIGIOUS FESTIVALS include: 10th February - Festival of St Charalampos, Angidia; 25th March - Festival of Evangelismou, Chalki; 23rd April - Festival of St George at Kinidaros & Potamia; Friday after Easter - Procession & pilgrimage of the Virgin of the Life-Giving Spring (Zoodochos Pighi), Koronos; 14th July - Religious procession & festival of St Nikadimos, Naxos Town; first

week August - Festivals & folk dances (dating back to the pagan cult of Dionysus).

TRANSPORT LINKS
Air The continued construction of an airfield will result in a regular domestic service.

Ferry Although Naxos is not quite such an important terminus as say, Paros, it is the spring-board for the scattered Eastern Cycladic islands of Iraklia, Shin-oussa, Koufonissi, Donoussa, Amorgos and Astipalaia. Ferry-boats connect daily to Piraeus (M); five days a week with Iraklia, Shinoussa, Koufonissi, Donoussa, Amorgos, Mykonos and Rafina(M); two days a week to Sikinos and Folegandros; with one boat a week to Astipalaia, Kalimnos, Kos and Rhodes.

Hydrofoil Two days a week the service docks to continue on to Ios, Santorini and Crete.

The ferries are met by a respectable number of accommodation owners, and the bus.

Mentioned by Homer (Zia or Zeus Island). Its mythological fame is due to Theseus, an Athenian hero and slayer of the Minotaur, leaving his lover, Ariadne, on the island whilst she was asleep. Ariadne, a Cretan princess and half-sister to the Minotaur, had aided Theseus to defeat the mysteries of the labyrinth. For whatever reason, she was abandoned, Dionysus Bacchus

(the god of wine) arrived on the scene and they fell in love. The Cretans were early inhabitants.

By the 7th century BC, Naxos marble was being sculpted for export far and wide. For instance the Delos Lions were created on the island, as were numerous Kouros (male statues). The 6th century BC ushered in a period of great affluence, despite which the

---

For greater detail acquire GROC's Candid Guide to The Cyclades Islands

islanders fell foul of internal strife. The island joined the Delian League but, on trying to resign, was taken over by Athens. From then on Naxos slipped into obscurity, a state of affairs that lasted until the arrival of the Venetians.

Marco Sanudo, a Venetian, established a strong family dynasty that lasted for 359 years, until the Turks captured the island. The Russians briefly ousted the Turks, but only for four years, between 1770-1774. The Turks regained their possession until the Greek War of Independence (1821-1827), after which Naxos joined the united nation.

Because of the island's mineral and agricultural resources, Naxos did not have to woo tourists. However, it has now jumped on the holiday bandwagon and tourist complexes are springing up all along the south-west coast, as well as at Apollonas.

MAIN PORTS & RESORTS
NAXOS The capital town and port is a busy, commercial seaport, with holiday resorts on either side. The one at the north end is still fairly small - more a residential suburb than a rowdy, package tour complex. However, the small town to the south, springing up behind Ag Georgios Beach is a veritable warren of holiday accommodation, both completed and under construction. It is now truly a tourist 'new town', with all the facilities, even a conference centre. Behind the waterfront an extensive, almost medieval Old Quarter stretches up the hillside. No whitewash here but, sadly, the shops and facilities are changing their character to satisfy 20th century demands.

Not only does Naxos town

possess one of the finest beaches of any Cycladic island, but the south-west coast of the island is almost one long, sandy beach. The town's prize is Ag Georgios Beach, bordered, at the near end, by package holiday hotels. This is a long, curving, sandy bay with a gently shelving sea bottom and very clear water, the first section of which is edged by a wall and a few spindly trees.

Possibly no other major island settlement is able to offer as much accommodation as Naxos but, due to the maze-like nature of the Old Quarter, locating many of the Rooms requires diligence. A number of the Esplanade cafe-bars, tavernas and restaurants present 'numbered' breakfasts.

Places of interest include:-
The Church of Myrtidiotissa Possibly the first island church seen by a visitor, as the little chapel picturesquely sits on a tiny islet to one side of the harbour.
The Catholic Cathedral A lovely building with a boldly domed roof in the rather small, claustrophobic Kastro square. It is located within the old walls, still only breached by the original gateways.
The Kastro There is not much of the original castle left. The only real evidence is the Venetian houses. Many of these, still emblazoned with heraldic devices, are built into the old walls, forming a picturesque ring of medieval buildings. Within these is a beautiful area, a jumble of paved streets, an ancient cistern, the Cathedral, the Museum, the Palace of Sanudo and other attractive buildings.
Chora The Old Quarter is quite extensive, radiating out from the epicentre of the steep, hilltop Kastro, around which the lanes,

alleys and arched walkways wind.
Museum It is rather tucked away
to the right of the Cathedral on the
main Kastro walkway. Now open,
after some years of restoration.
Temple It prominently caps **Palatia**
islet, around which the ferry-boats
steam. Not so much a temple,
more a single gateway, reputably
of the Temple of Apollo.

Abram Beach (20km from Naxos)
On the north-west coast. In the
summer-time, the river of this
agricultural valley is almost
stagnant. A chapel overlooks the
pebble beach and a sandy backshore, as does a pension.

APOLLANAS (30km from Naxos
Town) Situated on a northern bay
sheltered by high mountainsides,
this was once a lovely, sleepy,
archetypal island fishing boat
port. Unfortunately it is fast becoming a resort in its own right,
with vast amounts of building work
taking place.
 The bay is split into two by a
rocky projection, on which are
built four changing rooms. To the
right, is the main, wide, shingly
beach, with some kelp, stretching
away to the far edge of the bay.
The port and a small, sandy beach
are to the left. There is plenty of
overnight accommodation, with
Rooms to be found in most of the
back streets, as well as at least
three hotels. The Esplanade hosts
a minimum of four tavernas.

LIONAS (44km from Naxos
Town) Located on the north-east
coast. An oleander planted river-
bed tumbles down a steep gorge.

The beach at the bottom of the bay
is made up of large pebbles.

Ag Anna Beach (12km from
Naxos Town) Situated on the
south-west coastline. The lane
widens out and spills on to the
sandy, rather bedraggled, narrow
waterfront of this quaintly ethnic
location. Apart from a hotel, there
are several tavernas and over the
sand dunes to the south, a taverna
and unofficial campsite.
 The curving, narrow, sandy
foreshore, which doubles up as an
'Esplanade', stretches away to the
north of the quay, all the way back
to **Ag Prokopios**, some 3½km
from Naxos Town. To the south of
the quay, the bay curves quite
sharply around to a low headland
hill, topped by a small chapel.
This almost creates a lagoon, the
beach of which is sandy, if messy.
Continuing south along the rough
track, spills on to an immense
sweep of sandy beach, backed by
tufted sand dunes in which are set
clumps of low trees and gorse.
Effectively this stretches all the
way from the north, as far as
Pyrgaki, in the south-west, with
the occasional headland protruding
into the Aegean sea.

Pyrgaki Beach (21½km from
Naxos Town) The rocky coastline
is interspaced by three coves, the
first two pebbly, the last smaller
but sandy. This is more a map
place name, than a settlement,
despite which there is a very
smart, multi-cellular, elaborate
holiday complex set into the
sloping, arid hillside.

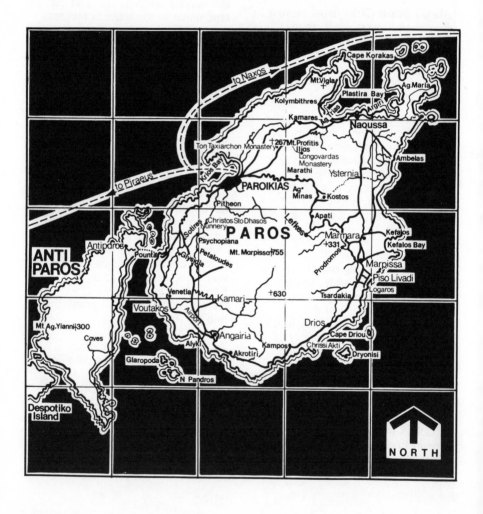

Illustration 24 Paros island

FACT FILE

IMPRESSIONS Travel agents & tourist offices; port bustle of ferry-boats; English spoken; Old Quarter; lack of mountains; cultivated countryside; indented coastline.

SPECIALITIES Marble quarrying; a red wine; agriculture.

RELIGIOUS FESTIVALS include: July - Festival of fish & wine; 23rd August - Festival, Naoussa; 24th September - Feast & festival, Panaghia Myrtidiotissa Thapsanon, Mt Ag Pantes.

STATISTICS Tel prefix 0284. The island is 21km from north-east to south-west & up to 16 ½km across, totalling some 190sq km in area. The population numbers about 7,000, of which some 3,000 live in and around the main port, town & Chora of Paroikias (Paros).

TRANSPORT LINKS
Air The airfield is almost the other side of the island, some 12km from the main town. There are at least four flights a day to and from Athens; three a week to Rhodes, and three a week to Crete, in the summer months.

Ferry Apart from being on the 'main line' route, linking Syros, Ios and Santorini, connections can be made with the Western chain (by small passenger ferries to Siphnos), to Naxos, for the scattering of Eastern islands (comprising Iraklia, Shinoussa, Koufonissi, Donoussa, Amorgos and Astipalaia), as well as Mykonos for the Eastern wing of islands (Andros and Tinos).

Ferry-boats connect daily with Piraeus(M), Naxos, Ios and Santorini; six days a week with Amorgos; four days a week to Koufonisi and Crete; three days a week to Ikaria, Samos, Astipalaia and Siphnos; two days a week to Sikinos, Folegandros, Donoussa, Shinoussa, Kalimnos, Kos, Nisiros, Tilos, Simi and Rhodes; and once a week to Anafi, Iraklia, Kastelorizo, Chalki, Karpathos and Kasos.

Hydrofoil Five days a week a craft continues on to Ios, Santorini and Crete; two days a week to Naxos and Mykonos.

Owners of accommodation, clamour for clients, swarming over the alighting passengers.

Apart from the usual Neolithic remains, the most interesting site is **Saliangos islet,** which is located north of Antiparos island, in the narrowest point of the channel between the two islands. Here has been revealed a complete Neolithic settlement, dating from 4000 BC.

During the years between 2000-1500 BC, the island traded extensively with Crete. Conquest by the Ionians resulted in the arts flourishing and a great age of prosperity with colonies being established on Thassos and the Dalmatian coast. Architochos, the poet who created *iambic* verse, achieved fame in both poetry and war,

For greater detail acquire GROC's Candid Guide to The Cyclades Islands

dying during a battle with the citizens of Naxos (654 BC).

Island marble was exported, far and wide. The general affluence continued through to the period of domination by the Romans. The island re-emerged into the spotlight of history with the establishment of the Cathedral Church of Panaghia Ekatontapyliani.

A savage raid by Arabs, in the early 9th century, left the island depopulated, until the arrival of the Venetians, in the early 1200s. During their rule castles were built at Paroikias, Naoussa and Kefalos. In 1537, the Turks launched a savage attack, finally capturing the island in 1560.

After the War of Independence, the Mykoniot heroine, Manto Mavrogenous, settled on Paros.

The countryside, in which are set some attractive, small villages, is absolutely delightful.

MAIN PORTS & RESORTS
PAROIKIAS (Parikia, Paros) The capital town and main port is low-lying and possibly the busiest Greek island ferry-boat port in the Aegean. The Esplanade has lost any charm it once possessed. Not all is dross - the Old Quarter that lies behind the Esplanade is still a lovely maze of lanes, alleys and steps. Naturally intensive tourism has proved very penetrative.

The town boasts two, or perhaps three, small beaches. To the south-west is a not-very-large, sand and shingle, fairly narrow beach of no great length but pleasantly tree-lined. The other two beaches are at the north-east, package holiday sector of the large, curving bay.

If by some mischance a traveller is not offered accommodation, a signboard lists many of the island's hotels and telephone numbers. A large number of the hotels are tour-operator booked, despite which, there are plenty of D and E class establishments, as there are pensions and Rooms. The Town proliferates an abnormally high incidence of 'low-life' eating places - despite which there are still a few middle-of-the-road, honest-to-goodness tavernas.

Places of interest include the:-
The Cathedral Church of Panaghia Ekatontapyliani (Katapoliani) The stories attached to the church are more interesting than the building itself. The most recent research suggests that the site is a very early place of Christian worship.

Legend suggests that the church was founded, in AD 326, by St Helena, the mother of Constantine the Great.

A clutch of 16th and 18th century churches surround the area of the Kastro, which sits atop the lowly hill named after the fascinating colonnaded Church of Ag Konstantinos. Additionally there are a number of enchanting, churches scattered about the town
Kastro Very little is left of this 13th century fort except a tower and a piece of wall which incorporates some rather strange, circular stones and blocks of varying thickness. The whole seems oddly incompatible, which may be explained by the fact that much of the original material came from the ruins of an ancient Temple.
Fountains The Chora has three lovely water fountains dedicated to the War of Independence heroine, Manto Mavrogenous.
Museum Adjacent to the school playground, across the way from the Church of Ekatontapyliani.

Krios Bay & Beach (3½km) The Krios beach water-taxi moors to the left of the ferry-boat quay.

NAOUSSA (Naousa) (11km from Paroikias Town) The heart of this northern fishing village is over a bridge spanning a wide, summer-dry river-bed. The outer harbour is formed by large boulders which stretch around the small headland, incorporating a ruined Venetian Castle. The agreeably messy main quay and inner harbour have an intimate, friendly atmosphere. The main harbour hosts modern tourist craft and yachts, whilst the small caique harbour is crowded by caiques. The tiny 'Old Quarter' is a charming maze of lanes.

The beach to the west of Naoussa is pleasant, if rather stony.

The other beach, to the south of the town, and officially designated the Town beach, is disappointing. The narrow shore is flanked by the peeling and unpainted backs of buildings.

There is an abundance of private houses with accommodation, as well as an adequate number of hotels. There are numerous eating establishments but, as for the accommodation, dining out is generally very expensive.

Kolymbithres (3km from Naoussa Port) Famed for the unusual wind and sea scoured rocks on the water's edge. The marshy land has a sandy foreshore almost continuously washed over by the sea.

AMBELAS (4km from Naoussa Port) Once simply a charming, east coast fishing hamlet, with a pleasant beach. The whole village is open and scattered, and there are Rooms as well as a hotel.

ALYKI (12km from Paroikias Town) Originally a south-west coastal area of salt pans and a small fishing boat port.

There are two hotels, a few cafe-bars, some tavernas, several restaurants, a disco and a lovely, tree lined sandy beach.

DRIOS (22km from Paroikias Town) On the western approaches to this attractive, hamlet of a Greek holiday resort, are a couple of hotels, as well as Rooms. The high, steep retaining wall on the small, shingle sand beach side of the road is planted with trees.

Chrissi Akti Beach (23km from Paroikias Port) This sweep of shore really is 'golden' sand. A couple of hotels and a restaurant cater for visitors.

LOGAROS (22km from Paroikias Town) A comparatively under-developed and sparse settlement, spread along a narrow bay and lovely, sandy beach. There are a few Rooms and tavernas with a 'huddle', at the tree edged, right-hand end.

PISO LIVADI (21km from Paroias Town) A pleasant, lively fishing boat port struggling to hold off the usual ravages inflicted by organised holiday firms.

The left-hand side is lined with a few, three storey tavernas and hotels. The right- hand side encompasses the beach, edged by some two storey taverna buildings, with Rooms, followed by a tree lined road. The beach is sandy with shingle.

There are many Rooms, tavernas and restaurants.

For greater detail acquire GROC's Candid Guide to The Cyclades

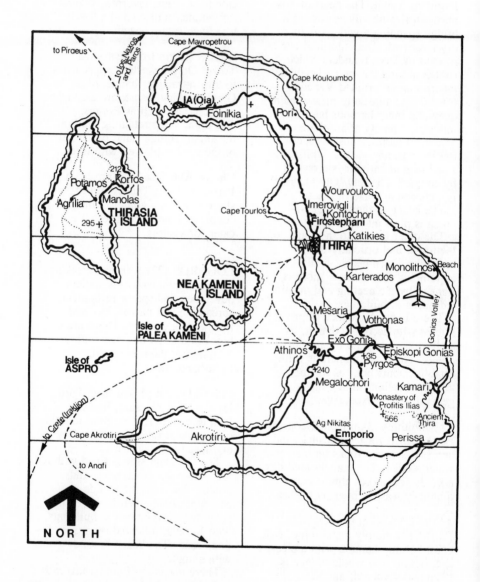

Illustration 25 Santorini island

FACT FILE	TRANSPORT LINKS
ALTERNATIVE NAMES Santorine, Thira, Thera	**Air** The airport is some 7km distant from Thira Town, close by Monolithos and the airfield is large enough for international flights to land. Domestic flight arrivals are met by Rooms and hotel owners. There are two flights a day to and from Athens; one a day to Mykonos; four days a week to Rhodes; and three a week to Crete.
IMPRESSIONS Stunningly dramatic coastline; country lanes; churches; barrel roofs; crowds of tourists; too few buses, ferries & taxis to cope with the demand; expensive services & supplies; cruise liners; duty-free shops.	
SPECIALITIES Excellent island wines; tomatoes; export of pumice stone, china clay & rock soil for cement making.	**Ferry** Most ferries dock at the new Port of Athinos, sometimes also calling in at the Thira Town and Ia (Oia) landing stages. Ferries daily link with Ios, Naxos, Paros and Piraeus(M); five days a week with Folegandros; four days a week with Crete; three days a week with Sikinos; two days a week with Syros, Milos, Siphnos, Serifos, Anafi, Kasos, Karpathos and Rhodes; and once a week with Chalki and Kimolos.
RELIGIOUS FESTIVALS include: 23rd May - Feast, Karterados; 19th-20th July - Festival, Profitas Ilias; 15th August - Feast, Episkopi (Mesa) Gonia; 1st September - Feast, Thira; 20th October - Festival, Ag Artemiou Church, Thira; 26th October - Festival, Ag Dimitriou, Karterados.	
STATISTICS Tel prefix 0286. The island, half-saucer shaped, is up to 17km long, between 1¼ & 12km across, and has an area of about 95sq km. Of a population of 7,500, approximately 1,500 live in Thira, the capital.	**Hydrofoil** Five days a week hydrofoils proceed to Ios, Paros and Crete; and two days a week go on to Naxos and Mykonos. The ferries are met by Room owners from all over the island.

Historically there were a couple of fundamental differences from the Cycladean island 'norm'. One was the Cretan, or more correctly the Minoan 'connection', which ended rather dramatically, in about 1520 BC. The other was the more than usually Machiavellian and multifarious in-fighting and coups of the medieval Venetian ruling families.

The Minoan link, and other interwoven items, fostered the possibility that Santorini was part of the lost city of Atlantis, popularised in the writing of Plato and Egyptian papyrists. Perhaps it was 'geological justice' that the island, originally formed by volcanic

For greater detail acquire GROC's Candid Guide to The Cyclades Islands

activity, some 20-25,000 year
ago, should be blown in half by an
enormous eruption, circa 1600
BC. After the eruption, the islands
of Santorini, Thirasia and Aspro,
as well as the enormous bay or
'caldera', were in position. Explo-
sions, eruptions and discharges
over the years eventually formed
the other offshore islands of Nea
Kameni and Palea Kameni.

Despite years of cruise liner
visits, serried ranks of backpackers
and swarms of package tourists,
the sheer beauty, the stunning vis-
ual effects of the cliff-hanging
towns and the loveliness of the
countryside continue to triumph.

Identification of the ports is a
help: Ia and Thira are ostensibly
similar, with the small, and pretty
harbour facilities nestling at the
bottom of steepling cliffs, but the
relative position of the islands of
Thirasia and Nea Kameni helps
selection, as does the reminder that
only Thira has a cliff-top cable car.

The most important, most often
used is:-

MAIN PORTS & RESORTS

ATHINOS (Athinios, Athiniou)
(some 6km from Thira Town) The
main port is a damned big quay
edged by unattractive, concrete
faced restaurant/cafe-bars. A
veritable swarm of hotel coaches
meet disembarking clients and, if
everything is in order, there will
be several island buses waiting.

THIRA (Phira, Fira) The capital,
and a port. Thira is possibly one of
the most amazingly and breathtakingly situated capital town's,
not only in the Cyclades but in
Greece. The rambling, brilliant
white buildings, spotted by the
occasional blue church dome, skirt

the cliff-top ranging along, the
multi-coloured and layered mountain edge circling the east of the
enormous caldera. The impact is
quite staggering. Unfortunately,
this riveting beauty has resulted in
an excess of tourism, which numbers include cruise liner passengers. These latter craft moor at the
foot of the Thira cliff-face and
disembark their clientele into
ship's boats. Once landed, a few
hire donkeys to climb the steep
zig-zag steps, but most use the
cable car. For many years the only
way from the harbour to the town
was via the 550/650 steps and a
band of donkey men still exercise
a firm monopoly on the path. The
affluent 'liner' clientele, emanating
an aura of wealth, have resulted
in the streets lining and parallel to
the top of the cliff, being jammed
with sleek boutiques, jewellery and
gift shops, the windows of which
shriek with inducements to pay by
credit card.

There is a wide range of hotels,
pensions and Rooms, most of
which are extremely expensive
and prices, in recent years, have
been increased by very large amounts. Few Thira eateries have a
patio, unless well shielded, as the
winds are very strong, and here
again prices are generally high.

Places of interest include the:-
Archaeological Museum and the
'Local''Museum.

Excursions The various travel
agents offer boat trips to the
Volcano on Nea Kameni island.
The 'round the bay' trips encompass the Volcano, the hot
springs on Palea Kameni and
either Manolas Harbour on Thirasia island or the northern port of

Ia. Round-the-island coach trips are good value.

Monolithos Beach (7km from Thira Town) The broad east coast beach is fine, black sand, enclosed by rocky moles. The foreshore is kelpy for a metre or so, after which the sea is very clear. The broad backshore is rimmed by groves of arethemusa trees.

KAMARI (10km from Thira Town) The package tourist development has ensured that this is a thoroughly horrid, expensive place. The road terminates at the right-hand end of the seaside village where a fleet of about twelve small fishing boats and caiques still pull up on the beach. The sea-bed is too steeply shelving for the comfort of young children. There are many hotels but, as with eating and drinking, they are costly.

Ancient Thira (2km) From the right-hand side of Kamari Bay, a very steep, winding, flint road, ascent ends on the saddle of a ridge. The site above dates back to the 9th century BC and was excavated in the 1890s.

PERISSA (15km from Thira Town)

Almost a 'mirror image' of Kamari, with the headland and main village to the left and the black, coarse, sandy beach curving away, to the right. There the similarities end, for Perissa is 'a Clacton' to Kamari's 'Frinton'. Certainly the resort is more Greek. There are Rooms, in addition to the to-be-expected hotels, pensions, restaurants and tavernas.

Akrotiri Excavations The discovery of this ancient town provided undeniable proof of the island's close connection with Crete and, as with Pompeii, the larvae and ash preserved many buildings, even multi-storey ones, in their originally constructed shape. The most dramatic finds were the frescoes and murals.

IA (Oia) (10km from Thira Town) A pretty, north coast, cliff-top edge village, from which stunning views, and a foot-of-cliff port. Ia evinces a slow, leisurely pace but is most definitely on the 'day-trip excursion' circuit. Old-fashioned, low-rise hotels, pensions, Rooms, restaurants and tavernas spread along the attractive High St, which teeters beside the escarpment.

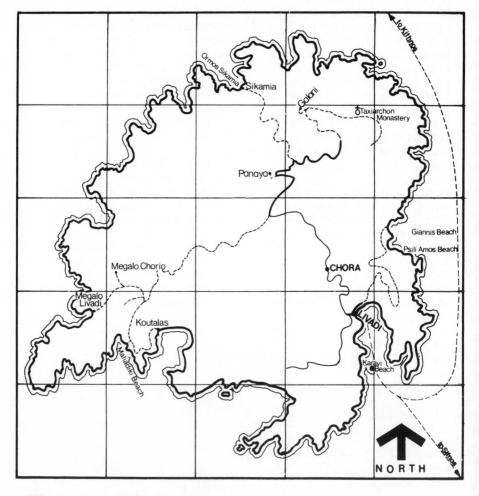

Illustration 26 Serifos island

FACT FILE
ALTERNATIVE NAMES
Seriphos

IMPRESSIONS Womens' bonnets (koukoula); beautiful butterflies & wild buddleia; unsurfaced roads; charter caiques & flotilla yachts; Greek holiday island; winnowing.

RELIGIOUS FESTIVALS include: 5th May - Festival, Ag Irenes, Koutalas; 6th August, Ag Sotiras, Kalo Amebli (south coast); 15-16th August - Feast & festival, Pirgos; 7th November - Festival, Monastery of Taxiarchon.

STATISTICS Tel prefix 0281. The circular island is up to 8km from side-to-side & top to bottom, withan area of 70sq km. The population numbers about 1200.

TRANSPORT LINKS
Ferry The boats here are not met by owners of accommodation. Seven days a week ferries proceed to Piraeus(M); six days a week to Siphnos and Milos; four days a week to Kithnos and Kimolos; two days a week to Ios and San- torini; and one day a week to Syros, Sikinos, Folegandros and Rafina(M).

Mythology informs us that Princess Danae and her son Perseus landed on Serifos, having been set adrift by her father. Perseus killed Medusa, the ghastly gorgon, at the request of the King of Serifos, who really wished to ravage Perseus's mother. Unfortunately for the King's designs, Perseus, enraged at his host's behaviour, held up the dead head of Medusa to the King and his court, who turned to stone.

Historically the island's existence was rather humdrum, following the usual Cycladean succession of overlords. The Romans sent exiles here, as they did to a number of other unprepossessing islands.

The mountains seem rather massive, old and rounded. The peaks are centrally located which, combined with the almost circular shape of the outline, gives a bloblike appearance to the island. The name is supposed to designate dry, which is probably why the map makers are so keen to detail a plethora of massive, but nonexistent rivers, in addition to innumerable paved roads - another figment of the cartographer's mind.

The lack of bus routes to other than the Chora, makes it difficult to connect with the two or three other extremely rewarding, but widespread seaside hamlets. Admittedly the roads are nothing more than rather fearsome tracks through the interior.

MAIN PORTS & RESORTS
LIVADI The port has a massive ferry-boat quay and the village spreads up the 'High' St. From hereon, all the way round to the far edge of the bay, is a spreadout, rather scrubbly and 'tacky' ribbon of development skirting the

---

For greater detail acquire GROC's Candid Guide to The Cyclades Islands

water's edge. This includes tavernas, restaurants, hotels, private
homes, discos, pensions, Rooms,
cafe-bars and a few shops, slowly
thining out the further round the
bay one progresses. The surfaced
quay road runs out on the main
square. The rest of the shore encircling 'Esplanade' is nothing
more than a dirt track, enhanced
by the number of mature trees
spread along the backshore of the
beach, which stretches almost the
full length of the bay. The nearside
is sand and fine shingle, whilst the
middle section is pebbly sand.

As the season progresses, and
accommodation gets scarcer, so
'wild' backshore camping increa-
ses. Rooms, at the height of season, are almost non-existent and
owners only accept pre-bookings
for a minimum of a week. Meals
tend to be expensive.

Psili Amos Beach (about ¾ hr walk
from Livadi Port) The rough track
passes by above the lovely, clean,
golden sand cove, with small arethemusa trees planted on the edge
of the low, sand dune backshore.
The sea is delightfully clean and
there is one taverna and a cafe.

Ag Giannis Beach Another fifteen
minutes walk on from, and larger
than Psili Amos. At the nearside,
the coarse sand beach blends into
large pebbles, backed by a grove
of trees. There are a number of
private dwellings.

THE CHORA (2km from Livadi
Port) If the ascent is made by bus,
this circles round at the top, north
end of the mountainside Chora.
The village is draped around a
precipitous hilltop, spilling over
and down its flanks.

There are a few Rooms, cafe-bars
and tavernas.

Ormos Sikamia (6km from the
Chora) A lovely and unspoilt,
north coast bay backed by extensive dunes, hosting groves of bam-
boos, with some plastic litter scattered about. The beach is sandy,
the sea clear and clean and the
backshore is a sand and pebbles
mix planted with occasional
clumps of trees. Apart from some
new buildings spread out amongst
abandoned, older dwellings, there
are no facilities and the 'High
Street' is nothing more than a
sandy track, winding between the
dunes and outcrops of bamboo.

All on the south-west coast are:
MEGALO LIVADI (7km from the
Chora) The stony backshore of the
mature, tree lined beach runs parallel to the sea's edge, taking in a
stony football pitch. The beach is
made up of a scrubbly foreshore
and a broad sandy strip. The landward side of the track is edged by
a hotchpotch of buildings, including a kafeneion, a store and a
taverna. At the latter they can
rustle up a nice lunch time snack,
but no accommodation.

KOUTALAS (7½km from the
Chora) This spacious bay is
divided by a large church topped
bluff, in the middle distance. Only
a scattering of buildings now
perch on the gentle mountain
slope, that hems in the narrow, tree
lined, shingle beach and small
pebble foreshore. The scant community of fishermen support a
'hillbilly taverna', the owner of
which is delighted to minister to
travellers' requirements, but there
isn't any accommodation.

CHAPTER 32

SHINOUSSA
(The Back Islands)

FACT FILE
ALTERNATIVE NAMES
Schinoussa, Skchinoussa,
Skinoussa

IMPRESSIONS Construction
work; a friendly but dwindling
population.

RELIGIOUS FESTIVALS include:
25th March, Theotokou, Messaria.

STATISTICS Tel. prefix 0285.
The population is about 190 & the
island has an area of 8.5sq km.

TRANSPORT LINKS
Ferry Shinoussa has a natural
harbour at Mersini Bay, where
several yachts are always moored. Ferries call in four days a
week, linking with Amorgos,
Iraklia, Naxos, Paros, Mykonos,
Syros, and Piraeus(M).
The quay has been 'under
improvement', for a number of
years. Mersini Bay has one
shingle beach and one narrow,
sandy beach. Besides the latter is
a large taverna with Rooms.
There is a second Rooms block in
a nearby orchard.
The (capital) village is not
visible from the port and is a hot,
fifteen minute, uphill walk.

The people of Shinoussa have long
been farmers and, as a result, the
population is dwindling fast. The
tourist facilities are well advertised
in an effort to stem the 'outflow'.

The town's nearest beach is fifteen minutes walk away, but the
island abounds in sandy beaches,
there being about nineteen.

SHINOUSSA The capital. Most of
the accommodation is spaced out
along the long main street of the
straggling island capital and an
assortment of cafes/bar/tavernas
serve whatever the ferry-boats
bring in, at a reasonable price.

Tsigouri Beach Of the selection,
this is the best shoreline, and happens to be the closest. It is fifteen
minutes walk and has a taverna
with a couple of basic Rooms.

Other beaches near Shinoussa
'town' are **Livadia** and **Almiros**.
Proceed to the end of the High
Street and turn right for Livadia.
This passes between wheat fields,
and is about a twenty minute walk
from the settlement's centre. Not
a very inspiring, narrow, sandy
and grassy beach, but the bay enjoys protected, calm waters. The
left fork leads down a stony track.
Where this ends climb over the
wall crossing a large wheat field
to the wild, sandy, 'Minoan-
flavoured' Bay of Almiros. This
choice is also twenty minutes
from the town.

To reach the beach at **Psili
Ammos** walk, for some forty-five
minutes, to the tiny hamlet of
Messaria. From there battle on for
another ten minutes for the beach.

For greater detail acquire GROC's Candid Guide to The Cyclades Islands

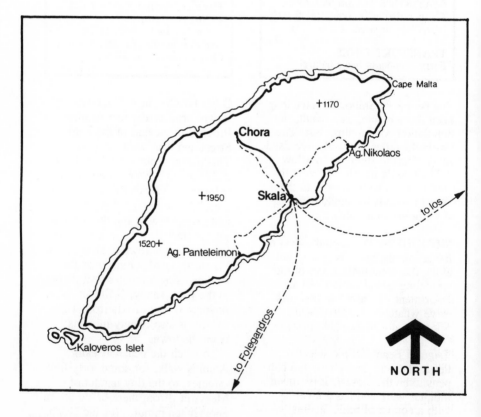

Illustration 27 Sikinos island

FACT FILE

IMPRESSIONS Dry, but comparatively verdant countryside; plentiful wells, but slimy water; donkey & mule trains; few tourists.

SPECIALITIES A highly resinated wine; *Xinogalo* - an island cheese.

RELIGIOUS FESTIVALS include: Friday after Easter - Festival of Zoodochos Pighi, Monastery of Zoodochos Pighi, Chora.

STATISTICS Tel prefix 0286. An area of about 40sq km, with a population of some 300, spread between the Port and the Chora.

TRANSPORT LINKS

Ferry To date, the quayside is too small for the larger boats which 'pull up' in the mouth of the harbour. Passengers are transferred to one of two 'pass-boats', in order to complete the journey.

Ferries sail five days a week to Ios, Santorini and Piraeus(M); four days a week to Naxos, Folegandros and Paros; three days a week to Milos, Siphnos and Serifos; two days a week to Crete, Kimolos, Kithnos and Syros; and one day a week to Anafi, Kasos, Karpathos, Chalki and Rhodes.

Accommodation is usually proffered by Room owners.

The island was settled in ancient times. About 4km south-west of the Chora is a 5th century AD church, built over a 2nd century BC temple of Apollo. To the north of the Chora, on the coast at **Palaiokastro**, are the indistinct remains of an ancient sanctuary.

Depending on the time of year, in addition to the scheduled ferryboats, there are a few trip-boats from Ios and Santorini.

The lack of a suitable landing place, at which even charter yachts can easily berth, has helped preserve Sikinos as one of those finds, a 'jewel of island uniqueness' set in the Cycladean sea beset by tourist hordes.

The symmetry of the port and its beach, bordering the lovely cove, is fully complemented by the 'old world', Chora of outstanding but simple agricultural beauty. To get to the upper village, the traveller is often faced with a climb of about an hour, as the new bus runs somewhat spasmodically. This service revolves around ferry-boat arrivals, and there are no taxis. Regretfully, the coming of mechanised transport has reduced the number of mule trains.

The dramatic landscape is colourful, almost verdant, with a surprising amount of agriculture. There are water wells, everywhere, which are constantly replenished by spring water trickling from the surrounding hillsides.

SKALA The harbour which is also known as Alopronia. This is more a semi-circular cove, with a caique quay and small settlement to the left, a broad, sandy beach to the centre, and a thin ribbon of development to the right. Prior to the preoccupation of the Colonels Junta with tourism, and the inception of widespread development of the islands, Sikinos was regarded as a rather uninteresting, forced port of call. Mind you that was in the days when Ios was described as 'lesser-known, quiet and off the beaten-track island!

The splendid beach fills the bottom of the bay. It is a comparatively generous sweep of sand and a backshore of pebbly sand on which are scattered some small craft, boat trailers and beer crates. A narrow, stone laid path sweeps up to the Chora. Further along is a dry river-bed, the other side of which is a flat grass field which has a marshy appearance. At the far end of the bay, the sea bottom is rocky and the narrow foreshore is big pebbles with a pleasant grove of trees on the backshore.

There are a few pensions, some Rooms, tavernas and a kafeneion.

THE CHORA/KASTRO (a one hour walk or quick bus ride from Skala) The upper, mountain community almost divides into two, sprawling and dipping down across a central, saddle ridge. Strictly speaking the right-hand village is the Kastro, the left-hand one is the Chora. Dominating the saddle, where the old path, as distinct from the old road, scrambles up to the Chora, is the school.

Truly, this must be one of the loveliest examples of an island 'working' town still extant. I stress working because agricultural pursuits take place almost to the core of the settlement. There are a number of now defunct windmills ranged along the escarpment, facing out over and high above the sea, beyond the tumbling, brown, parched mountainside. There is accommodation and a couple of very acceptable tavernas.

Hikers will be pleased to note that there are three or four excellent island walks.

FACT FILE
ALTERNATIVE NAME Sifnos

IMPRESSIONS Greek holiday resort; neat countryside; fanciful, ceramic chimney pots; clean & neat; green & cultivated; relatively unspoilt; dovecotes & windmills.

SPECIALITIES Pottery.

RELIGIOUS FESTIVALS include: 6th September - Feast & Festival, Taxiarchis Vathiou, Vathy.

STATISTICS Tel prefix 0284. Up to 20km from top to bottom & about 10km wide, with an area of some 74sq km. The population numbers approximately 2,000, of which 1,600 or so live in the capital of Apollonia & its satellite villages.

TRANSPORT LINKS
Ferry Ferries sail five days a week to Ios, Santorini and Piraeus(M); four days a week to Naxos, Folegandros and Paros; three days a week to Milos, Siphnos and Serifos; two days a week to Crete; Kimolos, Kithnos and Syros; and one day a week to Anafi, Kasos, Karpathos, Chalki and Rhodes. The boats are usually met by the owners of accommodation, as well as buses and taxis

---

Gold and silver mines gave the island great wealth, in antiquity, and resulted in Siphnos being the largest contributors to the mainland Delphi Treasury. Otherwise Siphnos generally followed the average, 'run-of-the-mill' history of the rest of the Cyclades.

The main areas of agriculture are neat and intensive, with many fields enclosed by stone walls. The valleys and river gorges are perhaps the most impressive, the cultivation being sprinkled with dwellings and magnificent castellated dovecotes, between which cascade 'rivers' of flowering oleanders. The initial impression of tidiness and well-being is reinforced throughout Siphnos.

Even the buses run on time on this well ordered and pleasant land, and the service is very extensive, despite which the island is fertile ground for walkers.

MAIN PORTS & RESORTS
KAMARES The main port is also a clean, orderly, fishing village seaside holiday resort, with an aura of wealth. It is impressively positioned in an amphitheatre of massive mountains inevitably crowned, here and there, by the occasional chapel. On the right, the horseshoe bay is bordered by a tree-lined Esplanade, backed by the nearly 900m high Mt Profitis Ilias; the bottom centre of the bay is filled out by a magnificent sweep of beach; and rocky cliff-faces blank off the left-hand side. The fine sand beach fills the bottom of the very long bay. It

For greater detail acquire GROC's Candid Guide to The Cyclades Islands

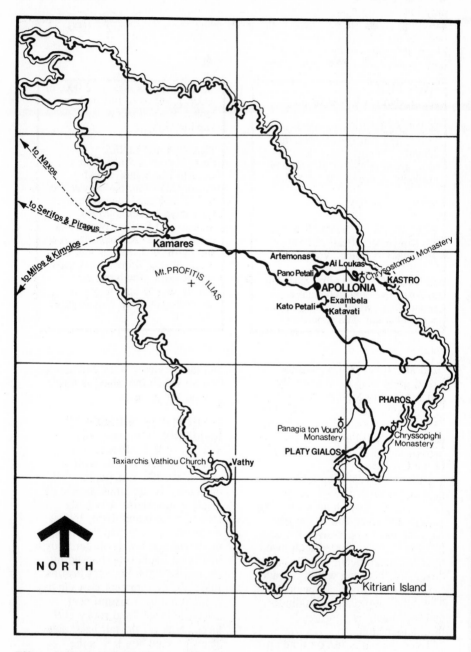

Illustration 28 Siphnos island

only has one shortcoming - the extremely slow gradient of the sea-bed. At the near side is a small block of beach showers, a facility necessary to cope with the backshore 'wild' campers.

The accommodation possibilities have increased over the years, so much so that there is enough to go round, even in the height of summer months. There are a number of acceptable eating places.

Trip boats depart daily to the attractive, simple, south-western harbour of **Vathy**, only otherwise accessible on foot.

APOLLONIA (5km from Kamares Port) The busy and active, centre-of-island capital is a town, rather than a Greek island Chora. The settlement is more a collection of hamlets and villages, spread across the ridge and saddle of a number of busy, neat, agricultural hills enclosed by tidy terraces.

Despite the height of summer tourist influx it remains unspoiled, but there are not as many accommodation or eating places as might be hoped.

Places of interest include a plethora of churches, as well as the Museum, but perhaps the biggest attraction is the opportunity to walk the many paths and tracks.

PHAROS (Faros) (7km from Apollonia) A small, sleepy, *ad hoc* holiday resort, with sufficient accommodation and tavernas.

The first beach, edged by some accommodation and tavernas, is small and sandy with a coarse sand sea-bed and a pebbly back-shore. From the far end of the waterside are steps that ascend to a pocket-sized, pretty 'Old Quarter' draped over a prominent bluff.

Hereon are several rudimentary Rooms overlooking the sea, on the tip of the headland.

PLATY GIALOS (Plati Yialos) (10km from Apollonia) The road parallels the long, flat sea-shore. The landward side is hedged in by stone-walled fields of olive trees and the plain is ringed by hills. The sea side of the road is fringed by a row of single storey dwellings, at least five tavernas, a restaurant, snackbar, tourist shop and a two storey hotel.

The left-hand side of the bay is bordered by a gathering of fishermen's cottages, with benzinas and a fishing caique or two anchored in the shallow water. The beach at this end is stony, with some kelp, whilst the sea bottom has a little biscuit rock and large pebbles.

KASTRO (3½km from Apollonia) The east coast Kastro was a medieval fortress and is an exceptionally beautiful, clean, whitewashed Chora, dramatically positioned on a promontory that falls away sharply, on either side, into the sea, way below. The streets are in terraced tiers, climbing the hilltop in the fashion of a layered cake.

The antiquity and continuous development of the site is no better evidenced than by the bits and pieces of ancient columns and headless busts haphazardly incorporated into the facades of various houses. There are a number of churches, as well as a Museum, but the original castle walls have all but disappeared.

The Kastro exhibits few concessions to tourism, despite which there are Rooms to rent, on the hillside, at the outset to the settlement, close to some windmills at the entrance to the village.

For greater detail acquire GROC's Candid Guide to The Cyclades Islands

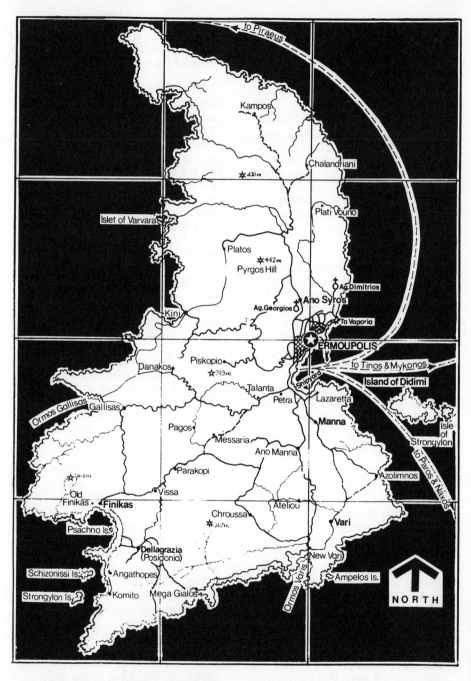

Illustration 29 Syros island

CHAPTER 35   SYROS

FACT FILE
ALTERNATIVE NAMES Siros

IMPRESSIONS Grand churches & mansions; shuttered houses with balconies; a rocky, bare island; a large shipyard; saline drinking water, in short supply.

SPECIALITIES *Loukoumes* (Turkish delight); nougat; Roman Catholicism.

RELIGIOUS FESTIVALS include: 25th September - The Virgin Mary, Faneromenis Monastery (Catholic & Orthodox procession); 26th October - St Dimitrios Church; end of October/early November - 'Apanosyria' Festival, Ano Syros; 27th December - St Stephen, Gallisas. There are also feasts at Kini & Finikas.

STATISTICS Tel prefix 0281. Syros, the legal & administrative

centre of the Cyclades, is about 18km from top to bottom & 10½ km wide, with an area of 87sq km. The population numbers 19,000, two-thirds of whom live in Ermoupolis, of which number some 1350 work in the shipyards.

TRANSPORT LINKS
Ferry The once pivotal role of Syros is highlighted by the island remaining on many schedules. Ferries connect daily to Piraeus (M), Tinos, Mykonos, Paros, Naxos; four days a week to Amorgos; three days a week to Ios, Santorini; two days a week to Astipalaia and Crete; and at least once a week to Sikinos, Folegandros, Anafi, Ikaria, Samos, Donoussa, Iraklia, Shinoussa, Koufonissi, Kalimnos, Kos, Nisiros, Tilos, Simi, Rhodes and Kastellorizo. The boats are met by owners of accommodation.

Mentioned by Homer as "abounding in pasture and wine, rich in sheep and corn", which it certainly isn't today. The island's history generally mirrored that of the rest of the Cyclades until, in 1207, Syros came under the suzerainty of the Duke of Naxos. In this period the medieval town of Ano Syros was built and became a stronghold of Roman Catholicism, a faith brought to the island by Genoese and Venetian merchants. During the Turkish occupation the islanders gained a rare number of concessions and flourished. This

may well have been a major factor in deciding the Syriots against physically joining the 1821 Independence uprising. Notwithstanding, they did help fund the struggle, in addition to taking in many thousands of refugees from other islands. The fugitives immediately constructed the new town and port of Ermoupolis, on the indeveloped area between the hill topped by Ano Syros and the sea's edge. Syros became the focal point for the combined industrial and shipping thrust of the new State. The immense wealth and culture,

For greater detail acquire GROC's Candid Guide to The Cyclades Islands

resulting from this prominence, bequeathed some magnificent private and public buildings, a very grand square, and a number of splendid churches.

The decline of coal vis-a-vis oil-fired power for ships, in the early 1800s, had far-reaching consequences for the island. The inevitable upshot was the slow but remorseless run-down in industrial activity and subsequent closure of many of the cotton mills, tanneries, iron-foundries, factories and warehouses.

MAIN PORTS & RESORTS

ERMOUPOLIS From a distance the twin hills overshadowing the capital and main port have an attractive look, even if the surrounding mountains are bare and unappealing. The one to the left is topped off by a Catholic cathedral and the one to the right by a blue domed Orthodox church.

Didimi islet stands off from the bay, often with a ship at anchor in the roads. The southern headland is named Lazaretta, and was once a quarantine stop - the origin of our word *Lazaretto*.

A closer inspection of the port does not present a pretty sight. To the left, the curve of the bay is occupied by the shipyard, a floating dock, as well as other industrial workings. The untidy buildings bordering the centre of the Esplanade, and parallel side-streets, conceal the glory of the magnificent main square. Moreover the three or four storey Venetian homes of the 'Upper Town' are also hidden from view. Unfortunately, many of the houses are shuttered and in partial ruins. To the east of the harbour peninsula are a few tiny, stony, pebbly beach coves.

There is plenty of accommodation available in the guise of a disproportionate number of lodging houses. These are, in the main, conversions of large, high ceilinged Victorian houses. The lower category hotels are splendid examples of a now almost bygone genre. Syros is remarkably short of above average tavernas or restaurants and prices are in the run-of-the-mill range. Mind you, the main feature of an Ermoupolis evening is to sit at one of the numerous cafe-bars, on the periphery of the main square, and watch the colourful and extensive *Ramblas*, which goes on for hours.

Places of interest include the:-
Church of Ag Nikolaos A beautiful, twin spired Orthodox Church, with a gold striped, blue domed roof, in front of which is a raised, tree planted garden.

A church and a cathedral dominate Ermoupolis, one each being mounted on top of the twin hills that tower over the port. On the left-hand hilltop is the old city of **Ano Syros**, founded in the 1300s, and the:-
Cathedral of St George A Roman Catholic place of worship dating back to medieval times.

The right-hand hill of **Vrontado** is topped off by the:-
Church of Anastasis This embraces the Greek Orthodox faith and possesses some fine icons.
Cemetery, British The well maintained cemetery is noticeable for its tall bell and clock tower.
Museum Exhibits include items from surrounding islands.
Plateia Miaoulis The magnificent, marble paved main square. The far side is edged by resplendent public buildings. including the Museum, Town Hall and Library.

In their basements are a row of smart cafe-bars facing out over the plateia, the tables and chairs of which are spread out beneath scattered trees and palms.

Theatre The Apollon is worth a mention as it is supposed to be modelled on La Scala, Milan.

Town Hall A well-proportioned, massive, neo-classical building which dominates the town's main square.

OLD VARI (10km from Ermoupolis Town) A pretty, interesting and squalidly attractive place to stay. The sandy beach of the small, enclosed cove has some rubbish on the foreshore and the sandy sea-bed is weedy. A fishing fleet is anchored at the far right of the bay. The left-hand headland is topped off by an impressive, if incongruous, castellated homestead.

A number of tavernas edge the backshore, planted with shady arethemusa trees, and there are a number of hotels.

DELLAGRAZIA (Posidonia) (12km from Ermoupolis Town) The colonial style settlement is very interesting, with some almost whimsical mansions, enclosed by large railings, once owned by wealthy shipowners. The streets are gracefully tree-lined.

ANGATHOPES (14km from Ermoupolis Town) The inhabitants obviously make an effort to keep the locale clean and tidy. The swimming is pleasant with an islet close to the shore and, tucked into the crook of the headland, a low, ugly, concrete box-like hotel.

FINIKAS (12km to Ermoupolis Town) The lovely, family holiday locations of Finikas and Dellagrazia almost run into each other. A curving, narrow, tree lined beach edges the bay-hugging road in and around which are spaced some hotels, bars, a mini-market, a number of Rooms and villas, as well as furnished apartments.

GALLISAS (9km to Ermoupolis Town) The broad, large, curving, gently shelving, sandy beach is edged by tufted scrub. To the left is a small boat quay and, beyond that, behind the church, is a nudist beach, a freshwater spring and a few caves. The latter continue to provide dwellings for the overseas summer season influx. There are Rooms, two campsites and one or two restaurant tavernas.

KINI (9km from Ermoupolis Town) The approach to the curving beach of sand, laced with pebbles, is spanned by two tavernas. To the left, over a small headland, is a sandy cove and to the right, the main body of the village. Several tavernas jut into the sea, and to the far right is a fishing boat mole and moorings.

Prior to the beach is a new, clean looking hotel, in addition to some Rooms.

Ia (Santorini) is the best point of departure for the ½hr excursion boat trip to Manolas Harbour, on the edge of Ag Nikolaos Bay, Thirasia. Nowadays, some five tavernas border the pebble beach at the foot of the steep, eastern island cliff-face. This escarpment is actually the western side of the Santorini caldera, thus the delightful 'Chora' village of **Thirasia** is a stiff 300 step climb. Fortunately, there is a cafe-bar at the top. Some 100m along the main thoroughfare is a taverna and mini-market, beyond which is a taverna with accommodation. The settlement, which houses some 230 inhabitants, is a splendid jumble of white and coloured, small cubes, haphazardly muddled together. Ag Nikolaos Church is similarly multi-coloured.

For a better beach, than the pebbles of the harbour, it is necessary to walk across the island, by a track, to the inland villages of, either, **Agrilia** or **Potamos**, and then strike out for the western coast.

Illustration 30 Thirasia island

FACT FILE
ALTERNATIVE NAMES Tenos

IMPRESSIONS Pilgrims; sick children; black-clothed crones; candles & *exvotos*; driving schools; Venetian dovecotes; (distinctive) church bell towers; wild passion flowers; ouzeries.

SPECIALITIES Religion; loukoumades; frontalia omelettes; Greek tourists & pilgrims; red, American style fire hydrants; green marble & stone masons.

RELIGIOUS FESTIVALS include:- 30th January - Festival, the Discovery, Panaghia Evangelistria (or Church of Megalochari); 25th March - Festival, the Annunciation, Panaghia Evangelistria; 23rd July - Festival, Ag Pelegia, Panaghia Evangelistria; 26th July - Festival, Isternia; 15th August - Festival the Assumption, Panaghia Evangelistria; 31st August - Festival, Isternia; 8th September -Festival, Kardiani, 4th September - Festival, Isternia; 11th November - Festival, Kardiani.

STATISTICS Tel prefix 0283. The island is 34½km in length, up to 14km wide, with an area of 194sq km. Esti- mates of population vary between 9,000 & 12,000, of which 3,000-4,000 live in the capital.

TRANSPORT LINKS
Ferry Rafina is the mainland port that serves Tinos, from whence daily inter-island connections are made. In the popular summer months, a daily ferry-boat operates out of Piraeus(M). Note that it is simply not worth travelling to or from the island in and around the most important 'holy' days. There are daily ferry-boats to Andros, Rafina(M) and Piraeus (M); ferries six days a week to Mykonos, and two days a week to Syros.

For a change, Tinos has an individual historical background, compared to the other Cyclades islands. The Venetians took the island over in 1207 and managed to beat the Turks, not succumbing to their general sweep of conquest until 1714. This extra period of stubborn resistance included repulsing nine or so specific assaults. The defenders' ability to resist owed not a little to the impregnability of the now all but vanished Exobourgo Castle, built close by an ancient city. The five hundred years occupation by Catholic overlords resulted in about one fifth of the population still being of that religious persuasion.

The island's supreme moment occurred when a nun, Sister Pelagia, of the Convent Kechrovounio, and later made a Saint, had a vision, in July 1822. In this, the Virgin Mary revealed where an icon, depicting her and the Archhangel, was to be found, in a field. Sister Pelagia's conviction must have been persuasive because excavations soon started but it was

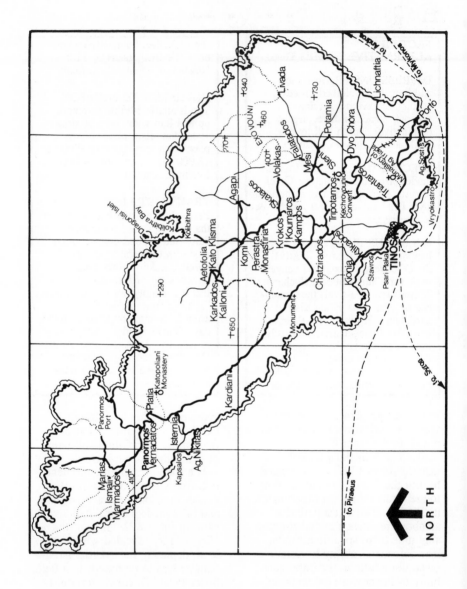

Illustration 31 Tinos island

not until early the following year that the buried 'treasure' came to light, close to the ruins of an old Byzantine church. Building the Church of Megalochari (Blessed Virgin), or Panaghia Evangelistria (Good tidings or Annunciation), commenced in 1832. Things never looked back and the island became the 'Aegean Lourdes'.

The main town and port is an appealing mix of old and new, whilst the forty or so villages of the hard-working agricultural communities are attractively spread out amongst the neat, country hillsides. There are a number of extremely inviting beaches and sufficient spots in which to hide away, as the urban Greek is not a great explorer. This latter fact accounts for the almost deserted nature of one or two seaside beauty spots, even in high season. The countryside has just the right mixture of soft mountains, verdant plains with golden green fields of hay, and rivers of olive trees. Churches and chapels vie with Venetian Gothic dovecotes for the available space.

MAIN PORTS & RESORTS
TINOS The capital and main port is a bustling, busy town with a Grecian bazaar, strident and swarming even on Sundays.

The town has two rather unsatisfactory beaches. One is a large, pebbly cove, the other, **Ag Fokas Beach,** is a narrow, tree-shaded, but also pebbly shore. There is yet another, not too distant option. The backshore is much broader than Ag Fokas but less shaded, although there are small arethemusa trees scattered about. This very long stretch of beach extends all the way to the large headland of **Vryokastro.** A hotel and pension

are constructed about the centre of the inland side of the backshore track. The shore finally peters out on the nearside of the conical Vryokastro headland. The track progresses over the bluff to a very small, quiet cove with a kelpy beach and stony sea bottom.

Though plentiful, accommodation tends to be expensive due to the all-year round numbers of Greek pilgrims, tourists and sick, many searching for a cure. In the town, the continuous flow of Greeks keeps prices high and the dining establishments rather 'typecast'. Generally there are few low price snackbars, some reasonable priced tavernas, and a great many expensive cafe-bars and waterfront taverna/restaurants.

Places of interest include the:-
The Panaghia Evangelistria The church dominates the town, topping the hill which overshadows the port. Once through the principal wrought iron gates, the main body of the church is reached across a colourful, pebble mosaic courtyard and up a majestic flight of marble steps. The dark interior is festooned with icons, masses of suspended lamps, candlestick and hanging exvotos, some of which depict the miraculous reason for their being donated.

Other buildings include a Museum, dedicated to island artists, and hung with their pictures and displaying various sculptures; a Byzantine Museum exhibiting mainly 18th and 19th century icons; and a picture gallery.

KIONIA (5km from Tinos Town) A small settlement, to the north of Tinos, that has 'benefited' from plush hotel development. The beach starts out sandy, with a pebble seashore. Towards the far end, beyond a low, small rocky promontory, both beach and sea bottom are sandy. The backshore is edged by a very smart hotel.

Ag Sostis Beach (7km from Tinos Town) A lovely, sweeping, sandy beach set in low-rise hills to the south-east. The backshore is edged by low dunes supporting small, sparse arethemusa trees. An out-crop of rocks divides the beach.

PORTO (Ag Ioannis) (17½km from Tinos Town) Despite the 'up-market' treatment, the beach is rather scrubbly, with some kelp heaped about, the sea bottom is sandy, whilst the low backshore dunes and the beach extend around the curve of the low head-land. There is a taverna with acc-ommodation, just beyond the turn-ing to the beach.

Kolibithra Beach (Kolympithra) 22km from Tinos Town) On the north coast, the large, broad, gloriously sandy beach, stretches away to the left. To the right-hand side is a swampy river running into the rocky edged Kolibithra Bay. The sea entrance almost seems to be blocked off by an islet. Around a bluff to the right is a deep-set, small, sandy beach cove spoiled by some tar. Above the cove, to the right, are six terraced-house apartments, a restaurant/cafe/souvlaki bar and, on the far side,

overlooking the edge of the beach, is an admirable, if rustic taverna.

AG NIKITAS (30km from Tinos Town) This north-west coast port was once destined for greater things in the sphere of tourism.
Out of the height-of-season hard-ly a tourist is to be seen, other than a few Greeks. To the right is a oversize commercial quay, a relic of the days when marble exporting was a viable proposition.

PANORMOS (Pyrgos, Pirgos) (33km from Tinos Town) A paved pedestrian way ascends past a small museum, to the pretty, pro-fusely flower and tree planted, higgledy-piggledy, a Chora. Herein, apart from the usual stores, shops kafeneions and tavernas, is a Rooms. The town is famous for the manufacture of sculptures and icons.

PANORMOS PORT (36½km from Tinos Town) A pleasant, quiet, rustic port, with a very large quay at the end of an equally large concrete road. To the left is a small, scrubbly beach. There are a side-by-side restaurant and a coffee-bar, a couple of stores and one gift shop. The few Rooms fill quickly when, vacancies occur.
The north-western end of the island is mountainous with a num-ber of hamlets and villages nestling here and there. The most renown-ed is **Marlas**, famed for its marble quarries and stone masons.

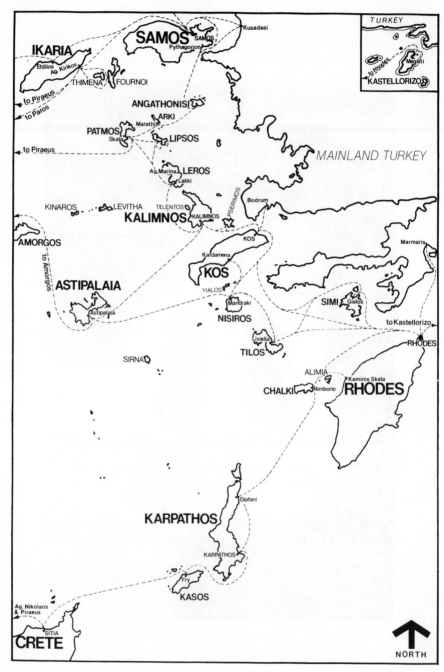

Illustration 32 The Dodecanese islands

PART FIVE

THE DODECANESE ISLANDS
(Dodekanes, Dhodhekanisos)

Dodecanese means the twelve islands, but confusingly embodies at least seventeen. Of all the islands and groupings, perhaps the Dodecanese can be 'all islands to all men' (and women!). From the monastic overlay of Patmos; the curious Italian art deco architecture of Leros; the bustling port activity of Kalimnos; the frantic package tourist hustle and bustle of Kos; the quaint island charm of Nisiros, the rather granite quietude of Tilos; the frenzied day-trip invasion of Simi; the old medieval city charm of Rhodes; the burgeoning desirability of Karpathos, to the forlorn, remoteness of Kasos. Other, smaller islands include Arki and Marathi, Angathonisi, Lipsos, Yialos, Pserimos, Chalki and distant Kastellorizo.

The history of the Dodecanese is one of almost constant invasion and conquest, starting with the Phoenicians, continued by the Minoans of Crete (2500-1440 BC), followed by the Achaians of the Peloponnese (1550-1150 BC) and then the Dorians from 1150-1000 BC. The Athenians took over in 480 BC, but the eminence of Rhodes was such that even Alexander the Great allowed the island to engage in flourishing trade with the Egyptians. The beginning of the end of this period of pre-eminence was heralded when Rhodes signed a treaty with Rome, in the second century BC. The Romans, to bring their wealthy and independent island ally into line, declared the Cycladean island of Delos a free port. From hereon it was downhill for Rhodes. The first thirteen hundred or so years of *anno Domini* were not to improve for the island, despite coming under Byzantium rule.

The proximity to the Turkish mainland, not unnaturally, resulted in the Dodecanese being strongly influenced, by their close neighbour. To add spice to the chronicles, the Knights of St John ruled over the islands, for some two hundred years, before finally being evicted by the Turks. The Knights' occupation resulted in their building fortifications on most of the islands. They repulsed two serious sieges, in 1444 and 1480, but fell in 1522 to the Turkish plenipotentiary, Suleiman 1st or The Magnificent.

Turkish dominance,over the Dodecanese islands, lasted 390 years but their influence would appear to have been restricted to a mosque here, and a minaret there. Arguably their 400 or so years of rule had less impact and influence than 31 years of Italian occupation, in the early 20th century.

The Turkish occupation ended in 1912, when the Italians drove them out of the Dodecanese. A number of international conferences failed to unseat the Italians who, on balance, must be considered to have benefited the islands during their occupation. The undue repression experienced throughout the Fascist part of this period should be weighed against the civil engineering, architectural and archaeological works put in hand by the Italians. Unfortunately the Second World War collapse of the Italians, in 1943, left a void, for which the German and British forces fought a number of bitter and costly battles, with much suffering incurred by the locals. After the collapse of the Third Reich, in 1945, the Dodecanese were freed by British and Greek troops, to be formally acceded to Greece in 1947.

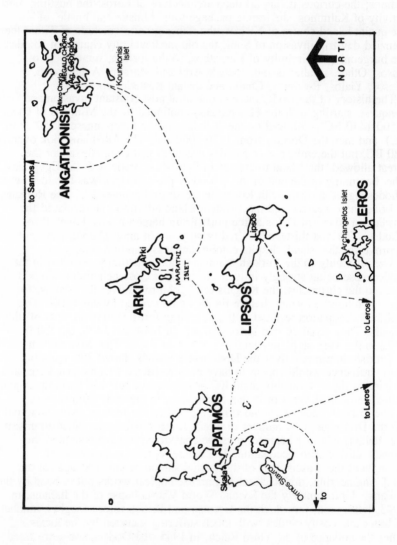

Illustration 33 Angathonisi, Arki, Lipsos &
Marathi islands

FACT FILE
ALTERNATIVE NAMES
Angathonissi, Agathonisi, Gaidaros, Gaidharos

STATISTICS
Tel prefix 0247. The island is about 2½km from top to bottom & 5km across, situated 25km from Samos and 35km from Patmos.

TRANSPORT LINKS
Ferry A weekly, scheduled ferry-
boat calls in, as does a twice weekly caique connection from Samos. A height of season trip boat comes from Leros - but not nearby Patmos, which is rather strange.

The once-a-week ferry proceeds to Pythagorion (Samos) and then runs south to Angathonisi, as well as Arki, Patmos, Lipsos, Leros, Kalimnos, Kos, Nisiros, Tilos, Simi and Rhodes.

A hundred and thirty one inhabitants populate this, the most northerly and remote of the Dodecanese islands. The true lover of Greece simply must visit. Despite its small size, the island community is vibrant and surprisingly healthy. Angathonisi does not emanate quite the same sense of doom as, for example, nearby Arki. This fortitude can be related to the fact that the population has remained relatively stable over the past twenty years.

There are three settlements on the island - **Ag Georgios**, the port, and the two villages of **Megalo Chorio** and **Mikro Chorio**. Megalo Chorio is on the mountainside to the right of the port, and Mikro Chorio, with only a dozen or so inhabitants, is to the left.

Accommodation is mainly to be found in the port, where there is also a swimming beach with clear seas. Although the few pensions and tavernas are down in the bay, most bona fide village life takes place in Megalo Chorio.

FACT FILE
STATISTICS
The island is some 5km long and 1km wide, located 17km from Patmos and 5km from Lipsos.

TRANSPORT LINKS A ferry-boat makes a once a week link. It calls in at Samos, then, on the return journey, Anga- thonisi, Patmos, Lipsos, Leros, Kalimnos, Kos, Nisiros, Tilos, Simi and Rhodes.

A gentle, hilly little island, covered with greenish scrub, but few trees. There is only one remaining settlement, **Port Augusta**, a cluster of primitive, stone-built dwellings around the inlet which makes up the island's harbour. Here, forty inhabitants struggle to keep the island alive.

Fishing is the sole source of income, whilst fish, eggs, goats milk and cheese are the only 'home-grown' produce. Everything else, including drinking water, has to be shipped in.

Accommodation is available, but not in private homes. There are a few bungalows for rent, owned by the same man who runs a restaurant/taverna.

If this sounds like Paradise, so it should. Visitors who stay can pretty well guarantee to be the only resident tourists, but perhaps a list of the non-existent facilities will not go amiss. There isn't: a beach (although of course bathing from rocks and rocky coves is possible); electricity (only oil lamps); drinking water 'on tap'; Post Office, shops or a bakery; transport; police station or policeman; nor does the island support a priest! The telephone is usually broken.

The locals are very kind and hospitable, and to those staying in the taverna-owner's rooms, the proprietor volunteers to supply any needs required. However do arrive prepared - with a phrase book and mosquito repellent!

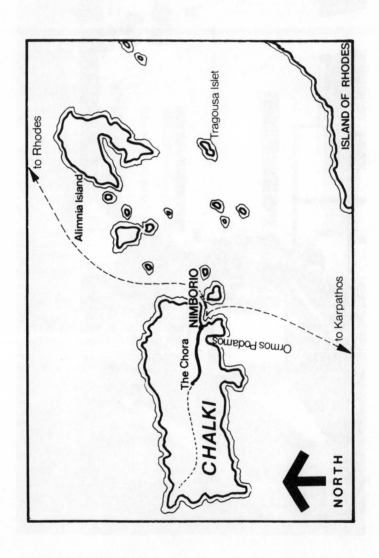

Illustration 34 Chalki island

FACT FILE
ALTERNATIVE NAMES Chalkis, Khalkia, Khalki, Halki

IMPRESSIONS Arid; grey & brown countryside quiet; no accommodation signs; very saline water.

RELIGIOUS FESTIVITIES include: 2nd August - Festival Ag Ioannis.

STATISTICS Tel prefix 0241. The island has an area of 28sq km & a population of about 340 people.

TRANSPORT LINKS

Ferry Only the smaller ferries can dock at the centrally situated ferry-boat quay.

Five scheduled ferries a week link with the other Dodecanese islands. A local caique runs a twice a week service to Kamiros Skala (Rhodes).

Owners of the already-full accommodation rarely meet the boats.

As would be expected, the island's history has mirrored that of nearby Rhodes. The Knights of St John built a Castle overlooking the old capital, the Chora.

It is rather a shock to find the island's limited accommodation occupied 'to capacity' by away-from-it-all package tourists.

Fortunately, the numbers are still limited, but it is not surprising those present are obvious, considering that the island's total population is under three hundred and fifty people.

Strangely, fishing remains a more extensive industry than tourism. Thus, those searching for an away-from-it-all package holiday, Chalki is a good out of the height of season bet.

MAIN PORTS & RESORTS
NIMBORIO (Emborio, Skala). The capital and port is charming and picturesque. The beach, some ten minutes walk away, is sandy, even if it has beach umbrellas.

An extremely odd, if not almost unique situation exists in respect of the letting of Rooms. As virtually all the available space is taken by package tour companies, it can be difficult, even outside the peak summer months, to find a bed. That which is available is over-priced and the very large hotel, at the far end of Emborio Bay, is often filled with conference visitors and closed to tourists. The plentiful tavernas are spread along the waterfront Esplanade.

Caiques run excursion trips to various island beaches, including **Areta, Kania, Trachia** and **Yiali**. The best beach is on the nearby islet of **Alimnia**, the site of a ruined castle.

The Chora The ruined, and now uninhabited, mountaintop Chora is about 1½hrs walk from the port. The castle, constructed on the site of an ancient acropolis, allows wonderful views over the sea and the rest of the island.

For greater detail acquire GROC's Candid Guide to Rhodes and The Dodecanese Islands

Illustration 35 Kalimnos island

FACT FILE

ALTERNATIVE NAMES
Kalymnos, Calymnos

IMPRESSIONS Larger & livelier than expected; scooters & motorbikes; a warren of back streets; arid, bare mountains; almost luxuriant valleys; preponderance of men; trees, flowers & fishing boats; gritty, saline water.

SPECIALITIES Sponges, divers & honey.

RELIGIOUS FESTIVALS include: 10-20th April - Blessing the fishing boats - Kalimnos Town; 27th July - Festival Ag Panteleimon.

STATISTICS Tel prefix 0243. The island is up to 21km long & 13km wide. Most of the 13,000 population live in or around the capital.

TRANSPORT LINKS
Ferry There are ferries to Kos and Rhodes on at least five days of each week; links to Leros, Patmos and Piraeus(M); some six days a week; two craft a week to Nisiros, Tilos and Simi; with one a week to Lipsos, Arki, Angathonisi, Samos, as well as Karpathos, Kasos, Crete, Astipalaia, Amorgos and Paros. During the summer months, an excursion boat makes daily sorties to nearby Pserimos island.
    Room owners meet the ferries.

Geographically a large island but, due to the mountainous nature and inaccessibility of much of the land, it appears to be a small location.

Kalimnos Town particularly, and the island less so, may come as a surprise, if not a shock. It's development as a holiday location has been so rapid that even books up to a few years old 'chatter on' about apparent poverty, the crippling effect of sponge diving, the unpreparedness of the island for tourism, the comparative peace and quiet, and more....

In reality, any poverty has been masked by a blanket of recent wealth attributable to the general rise in Greek affluence and tourism, in particular. Forget peace and quiet as the town absolutely hums, and the air is rent by the scream of high powered, noisy motorbikes, which are absolutely everywhere. No side-street can be considered safe from their intrusion, at any time of day or night, although there is supposed to be a ban on the night-time auditory assault.

The hills are too bare to be beautiful, except during the spring explosion of flowers, but individual areas are outstandingly lovely.

MAIN PORTS & RESORTS
KALIMNOS (Pothia) The capital town and port is much larger and livelier than would be imagined from reading the average travel book. The quayside absolutely throbs at night but, despite the overlay of tourism, much of old Kalimnos is still in evidence.

The Esplanade hotels tend to be hidden behind the profuse cover of the roadside trees and, as their signs are poorly illuminated, it is necessary to keep a sharp eye open for their whereabouts. There are cafe-bars almost everywhere, as well as one or two tavernas.

Places of interest include the:-
Ag Christos Church Sited on the imposing main square, which is edged by a long municipal building (occupied by the Police and Customs offices) and a clock tower.

This large church is not only strikingly beautiful but has attracted the interest of native and expatriate Greeks, mainly originating from Kalimnos, who have given of their time to redecorate and refurbish the internal decorations and icons.

KANTOUNI (6.5km from Kalimnos Town) This village is almost entirely a Greek holiday resort. The long, sandy beach only has a couple of restaurants and cafe-bars, as well as a hotel.

The impressive sweep of beach heads off northwards, past two chapels. The north side of an enormous rock, set down firmly on the surrounding terrain, is a hamlet and a little square set above the sea. The sandy beach below is small and rather seaweedy.

MYRTES (7.5km from Kalimnos Town) This seaside village marks an outbreak of 'pure', package holiday tourism. The pretty, tree lined avenue is spanned by various establishments. A number of hotels are supplemented by Rooms. Apart from various excursion boat trips, including a twice daily connection

to Leros, there are caiques which make the short crossing of fifteen minutes or so to:-

TELENTOS (Telendos) ISLAND More truly a sunken mountain than an island, it was probably connected to the main island, until an earthquake rent the two apart. There is almost certainly the remains of a submerged village in the channel. On the shore of Telentos, facing Kalimnos, is a small settlement with a population of about 100. A couple of beaches, a few tavernas, accommodation at two pensions, Roman remains and a medieval castle make this an almost ideal get-away location.

MASSOURI (8.5km from Kalimnos Town) A more 'developed', if neater location than Myrtes with some 'pubs', a number of villas, hotels, tavernas, moped hire and a disco.

EMBORIO (20½km from Kalimnos Town) The village is clean, ethnic, and 'old Greek', spaciously laid out with a central, small T-shaped quay. The latter projects from a fairly long, shallow, clean, stretch of pebble beach with a little sand and prettily shaded by mature trees. A few Rooms hide away in the settlement and there is a convenient backshore taverna.

VATHIS (8km from Kalimnos Town) A small port stripped of all the non-essentials. There are a number of kafeneions, two tavernas and a hotel. The sea surges into the fjord-like inlet, which terminates at the narrow, squared-off harbour.

FACT FILE

ALTERNATIVE NAME Scarpanto

IMPRESSIONS Island charm; dwellings dotted about; wealthy villages & returned expatriates; many white chapels; wind tortured trees.

RELIGIOUS FESTIVALS include: 28-29th August - St John the Headless, Avlona.

STATISTICS Tel prefix 0245. Nearly 50km long, up to 12km wide (& down to 4km narrow), with an area almost as large as the island of Kos. The population is only some 5,500, of which about 1,500 live in the capital, Karpathos (Pighadia).

TRANSPORT LINKS

Air The messy, not inconsiderable airfield is located some 15km from Karpathos Town. There are at least two flights a day to Rhodes, four a week to Sitia (Crete) and two a week to Kasos.

Taxis are *in situ*, whilst Olympic Airways operates a coach service to Karpathos Town.

Ferry The quay allows all-weather docking. There are ferries to Chalki and Rhodes two days a week, as well as boats to Crete, some Cyclades islands and Piraeus (M) on three days a week.

Overshadowed by its larger and more populous neighbours, the history of Karpathos follows closely in their footsteps. Findings of antiquity are few and far between, but there is evidence of a number of important, ancient sites. An idiosyncrasy was that the Knights only stayed two years, handing the island back to the previous overlords, the Venetian Cornaros family. The Turks took over in 1538.

The island's charms and attractions are now well-known but until recently, Karpathos was a lovely, relatively undeveloped island, with all the classic ingredients of a 'find'. These included inhabitants who made few concessions, but are still welcoming to visitors, and roads that tumble through stunning countryside, only to arrive at very little or nothing, and this after heading for a name on the map as large as a house.

A curious inheritance law, shared with the islands of Leros and Simi, is that the eldest daughter, not the eldest son, is the rightful heir. Reputably this quirk encouraged the males to emigrate, in order to make their fortunes elsewhere in the world. Certainly Karpathos is an island where the returning expatriates have resulted in 'North American' being the second language, as well as the presence of a disproportionate number of ladies' hairdressers.

MAIN PORTS & RESORTS

KARPATHOS (Pighadia). The capital town and main port edges a large and lovely bay, flanked by mountainsides to the north, with a

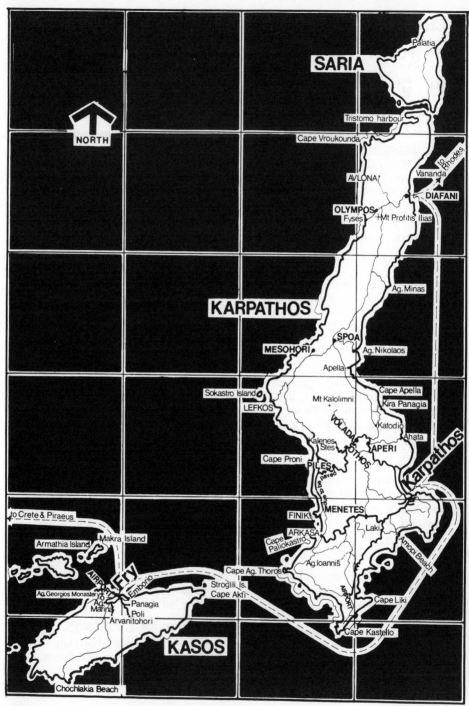

Illustration 36 Karpathos island

small islet set down in the middle of the inlet. The town gives an impression of being comparatively new and indeed much additional development is underway.

There is a small, rather littered strip of sandy beach, close to the town clock, but the main beach is a fifteen minute trudge to the west and takes in two bays. The first, smaller bay has a steeply climbing, sandy shore. To the left, beyond a mini-headland, is a much larger, curving, sandy foreshore encircling an adjoining bay.

At the height of the season, Rooms can be difficult to find at any one of the very good places available. There are some splendid restaurants and tavernas.

Amopi Beach (8km from Karpathos Town) The road peters out on the edge of the lovely, sandy beach and tiny bay. A number of small neat holiday flats have been built on the edge of the foreshore, with more under construction. There are Rooms and a couple of taverna/restaurants.

LEFKOS (26km from Karpathos Town) The road reveals a fantastic view over a long, sandy beach set in a deep bay, with a few white, square homesteads scattered about, and a chapel on the headland.

The road runs out on a grassy headland, on all sides of which are sandy beaches. The sea is brilliantly blue and clear and this is a superb, five star location with miles of sandy beach and rocky, sea-washed islets. One of the two tavernas rent Rooms.

OLYMPOS (44km (eastern route) from Karpathos Town) The village lies to the left, around and surmounting a hill-top on the side of the mountain. First impressions include the village women attired in their distinctive head-dress and costumes, the many churches, rich soil and a general air of neatness. The inaccessibility of the village, until comparatively recent times, has preserved an ancient way of life in a 'kind of' time-warp. The houses reputedly retain an affinity with those of Homer's day, the give away indicators being the sectioning into three, the solid timber doors with wooden keys and locks, and the colourfully painted verandas. The house interiors are singular, more especially the front rooms dominated by a balcony bed or furniture, including carved dressers.

There are simple Rooms, a couple of small pensions and a modest hotel.

DIAFANI (49km from Karpathos Town) This is the island's second port. and the flavour is rather Turkish. The women, of gypsy appearance, dress in traditional costume, woollen leggings, leather boots and jewellery, including large, gold, dangly ear-rings. The pint-sized finger quay can only accommodate the smallest inter-island ferries. The larger boats, when and if they stop, employ a local boat owner to ferry passengers, their goods and chattels to and from the shore. There are some four hotel/pensions and numerous tavernas.

The pebble and sand beach stretches to the right of the quay, whilst there is another agreeable beach at Vananda, about ½hr to the north of Diafani.

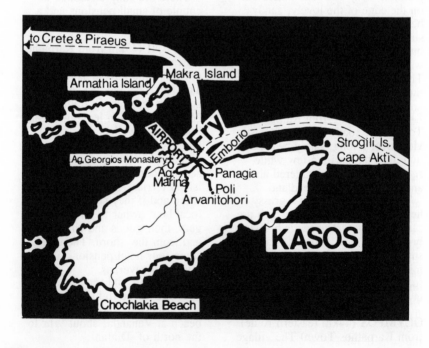

Illustration 37 Kasos island

FACT FILE
ALTERNATIVE NAMES Kassos

IMPRESSIONS Stones, boulders & more stones...; barren & messy; depopulated; very friendly, welcoming people.

SPECIALITIES Suez Canal pilots &, of course, the Holocaust.

RELIGIOUS FESTIVALS include: 6/7th June - Celebrations in memory of the 'Holocaust', Kasos Town.

STATISTICS Tel prefix 0245. Length 18km, up to 7km wide, & a population of about 1,200.

TRANSPORT LINKS
Air The neat, little, earth airfield is some 15 minutes walk from

Fry.Passengers are expected to walk into town. There are two taxis, but one is usually broken down and the remaining driver is pretty busy shuffling locals about. For some reason the bus does not include the Airport on its scheduled route. There are six flights a week to Rhodes, as well as two a week to Kasos and Sitia (Crete).

Ferry The smaller ferry-boats still dock at Emborio Port, whilst the larger ferries berth at the town finger pier. Three days a week, ferries connect with Crete, some Cyclades islands and Piraeus (M); twice a week with Karpathos, Chalki and Rhodes; and once a week a craft runs the length of the Dodecanese islands.

Being so adjacent, it mirrors the events of Karpathos island, with some notable exceptions. The inhabitants once numbered about 20,000 people, but now only about 1,200 soldier on. Apart from the unattractive nature of the place, depredation of the population was carried out by the Egyptians, who razed the island to the ground, in 1824. This event is still referred to as the 'Holocaust'. Apart from killing the menfolk and setting fire to the villages, the Egyptians carried off 2,000 women and children to slavery. Such are the vagaries of history, that only thirty five years later almost 5,000 Kasiot men arrived in Egypt, to assist in the construction of the Suez Canal! This had an interesting spin-off, in

that many of the Kasiots became Suez pilots, resulting in a once sizeable Greek community at Port Said. Some years later, a number of the more far-sighted citizens used their initiative, realised the advantages of steam, and were amongst the first Greeks to opt for and operate steamships, in preference to sail. There are now few tangible remains of the resultant family fortunes because they also had the foresight to emigrate, once again. There is a local saying that if all the Kasiot shipowners were to return, then they would circle the island, three times.

Nowadays many of the inhabitants commute to North America, for months at a time. It is wise counsel, as on Karpathos island, to

For greater detail acquire GROC's Candid Guide to Rhodes and the Dodecanese Islands

voice any adverse comments in a *sotto voce,* as most of the locals understand of English.

Plus points include the unfailing friendliness of the islanders and the fact that Kasos undoubtedly remains untouched by tourism.

MAIN PORTS & RESORTS
FRY (Phry, Fri, Ophrys). The capital town and port where a finger pier has been constructed, adjacent to the settlement. The beach is a small patch of large pebbles, nestling between large slabs of shelving lava rock, covered in a fine down of dead seaweed, bits of tar and a fair sprinkling of flotsam and plastic. There is a better prospect, some way beyond the airport strip, west around the headland. This is close to Ag Georgios Monastery where, incidentally, visitors can stay at night, for 'free'. The 'recognised' beach is sandy and set in pleasant surroundings but is located on the nearby **Armathis island**, which can only be reached by using a local caique. The sea journey takes 15mins. A few rave on about the three hour distant **Chochlakia Beach**, way down at the south-west end of the island.

There are Rooms hidden away, here and there, a substantial, if provincial, homely hotel and a couple of tavernas.

Emborio Port The ferry-boat harbour which is rather squalid and untidy. The sea leg of the too-small port is closed in by an oversized commercial quay.

The larger fishing boats berth in one crook of the harbour wall and a thin stretch of beach runs down to the other angle. Pretensions to grandeur are evidenced by a scruffy public garden, a municipal toilet block, which is 'kept' in an indescribable condition, and a rather avant-garde, but unused, column mounted port office.

FACT FILE
ALTERNATIVE NAMES
(Kastelorizo, Kastellorizon, Kastelloriso, Castelorizo, Megisti.

IMPRESSIONS Attractive port; bygone affluence; crumbling houses & ruins; crystal clear seas; inexpensive seafood; fiercely Greek.

SPECIALITIES Seafood; stravo & katimari, two pastry sweets made with honey & nuts.

RELIGIOUS FESTIVALS include: 24th April - Feast of St George, at the two large churches in Megisti (both named Ag. Georgios) & the Monastery of Ag Georgios, in the mountains; 21st May - Ag Konstantinos (the main Church on Horafia Square); 20th July - Festival, Profitias Ilias.

STATISTICS Tel prefix 0241. The island is about 6km from top to toe, up to 3km from east to west, with an area of 9sq km. The population numbers about 250. Kastellorizo is the most easterly of the Greek islands & lies only 2km from the Turkish coastline.

TRANSPORT LINKS
Air The little airfield is situated on top of the island, about a ten minute drive from the town. There is a waiting room and not much else. A minibus meets the plane, otherwise it is a very hot, long walk. Three flights a week connect with Rhodes.

Ferry The ferry-boats dock at the quay, to the left of the deep bay in which the port and town is set. As the Rhodes ferry calls only twice a week, it is met by most of the population, including owners of accommodation.

Mentioned by Homer, the island's first named settler was supposed to be a King Meges from Echinada, who may have given the island its alternative name of Megisti. On the other hand, Megesti (or Megiste - the largest) probably relates to the fact that Kastellorizo is the biggest of a small archipelago of some other ten or twelve uninhabited islands and islets. The island sent ships to Troy and has been inhabited since Neolithic times. The Dorians first built a fort, where the 'Red Castle' now stands, and also constructed an ancient acropolis at Paleokastro, the walls of which are still visible.

The island fell under the rule of Rhodes for much of its history, with the Knights of St John reconstructing the Castle in the 1380s. The red rock used in the building of the fort's wall resulted in the island's current name, Kastellorizo (from the Italian Castello Rosso or Red Fortress). In 1440 it was occupied, for the first time, by the Turks, followed by the King of Naples, in 1450. By 1523 the island was made part of the Ottoman empire, though the Venetians settled Kastellorizo for two periods, in 1570 and 1659.

For greater detail acquire GROC's Candid Guide to Rhodes and the Dodecanese Islands

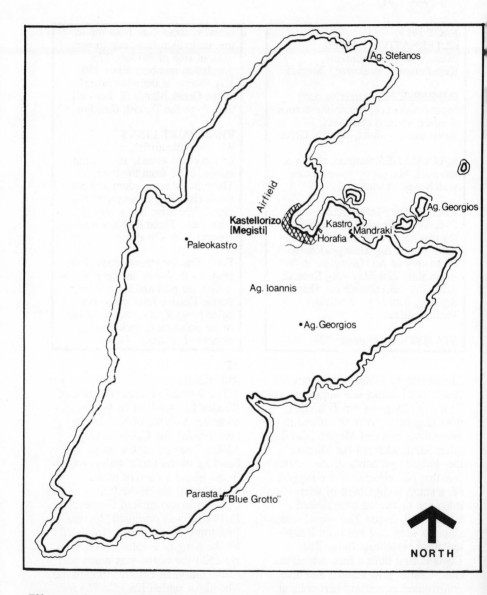

Illustration 38 Kastellorizo island

Kastellorizo took part in the War of Independence, in 1821, being the first Dodecanese island to revolt, but in 1833 was handed back to the Turks, in exchange for the island of Evia. The islanders prospered greatly, as shipowners, towards the end of the 19th century - the period of Kastellorizo's supreme affluency, when many of its big houses were built, and between 15,000 and 17,000 people lived on the island.

The First World War heralded the outset of the island's modern tragedy, and in 1927 a great earthquake destroyed many more buildings. Despite which, during the 1930s, Kastellorizo enjoyed a short autumn of prosperity. The outbreak of the Second World War marked the beginning of the end. The popuuation were evacuated to Egypt by the Allies, who then occupied the island. Prior to the remaining islanders' return, the town and port was burnt down and ruined beyond recognition.

It is said that the expatriate islanders consider themselves Kastellorizons, first and foremost, and natives of their country, second.

Kastellorizo remains a very quiet, unspoilt location. Admittedly there are no beaches, but there are plenty of rocky coves for bathing and the fish-filled seas are amazingly clear. The people certainly are friendly and helpful.

MAIN PORTS & RESORTS
KASTELLORIZO (Kastellorizon, Megisti). The capital town and only port, the initially attractive appearance of which belies the fact that most of it has been ruined.

Although finding accommodation is usually no problem, mid-July to mid-August can prove rather difficult. There are some excellent tavernas but they are not as inexpensive as might be imagined. This is because they not only cater for yacht owners, but all supplies now have to come from Rhodes, fraternisation with adjacent Turkey now being firmly forbidden by the authorities.

Places of interest include the:-
The 'Red' Castle The structure was originally built in Doric times and is believed to have given the island its name, when rebuilt by the Knights of St John, around 1380. The Greek flag still flies proudly from the hilltop tower.
Museum Very pleasantly laid out.
The Lycian Tomb The tomb is distinguished by a heavy stone entrance, beyond which can be seen the actual digging. It is the only such tomb in modern Greece.
The Mosque The two hundred year old Turkish Mosque is situated on the quayside.
Caique Trips These are available around the island, to other nearby islets and, most commonly, to the 'Blue Grotto', on the east coast.
The Blue Grotto is certainly not to be missed. The caiques take about forty minutes to reach the cave. Once inside, the chamber opens out into a vast cavern. There are stalactites and a 'resident' pair of seals, who continue to breed here.

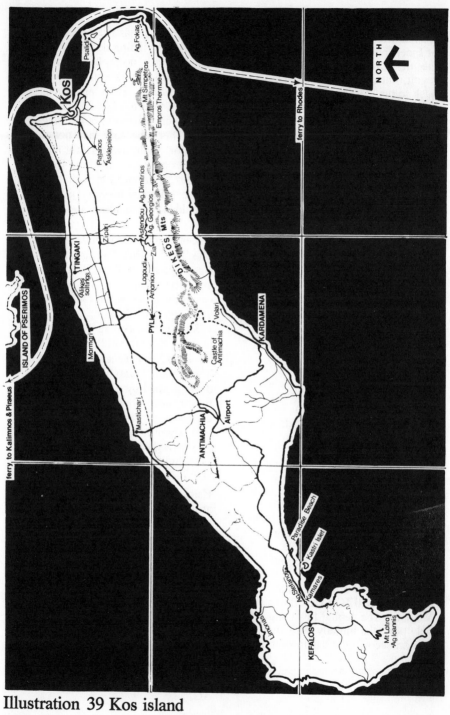

Illustration 39 Kos island

FACT FILE
ALTERNATIVE NAME Cos

IMPRESSIONS Mass tourism; the 'Costa Brava' of the Greek islands; bland, unexceptional, but expensive food & dining places; verdant growth; oleanders & bougainvillea; marvellous ruins.

SPECIALITIES Cheap alcoholic spirits & perfumes (as for Rhodes).

RELIGIOUS FESTIVALS include: 24th June - Fire of St John; 30th July - Festival of St Apostle, Antimachia; August - Festival of the Oath of Hippocrates, Asklepieion; 6th August - Saviour's Metamorphosis, Kos; 7th September - Festival of St Virgin of Tsukanon, Kardamena.

STATISTICS Tel prefix 0242. The second largest of the islands in this group (to Rhodes), being 45km from tip to toe, & up to 10½km at the widest point. Out of a population of 18,000, about 8,000 live in the capital.

TRANSPORT LINKS
Air The airport is located in approximately the centre of the island. Arrivals by Olympic Airways can catch the airline bus, package tourists are collected by their holiday companies' transport, but freelance travellers are at the mercy of taxis or can walk to the adjacent village of Antimachia, where a scheduled bus service stops. Kos enjoys at least two flights a day to Athens, one a day to Rhodes; two a week to Leros, one a week to Samos and Thessaloniki(M).

Ferry The ferry-boats dock alongside the narrow access of the almost circular harbour, close by the Castle. There are six ferries a week to Kalimnos, Piraeus(M) and Rhodes; five boats a week to Leros and Patmos; three a week to Nisiros, Tilos and Simi; and one connection a week to Lipsos, Arki, Angathonisi, Samos, Astipalaia, Amorgos, Paros, Chios, Lesbos, Limnos and Kavala(M). Owners of accommodation meet the ferries.

Hydrofoil In the summer months, weather permitting, there is a two/three times a week connection to Simi and Rhodes, as well as Leros and Patmos.

The geographical proximity has resulted in much of the island's history paralleling that of Rhodes. Alexander the Great occupied Kos, in 336 BC. On his death, the Egyptians took over and their rulers, the Ptolemies, visited, as did Cleopatra. The Romans held sway until the Byzantine Empire took over, only for the Saracens to sack the place, in the 11th century. It took the Knights six years longer to conquer Kos than it did Rhodes, but they still lost it to the Turks at the same time as Rhodes.

Earthquakes wrought havoc during the last century BC, early AD, added to which Kos Town

For greater detail acquire GROC's Candid Guide to Rhodes and the Dodecanese Islands

and harbour were badly damaged by tremors as recently as 1933.

Nowadays the holiday centres are equally spread throughout this green and pleasant land, from Kos to Kefalos, from Kardamena to Mastichari. The only locations that the developers have left unsullied are the eastern side of the Mt Dikeos range and the area to the west of Mt Latra.

MAIN PORTS & RESORTS
KOS The capital town and main port. Unlike Rhodes, the smaller harbour is wholly and attractively enveloped by the town. Furthermore, the fortress picturesquely borders one edge of the port.

The quayside and its immediate surrounds are a gathering place for the marina jet-set whilst the inner town, abounding with archaeological ruins, has an almost tropical milieu. This impression is heightened by the huge palm trees, the giant, colourful, luxuriant bougainvillea, oleander and jasmine that burgeon forth. The outer town has a prosperous, suburban ambience.

The nearest beach to the harbour is a narrow, small pebble and sand, rather grubby strip, in the shadow of the Castle walls. Another easily reached and convenient spot, is to one side of the seafront building in which is situated the Police officers' club. To the north is a long, clean, shelving beach of coarse grained sand.

There is any amount of accommodation, but the town is singularly bereft of even good, let alone outstanding eating places.

Places of interest include the:-
Ancient Agora & Port Quarter A number of interesting exhibits, dating as far back as the 4th century

BC. Interestingly enough, it was an earthquake in 1933 that destroyed many medieval buildings and thus enabled the eager Italian architects to get to work.

Close by the north end of this site is the:-
Square of The Hippocratic Plane Tree The lovely plateia is dominated by an extremely old and 'arthritic tree', the branches of which are supported at every possible point. The buildings in and around the square are of a most diverse and dissimilar architectural milieu, and include:-
The Mosque of the Loggia-Hatji-Hasan Built in the late 1700s, the pleasant flight of marble steps, a splendid minaret, as well as the coloured stones, used in the construction make an impressive sight.
The Castle of the Knights An imposing Crusader castle, the walls of which are in a surprisingly good state of repair. The Avenue of Palms was originally a moat.

The main square has a number of interesting features including:-
The Museum A rather bland, small, yellow building of Italian construction, with an interesting collection of statues.
Deftedar Mosque Creates an island site towards one corner of the square. Various tourist shops are incongruously let into the building.

Behind the Mosque is the very pretty, if isolated, flower covered medieval **Gate of the Forum.**

Elsewhere particularly rich archaeological pickings include the:-

Temple & Altar of Dionysos Dated 3rd century BC, opposite which is the:-
Casa Romana The 3rd century AD

remains of a Roman house, super-imposed on the ruins of a larger Greek mansion, dated between 50-30 BC.

Acropolis An old site, with a minaret now in position.

Roman Road A stretch of paved way, edged by the remains of Roman built houses.

House of Europe Famous for its mosaics.

Hereabouts are the ancient remains of:-

The Nymphaeum, The Xystos (gymnasium), baths, latrines, taverns and more mosaics.

Ancient Odeion A theatre, approached and framed by a deliciously cool avenue of stately cypresses. Although extensively restored it is a beautiful construction, in a lovely setting, and is occasionally used for modern-day productions.

The Asklepieion (4km from Kos Town) The inland Sanctuary is named after the God of healing and is considered to have been constructed, after the death of Hippocrates, in the 4th century BC, on the site of sacred ground.

TINGAKI (11km from Kos Town) An exceedingly smart, small, but very pleasant, if crowded, north coast resort. To the right of the central grove of trees, up-market hotels edge the broad, sandy beach. There are seven or eight hotels, pensions and Rooms.

MARMARI (15km from Kos Town) A burgeoning beach resort hosting a very expensive hotel.

MASTICHARI (30km from Kos Town) The comparatively massive port facility services excursion craft connecting to the islands of Kalimnos and Pserimos. Around the corner is a broad, sandy, beguiling beach, with a beach shower close to a scattered grove of trees. A number of acceptable restaurants string along the back-shore. The package hotels and pensions are underpinned by numerous Rooms.

KARDAMENA (27km from Kos Town) Those holiday-makers who expect to find an attractive, south coast fishing community and village, a quiet backwater steeped in a centuries-old way of life, will be in for a big shock. Even the original core of the village is now hard to detect, as 'Costa del Greco' has overlaid the place. The shoreline is a long, beguiling stretch of beautiful sandy, if crowded beach.

Most of the hotels and pensions are block booked by package tourists. Even so the buses are still met by owners of accommodation who offer pleasant, if pricey Rooms. There are a number of reasonable snackbars, tavernas and restaurants, in addition to the glut of cocktail bars, pubs and discos.

Paradise Beach (approx 35km from Kos Town) For once the descriptive adjective, paradise, does not belie the long, lovely, crescent-shaped, sandy beach.

AG STEFANOS The views from the hillside above the village are breathtaking. Mt Latra rears up in the middle distance, Nisiros island crouches on the far horizon whilst, on the left, is an incredible *Club Mediterranee* complex. Down below, close to the shore of the long, gently curving, sandy bay, is the islet of **Kastri**, capped by a diminutive chapel. There is some accommodation, as well as plenty of dining possibilities.

For greater detail acquire GROC's Candid Guide to Rhodes and the Dodecanese Islands

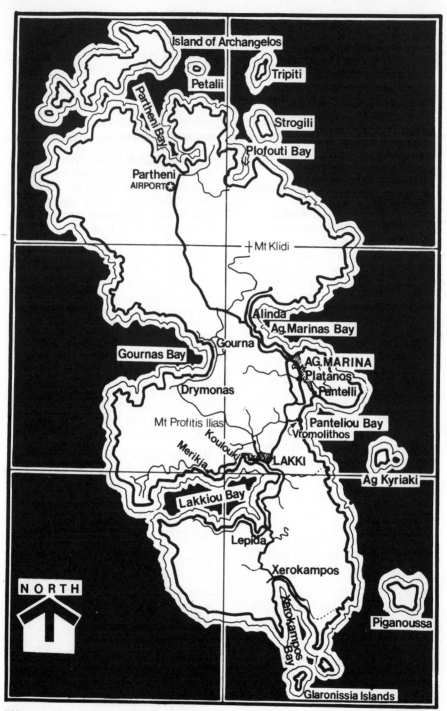

Illustration 40 Leros island

FACT FILE

IMPRESSIONS Faded, 1930s Italianesque buildings; palm trees; fencing & barbed wire; green beehives; little agriculture.

RELIGIOUS FESTIVALS include: Sunday before the Shrove Monday - Carnival; 26th September - Second World War commemoration, Lakki.

STATISTICS Tel prefix 0247. The population of some 8,500 live on an island savagely indented by the sea. Leros is about 15km long & between 11½km & 1¾km wide.

TRANSPORT LINKS
Air The strip, close by the northern village of Partheni, allows an adequate service. There are at least five flights a week to Athens and two a week to Kos.

Ferry The quay is sited towards the west of Lakki Port. Five ferries a week connect to Patmos and Piraeus (M), as well as Kalimnos, Kos and Rhodes. One boat a week links with Lipsos, Arki, Angathonisi and Samos, as does a craft with Nisiros, Tilos and Simi.

Arrivals are offered accommodation, whatever time of night the ferry docks.

Hydrofoil In the summer months, weather permitting, a hydrofoil services runs two/three times a week to Patmos, as well as Kos, Sami and Rhodes.

A Homeric island, much of its history is shared with the rest of the Dodecanese.

During the Second World War, Leros was the scene of a very bloody campaign in which some 5,000 British troops were cut down during German parachute assaults. The island and the islanders have not yet been overwhelmed by package tourism. Leros is more a holiday resort of the *cognoscenti*, than the mob, but development is taking place at the seaside villages of Alinda and Xerokampos.

MAIN PORTS & RESORTS

LAKKI The main port edges a section of a rather strange, huge bay. To those surprised that Lakki is not the capital, it only has to be realised that the Italians were almost wholly responsible for the harbour's development, in conjunction with the massive port facilities across the bay. Lakki is a horribly magnificent, if faded and crumbling concrete monument to the Mussolini inspired, Italian dream of a Mediterranean Empire.

There aren't any beaches in the port, it being necessary to walk 1km, to a tiny, tree lined lido at **Koulouki**. There is a snackbar and a very small, narrow strip of sandy beach. A further 1½km leads to **Merikia**, a rather strange but pleasant area by the sea's edge, set amongst a grove of trees in which are a number of large, ruined buildings.

Certainly considering it's loca-

For greater detail acquire GROC's Candid Guide to Rhodes and the Dodecanese Islands

tion, it is surprising that there are so few hotels, pensions or Rooms. And if Lakki lacks breadth of accommodation, then eating places are almost non-existent.

PLATANOS VILLAGE (3.5km from Lakki Port)

The inland capital built on and over the crest of a ridge. To the north the ground falls away towards the port of Ag Marina and to the south towards the fishing hamlet of Pantelli.

Platanos village is dominated by a castle, in the shadow of which is a pretty, small, main square. The large, almost disproportionately large, Town Hall occupies one side of the square, whilst a few kafeneions, tavernas and Rooms take up the other flanks of the plateia, and surrounding lanes.

The Kastro The view is remarkable. Originally a Byzantine fort, it was taken over by the Knights. The church inside the entrance has been rebuilt.

AG MARINA (about 4½km from Lakki Port)

The island's second port and original harbour of the island. Fortunately the relevant authorities have decided to preserve the tree lined, quiet village, which is a perfect example of its genre. A narrow, pretty little lane edges the sea and a small beach.

PANTELLI (about 4½km from Lakki Port)

This fishing hamlet is a lovely, small seaside settlement, with a fine shingle, sandy but rather limited and narrow beach. Working caiques are moored haphazardly to ramshackle finger piers which jut out from the ragged waterfront. A couple of tavernas attractively border the backshore and there are several pensions, as well as Rooms.

VROMOLITHOS (2km from Lakki Port)

An east coast hamlet which spreads along a pretty, sheltered, curved bay with a tree shaded, stony foreshore. The shingly beach is narrow to the right, but pleasantly opens out, to the left. There is a hotel, some Rooms, a taverna and a coffee bar.

ALINDA (7km from Lakki Port)

Still a pleasant location but, even out of the height of the season months, the very narrow beach is rather crowded. The bay is made up of numerous, tiny, fine shingle and sandy beaches backed by an admixture of spaced out kafeneions, pensions, hotels and houses.

XEROKAMPOS (4½km from Lakki Port)

This south coast village spreads its way down to a sleepy, quiet and lovely bay, with a pebbly beach stretching either side of a rustic taverna. The beach to the left is slightly oily, kelpy, and the water muddy. There are Rooms close to the beach.

GOURNA (10km from Lakki Port)

A west coast hamlet which spreads round the mainly rocky but pretty bay. There is a small stretch of narrow, pebbly beach, and a chapel, idyllically set on an islet, close by the shore. There are no facilities.

PARTHENI (12km from Lakki Port)

A north coast, rather rustic location edging an inlet of the bay of Partheni, the shoreline of which is somewhat marshy.

FACT FILE

ALTERNATIVE NAMES Lipsi, Lipso, Lipsoi

IMPRESSIONS Quiet; fishy; blue & white churches; vivid town.

SPECIALITIES Woven carpets.

RELIGIOUS FESTIVALS include: 24th August - Festival of the Madonna of Charos Chapel.

STATISTICS Tel prefix 0247. The island is about 8km long &, at the narrowest point, only 1km wide. There are about 650 people.

TRANSPORT LINKS
Ferry Both a weekly scheduled ferry-boat, and a summer months daily excursion craft from Patmos call. The ferry-boat links with Patmos, Arki, Angathonisi and Samos, before running south to Rhodes via Leros, Kalimnos, Kos, Nisiros, Tilos and Simi.
   The boats are met by jeeps and Datsun trucks, with wooden boards on top indicating the name of the beach to which they will transport passengers. Before leaping in, it is wise to note that only Katsadia Beach has any kind of facilities - a taverna with Rooms. These vehicles are the island's only transport.

Historically the island was been inextricably linked to Patmos, the Monastery of which owned Lipsos for some six hundred years.

Lipsos is usually lumped in with the islets of Arki, Angathonisi and Marathi. Visitors to this pretty, idyllic spot, won't be the only foreigners present, as quite a few island aficionados have already sought out the place. Lipsos is rather more down the road to tourist development, than the other three, and should be visited before this activity takes a firm hold.

MAIN PORTS & RESORTS
LIPSOS The port and small fishing village is the only settlement, and is very attractive, with a Cycladean type, large, blue domed church dominating the scene.

Lipsos has one modern hotel, which caters for 'away from it all' package tourists, as well as a small selection of tavernas. A further five pensions offer reasonably priced accommodation.

Katsadia Beach Apart from the jeep ride, it is a twenty-five minute walk through fertile countryside and over a hill, from whence the track drops down to the wide, picturesque bay with a narrow, golden sandy beach.

Rooms and food are available from an extremely primitive taverna. There isn't any electricity, and only water from the well, but the meals are tasty and inexpensive.

For greater detail acquire GROC's Candid Guide to Rhodes and the Dodecanese Islands

CHAPTER 48

FACT FILE
STATISTICS Tel prefix 0247. The island is approximately 1km 'round', some 4km from Arki and 14km from Patmos.

TRANSPORT LINKS
The only transport link is a small, 'scheduled' passenger caique that runs daily from Patmos, weather conditions permitting.

This low-lying, little islet boasts one family. They live here for the summer months in order to run the clean, and very modern taverna and accommodation.

Marathi is a super place to stay for those who desire peace, seclusion, comfort, good food as well as a long, sand and shingle beach. This shoreline edges a very clear sea.

FACT FILE
ALTERNATIVE NAMES Nisyros, Nissiros

IMPRESSIONS Crumbling, Italian built municipal buildings; friendly inhabitants.

SPECIALITIES Sumada, an almond cordial, diluted with water to drink.

RELIGIOUS FESTIVALS include: 20-21st June - Festival of Ag Nikitas, Church close to the harbour; 15th August - Festival of Panaghia - Monastery of the Lady Virgin of the Rocks.

STATISTICS Tel prefix 0242. The island is almost circular, being 10km wide & 8km long. Of the 1300 population, some 800 live in Mandraki Town & Port. The island's central core is a bubbling volcano, recessed in a circular crater, some 4km across.

TRANSPORT LINKS
Ferry A 'reasonably' irregular inter-island service is backed up by daily caique trip boats from Kardamena (Kos), in addition to excursion craft from Kos Town. At least three scheduled ferries a week connect to Tilos, Simi, and Rhodes, as well as to Kos, Kalimnos; once a week with Lipsos, Patmos, Arki, Angathonisi and Samos, as well as Astipalaia, Amorgos, Paros and Piraeus(M).

The island's history is as for other islands in the group.

Due to a lack of facilities, Nisiros has remained a day-trip location. The curious make excursion boat visits in order to view the volcano. There are no other 'attractions', to swell the present numbers of daily tourists.

The volcano visitors are jammed into one of two buses that marshal on the harbour quay. These crawl and steeply wind their way up the extensively terraced, thickly tree planted and green mountain slopes. The road breasts the rim of the large, cultivated but parched looking sunken plain, which edges the core of the volcano, and the buses descend, on an unmade road, into the very large crater, to one side of which is the epicentre of the sulphuric activity.

Overlooking the site are the two crater-edge villages of **Emborio** and **Nika**.

Emborio is nearly deserted and much of it is in ruins. Nikia is more attractive, alive and closer to the rim of the volcano. Both villages enjoy magnificent views of Nisiros, the adjacent islands of Tilos, Yialos and Kos, as well as the Turkish mainland.

MAIN PORTS & RESORTS
MANDRAKI The capital village and port is a strange, many faceted, strung out locale. The immediate approach from the harbour is shabby, unprepossessing and dusty, and is followed by a narrow lane, toy-town milieu. That sector which climbs the hillside takes on

---

For greater detail acquire GROC's Candid Guide to Rhodes and the Dodecanese Islands

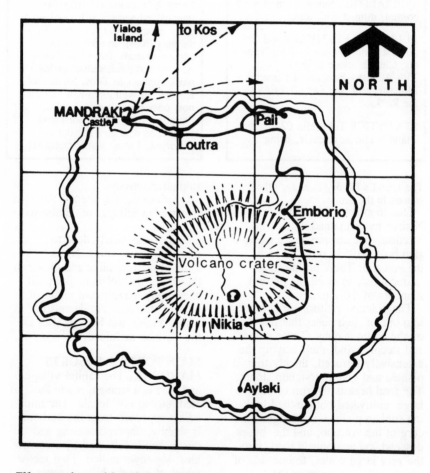

Illustration 41 Nisiros island

a Greek Welsh village quality. The terraced houses, and their small flights of steps, edge the very narrow alleys. The women sit on their doorsteps, dressed in traditional costumes, knitting and gossiping.

There is a small beach, two-thirds of the way to the harbour. It is messy, kelp covered and rather cluttered with 'this and that'. To the left of Mandraki Town is the unusual **Koklaki beach**, which is not so much a beach, more a small bay of large pebbles and stones.

The town actually takes on the character of a vehicleless, French Dordogne village and the grand Town Hall is followed by a tree shaded square, edged by cafe-bars. This is a lovely location, with more than sufficient accommodation and a fairly wide variety of eating places, one or two of which are excellent.

Places of interest include the:-
The Monastery of the Lady Virgin of the Rocks The religious house is perched on the cliff-edge overlooking the town, and reached via a steep, narrow flight of steps. A signpost points the way. Unusually the door is often left open, to allow an inspection of the lovely, 'standard', rich and dark Byzantine monastery interior.
The Castle The fortress, which dominates the hillside headland, to the west of the town, is accessed by the next flight of steps up from those to the Monastery. The ruined, large hewn block, fort walls, up to three metres thick in places, allow magnificent views.
Town Museum This tiny, two storey Dickensian house is situated in a quaint corner, opposite a restored Byzantine church
Yialos islet Yialos is about a twenty minute boat trip from Nisiros. The odd appearance is due to continued, extensive surface mining for building materials.

LOUTRA (2km from Mandraki Town) A rather strange hamlet with a large seafront building, partly in ruins which houses a small and rather incongruous taverna. Next door is a very big, warehouse-type construction, a thermal spa. Rooms are available for patients who bathe in the hot mineral waters.

PALI (4km from Mandraki Town) A very spread out fishing hamlet. To the left is a rocky breakwater forming a large caique harbour. Pali has Rooms, a couple of tavernas and a smart hotel. From Pali, a straight track edges a long, volcanic sand, but littered beach. To the right spreads ramshackle, sprawling, dwellings and scatterings of the village's outskirts.

For greater detail acquire GROC's Candid Guide to Rhodes and the Dodecanese Islands

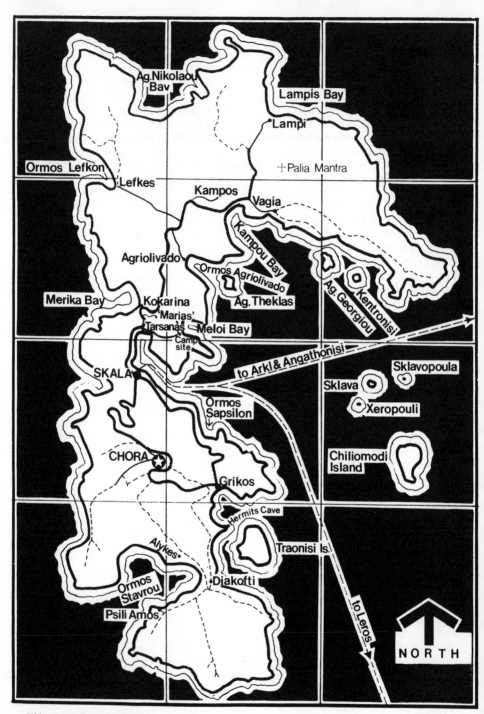

Illustration 42 Patmos island

FACT FILE
IMPRESSIONS Cruise ships; tourists; neat farming-country.

RELIGIOUS FESTIVALS include: 6th March - Festival in memory of the death of the Blessed Christodoulos, The Monastery; 21st May - Saint's day, The Monastery; 15th August - Festival of the Panaghia Church; 21st October - Festival to celebrate the return of the bones of the Blessed Christodoulos from Evia (Euboea). The Monastery also celebrates the national holidays & religious festivals, in very grand style, including the Orthodox Easter & the 'Washing of the Feet', on Maundy Thursday.

STATISTICS Tel prefix 0247. The extremely indented island is 14km long, & up to 8km wide. In excess of 2,000 of the total population of 3,500 live in Skala Port & the Chora.

TRANSPORT LINKS
Ferry Five ferries a week link with Piraeus(M); four a week to Leros, Kalimnos, Kos and Rhodes; one a week to Arki, Angathonisi, Samos, Chios, Lesbos, Limnos and Kavala, as well as Nisiros, Tilos and Simi.
  The boats are met by a swarm of people, many offering Rooms.

Hydrofoil A summer months, weather permitting, two or three times a week service to Leros, Kos, Simi and Rhodes.

Unusually for the Dodecanese, the history of Patmos does not mirror that of the other islands. The reason lies in the Romans exiling St John the Divine to Patmos, in about AD 95, where he experienced a revelation. Some hundreds of years later one of St John's admirers transcribed his 'memories' of the Saint. Pirates kept the island clear of pilgrims, until 1088, when the Blessed Christodoulos received the sanction of the Orthodox Church to build a monastery in honour of St John. The fame of the religious order protected the fortified Monastery, if not always the island, from the worst depredations of the various overlords. The latter included the Venetians twice, a Pope, and the Turks.

The latter lost possession for a number of years, after the 1821 War of Independence, took it back, only to be followed, in turn, by the Italians and Germans.

One of the reasons for the Monastery's continued wealth and prosperity was that it owned a fleet of ships, even whilst, ostensibly, under the rule of the Turks. The captains of the ships were in the habit of commissioning stylised, pendant jewellery symbolising their sailing vessels, with baubles hanging down to represent the keels. Some of these renowned pieces are displayed in the Monastery museum, or Treasury.

The countryside is neat, busy

---

and pretty. The heavily indented
coastline has resulted in a disproportionately large number of bays
for an island as small as this.
Unfortunately few are outstanding
and the cruise ships dominate the
island's economy. At the height of
the summer season, the liners
literally queue to get into the port.

MAIN PORTS & RESORTS
SKALA The port with the main
body of the harbour village spilling
off the enormous quay that
dominates the south side.

The sandy and narrow beach
edging the tree lined Esplanade,
with a steeply shelving sea bottom, runs out on a small bluff.

Rooms owners compete for business, in order to fill their accommodation. In addition to the hotels,
pensions and Rooms, there are
sufficient dining establishments.

Chora & The Monastery (some
6km) The old town is a clean,
rather antiseptic, whitewashed
Chora, dominated by the fortified
Monastery of St John the Divine.

The monastery is a 'five star',
'fully operational' establishment -
an attractive and imposing building with magnificent views, not
only out over Patmos, but as far
as and including Samos to the
north, Naxos to the west, Kos in
the south and Turkey to the east.

GRIKOS (3km from Skala Port) A
pleasant, if rather 'dead', south-
east coast location. That is not to
say that Grikos is not nice and
quiet, despite the tourist facilities.
The settlement edges a large, curving cove, the road to which runs

out on the backshore. On the
immediate left is a restaurant and
thirty paces to the right is another,
as well as a small quay. The beach
to left and right, is rather dirty and
very seaweedy, but, further to the
right, the fine shingle becomes
clean. Several hotels look after the
accommodation requirements.

To the north of Skala are a number
of locations including:-
Ormos Agriolivado (4km from
Skala Port) The first section of the
beach is boulderous, with earth
spoil forming small swamps,
whilst the rest of the beach is
shingly sand..

The foreshore is edged by tamarisk trees with whitewashed trunks
and there is a small beach bar.

KAMPOS (5km from Skala Port)
A hilltop village with a cobbled
square edged by a church.

ORMOS KAMPOU A pleasant,
shingle beach with three tavernas,
as well as some pedaloes and
one-man sailing boats for hire.

VAGIA A small, peaceful, shingly
beach off which are anchored local
fishing boats.

LAMPI (9km from Skala Port)
Renowned for the coloured stones
of the very clean, shingle beach. A
taverna offers accommodation.

The delightful, sandy beach is
'serviced' by four tavernas, three
pensions and a general store. Half
an hours walk from the port are
another two sandy and pebble
beaches, to which 'resident' tourists tend to escape for the day.

FACT FILE
STATISTICS Tel prefix 0243. The island has an area of some 15 sq km and a year-round population of about 600

TRANSPORT LINKS
Day in, day out, during the summer months, excursion caiques bring a shoal of day-trippers from Kalimos & Kos.

The supposed tranquillity of the island is disturbed by the flood and ebb of day-trip tourists. Outside these intrusions, the inhabitants relapse into a placid existence.

The sole settlement is Pserimos hamlet, a cluster of pretty houses and pension-cum-tavernas, edging the delightful bay. The dwellings are looked over by a church, its separate campanile bell tower and the island's cemetery.

Half an hours walk from the port are two, more sandy and pebble beaches, to which 'resident' visitors tend to escape for the day.

Once the excursion craft, and their human cargo have departed, Pserimos reverts to the wonderful night-time Greece of yesteryear. An island calm descends, only broken by the clink of glasses, snatches of conversation, washed over by the sound of seabreezes, sheep bells and wavelets breaking on the shoreline.

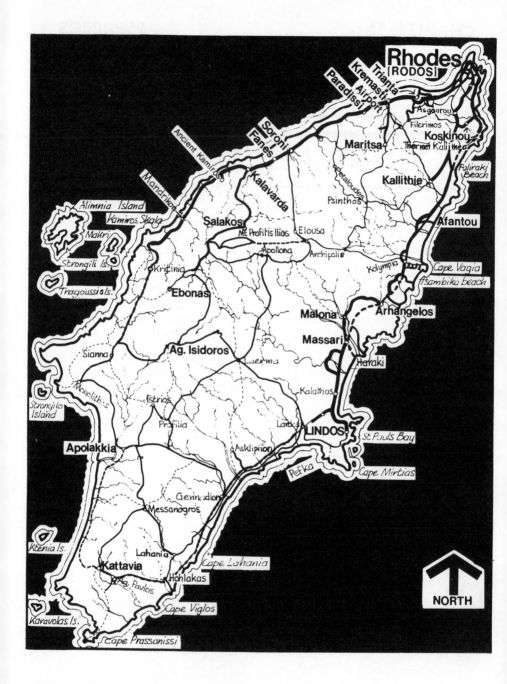

Illustration 43 Rhodes island

FACT FILE

ALTERNATIVE NAMES Rhodos, Rodos

IMPRESSIONS Mass tourism; an unrivalled, medieval Old Quarter; soft, agricultural country- side; a lack of churches & donkeys.

SPECIALITIES Fur coats; pasta dishes; duty-free spirits.

RELIGIOUS FESTIVALS include: 7th January - Feast of St John the Baptist; 23rd April - Feast of St George, Afantou; 15th June - Ag Amos, nearby Faliraki; 17th June - festival at Asgourou, Koskinou & Paradissi (Paradision); 29th-30th July - Ag Soulas, Soroni; 6th-31st August - dance festivals at Ebonas, Kallithea & Maritsa; 26th August - Ag Fanourios, Rhodes Old Quarter; 8th September - Fertility festival, Tsambika Monastery; 14th September - Feast, Apollona, Damatria & Malona.

STATISTICS The island, largest of the Dodecanese, is 77km long, up to 37km wide, with an area of some 1400sq km. There is a population of 80,000, of which about 35,000 are domiciled in the capital.

TRANSPORT LINKS

Air The airport is some 13km from the city, on the west coast, immediately prior to the village of Paradissi (Paradision). There are at least four flights a day to Athens; daily flights to Crete, Karpathos, Kos, Mykonos; five flights a week to Kasos; four flights a week to Santorini and Thessaloniki(M); three flights a week to Kastellorizo and Paros; and two flights a week to Lesbos. A bus service and taxis connect the airport to Rhodes City.

Ferry The main inter-island ferries berth in the Commercial Harbour, whilst the smaller, island excursion/trip boats dock in the Mandraki Harbour. Apart from daily ferries to the other Dodecanese islands, the Cyclades and Piraeus(M), there are boats at least days a week to Crete and two days a week to Kastelorizo.
    Accommodation is offered to arrivals at both the bus terminals and the ferry-boat harbours.

Hydrofoils A summer months, weather permitting, daily service runs to Simi, with a two or three times a week connection to Kos, Leros and Patmos.

Rhodes must vie with Corfu as the most international holiday target of all the Greek islands and the constant coming and going of aircraft is supplemented by a tidal wave of cruise liners.
    Perhaps the most unacceptable manifestations of tourism are to be observed in the Old Quarter High Street of Rhodes City. The length of this pedestrian way is lined with predatory shopkeepers, selling furs and other 'touristabilia'. On the other hand the mass market, tourist packaging of Lindos or the wall-to-wall, high-rise hotels of Faliraki Beach may be regarded as better (or worse)

For greater detail acquire GROC's Candid Guide to Rhodes and the Dodecanese Islands

examples. To counter the excesses of the holiday industry, it is only necessary to wander through the quieter backwaters of Rhodes City Old Quarter or visit most of the island south of a line drawn from Monolithos Castle, in the west, to say Gennadion, on the east coast.

Rhodes is an attractively verdant and pretty island of comparatively low mountains and relatively flat land in nearly all the areas bordering the coastline.

The richness of the architecture owes much to the Knights, some to the Turks, and a lot to the Italians.

MAIN PORTS & RESORTS

RHODES (Rhodos, Rodos) Tel prefix 0241. The capital city and main port. Really two towns, one the large, rambling, medieval Old Quarter encircled by the other, the new development - New Town or Nea Chora. The flourishing Old Quarter appears to be a maze of incoherent, directionless, narrow lanes, passages, alleys and streets. These wind their way in between a glorious admixture of dwellings of all descriptions, shapes and sizes, as well as squares, churches, mosques and minarets, all crowded and packed inside the great walls encircling the Old Quarter.

Both New and Old town are, on the east side, edged by the waterfront Esplanade. In Mandraki Harbour, small inter-island ferry-boats dock, as well as fishing caiques and private yachts. The substantial mole, closes off the eastern side of the Harbour. Three windmills, now refitted with sails, still remain standing on this mole, as does the Fort of St Nicholas.

Beyond St Paul's Gate, the quay road borders the Commercial Harbour and is edged by massive fort walls pierced only by the Marine

and St Catherines Gates. The first, north section of the Commercial Harbour is host to local craft, whilst the east side is utilised by the larger, inter-island ferry-boats and cruise liners. The most southerly harbour is Acandia, where the hydrofoils berth, beyond which the City degenerates into an industrial mess, or 'East End'.

North of Mandraki Harbour, Rhodes peaks out to a narrow bluff, Sandy Point, around which the most popular beach wraps itself. The west shore is narrow and more pebbly, edged by a busy main road, bordered by high-rise buildings in amongst which are a sprinkling of hotels.

The prodigious number of tourists places a great strain on accommodation, at the height of the season. Most of the hotels are located in the New Town, but are tour operator, block booked, whilst most of the Rooms are scattered about the Old Quarter. There is no shortage of eating places, in fact there is a surfeit of average and expensive establishments.

Places of interest include the:-
Orthodox Cathedral of St Mary, Old Quarter This 13th century Byzantine church, became the first Cathedral of the Knights, was converted into a mosque and is now a Byzantine Museum.
Hospice of St Catherine, Old Quarter Built, in 1392, to provide accommodation for pilgrims.
Church of St Fanourios, Old Quarter Gates, Harbours & Walls The Walls of the Old Quarter are continuous and there are two guided tours a week. The medieval military wall, towers, gates and ditches were built, and the moats excavated, by the Knights. After 1465 the fortress was divided into

eight sectors which were allocated, for defence purposes, to the eight Tongues, or nationalities.

Mandraki Harbour At the narrow entrance are two pillars supporting, respectively, a statue of a stag and a doe.

It is popular belief that, the Colossus of Rhodes stood in the place of the more modest, modern-day pillars. One of the Seven Wonders of the Ancient World, the bronze statue of the Sun God Apollo, or Helios, was some 30m tall. Unfortunately, about 70 years after its erection, an earthquake brought the remarkable statue to its knees, the broken remains lying around for eight hundred years.

The landward side of the Harbour 'benefited' from the Italian treatment. The guide books tend to be dismissive of the majestic, 1930s, 'neo-municipal' Italian architecture, which includes the Harbour Master's office, the Post Office, the Town police, the Town Hall, two theatres, Government House and St John's Church.

One building in this vicinity, not reconstructed or newly built by the Italians, is the delightful and elegant **Turkish mosque of Murad Reis**, and its cemetery. The minaret is particularly attractive and the tree shaded burial ground is littered with distinctive and quaintly carved headstones.

The Knights Quarter The attractions include the:-

Palace of the Grand Masters A splendid and imposing pile which is not surprising as it was completely rebuilt by the Italians. The Knights originally completed this magnificent edifice in the 14th century. It served the dual purpose of a fort, in time of war, and the home of the Grand Master, in times of peace. It was during the

rule of the languid Turks that the Palace acceleratingly deteriorated, which dilapidation climaxed in a horrendous explosion in 1856.

Street of the Knights An almost unbelievably quiet, almost stately, cobbled lane. The Knights were divided into the Tongues of their native language and each one had its own hall of residence, or Inn. The large Inn of France is well endowed with various coats of arms and is probably the most eye-catching of all these buildings.

It is thought that the ground floor of the Inns were utilised as stables for their animals, or as warehouses, the first floors being accessed by open stairs. The Turks, festooned them with wooden, upper storey balconies.

Hospital of the Knights Completed in 1489, it is now the Archaeological Museum.

The Museum of Decorative Arts This building was probably an Arsenal at some time.

The Municipal Art Gallery Mosques (& the Turkish Sector of the Old Quarter) The most noteworthy of the mosques was the:-

Mosque of Suleiman Constructed in honour of and, no doubt, on the instructions of the Turkish Conqueror, in 1522.

Turkish Baths Built in 1765, the old marble floor of the rebuilt building remains.

Ibrahim Pasha Mosque Originally built in 1531, it was restored by the Italians, in the 1930s, who also rebuilt the minaret.. A large plane tree alongside the building is said to have been the site for summary executions, during Turkish rule.

Son et Lumiere The performances take place in a municipal garden.

Theatre Performances of Greek folk dances and songs are enacted.

Down the east coast are:-

For greater detail acquire GROC's Candid Guide to Rhodes and the Dodecanese Islands

AG MARINA (4½km from Rhodes City) The not-so-smart seaside expansion, almost part of the 'down- town' Rhodes City, has a slightly tatty milieu. The beach is sandy, with a 1930s lido building, showers and sun umbrellas.

THERMEI KALLITHEA (10km from Rhodes City) Edging a bay, with a sandy area dotted with sun umbrellas and separated by rocks from the sea. The North African appearance of the buildings is a result of a whim of the Italians, who built the complex, in the 1920s, as a health resort and watering place.

THE PETALOUDES (The Valley of the Butterflies - 25km from Rhodes City) This inland site is an extensively foliaged defile, down which a rivulet tumbles in a series of rock pools and waterfalls. The season for the butterflies is between June and September.

Also on the east coast are:-
FALIRAKI BEACH (15½km from Rhodes City) A long, gently curving, fine shingle and very sandy beach, with a number of massive hotel complexes. These are flanked by clear beach on either side. The far end of the crescent of the bay slides into a less smart, international mix of small hotels, villas and shopping precincts.

Afantou Beach (22km from Rhodes City) The beach is edged by a long, straight, narrow road.

KOLYMPIA (Kolibia - 26km from Rhodes City) To the right of the Cape Vagia headland, a track proceeds to a large pleasant bay with fine shingle edging a sandy seashore. To the left of the headland, is a small caique pier and repair yard. This is flanked by a taverna and a slab rock seashore, edged by a small, narrow, fine shingle beach.

Tsambika Beach (31km from Rhodes City) A very large, scrub clad plain backs a long and beautifully sandy beach. The extremely popular, large bay is edged by cliffs with the sand blown high up the almost vertical rock face.

STEGENA (35km from Rhodes City) The road descends to this delightful straggling village, made up of adobe style buildings, set on the near side of a pretty bay. The roadway borders a fine shingle, sandy foreshore, which gives way to a tiny, smooth pebble sea-bed. A small, unpretentious restaurant offers Rooms.

HARAKI (43km from Rhodes City) A not very large, comparatively quiet, lovely seaside village with a slender, clean, curving, almost circular pebble beach to the north side of a headland. The tree lined Esplanade sweeps round to a sandy, shingly beach. There are a few tavernas and Rooms.

Haraki Beach The shoreline is overlooked by the ruined Castle of Feraclos, set on a low promontory to the south side of the headland. The crystal clear sea more than makes up for the pebbly beach.

LINDOS (56km from Rhodes City) Certainly a breathtakingly beautiful sight from whence the road crests the last rise and Lindos and its Acropolis hoves into view.
  The old village is entered from the far side of a square, whence the visitor is absorbed into whatappears to be one huge maze of a bazaar. The tiny alleys are too narrow for mechanised traffic,

only the clip-clop of donkeys' hooves breaking through the ceaseless babble of human voices. Around the periphery of the village, off the well signposted 'beaten track' to the steps climbing towards the Acropolis, are some winding lanes still devoid of commercialism, with hardly a bar or taverna in sight! The small bay of the Grand Harbour has a modest sweep of very crowded beach.

Traditional food shops and stalls have almost all been displaced by a rash of cocktail bars, fast food establishments, 'pubs' and tourist shops. As most possible locations are block-booked by the package tour operators, that accommodation available is very expensive and usually full.

Places of interest include the:-
The Acropolis A splendid situation but around which the Knights draped castle walls, over and around earlier Byzantine fortifications. The Acropolis overlooks an:-
Ancient Theatre Not a lot left, apart from some of the seating and gangways, and:-
St Pauls Bay A small, almost circular bay surrounded by bare rock. This is supposedly the spot where a bolt of lightning caused the rock to split asunder. The lagoon became a harbour, thus enabling a storm tossed boat, in danger of capsizing and bearing St Paul, to reach safety.
Church of the Assumption of the Madonna Sited close to the middle of the main village. Possible older than the inscription of 1484-90, for these dates may refer to a period of rebuilding by the Knights. The external appearance, pure, simple Byzantine, with the red tiled, domed, seven sided cupola off-setting the white walls, starkly contrasts with the dark gorgeousness of the interior, the frescoes, the wooden screen and Byzantine icons.
Houses of Lindos The interiors are often distinctive, possessing decorated, lofty wooden ceilings and mosaic floors. Later houses, dating from the 16th and 17th centuries, sport an unusual family bed arrangement. The bedstead is raised on a platform, set under an arch, in the main room, and reached up a low flight of steps.
Tomb of Kleoboulous A tentative connection to a 6th century BC tyrant leader of Lindos, who ruled for 40 years and was one of the Seven Sages of the ancient world.

PEFKA (58km from Rhodes City) The houses are widely spread out over a small but wide lowland, the low cliffs of which line a splendid, gently curving bay. The very sandy, narrow beach, has a sprinkling of beach umbrellas. There are a few Rooms, a pension, a general shop and kafeneion, as well as a beach cantina.

GENNADION (70km from Rhodes City) Opposite this unpretentious village is a track which runs down to a sandy beach.

Plimmiri Bay On the right is a beach of shingly sand and pebble.

On the west coast are:-
FANES (26km from Rhodes City) At the far end of the village is a track which traipses across a windswept stretch of open coastline to a narrow, stony beach. Attractive in a slightly unkempt fashion. A hotel is supplemented by several restaurants.

Ancient Kamiros (34km from Rhodes City) The Ancient City lies in a large, shallow, saucer shaped

For greater detail acquire GROC's Candid Guide to Rhodes and the Dodecanese Islands

depression set in the gentle hillside. The site, dating, in part, to
the 6th century BC, was discovered in 1860.

KAMIROS SKALA (48km from
Rhodes City) A fairly pretty location with some three tavernas and
a pension. The activity in and
around Kamiros Skala is generated
by the 'Chalki island connection'.

Paradise Beach A five kilometre
dirt road loops steeply down
through extensively pine forested
hills to a small, remote settlement
on the edge of the coast. There
are two taverna/pensions, the remains of a lookout tower, a strip
of large pebble sea-shore and a
small caique quay.

SIANNA (75km from Rhodes
City) A pretty, working village
hanging on to the hillside with
many kafeneions and a glorious
view down along the distant coastline of Apolakkia Bay.

Monolithos Castle (82km from
Rhodes City) The fort nestles

neatly on the top of a 250m high
pillar of rock which rises needle-
like out of the plain, in the middle
distance. There is a vast backcloth
of blue sea in which is set the
rocky headland of Armenistis and
a small island off the Cape.

APOLAKKIA (91km from Rhodes
City) An inland agricultural settlement with few concessions to other
than the locals' pursuits. There is a
periptero, several pensions, a hotel
and a couple of tavernas, as well
as a petrol station.

The west coast road turns back
towards the coastline. The first
stretch of the road is edged by
dunes of rocks, followed by dunes
of sand, scrub trees and ravines
surrounded by wild countryside.

Skiada Monastery (102km from
Rhodes City) The monastery is set
in perfect island scenery, with
magnificent sea views.Sometimes
ccommodation is available from
the caretakers, but not food.

FACT FILE

ALTERNATIVE NAMES Symi, Syme

IMPRESSIONS A breathtakingly beautiful island port; a trip boat paradise; shortage of accommodation & water.

RELIGIOUS FESTIVALS include: 7th-9th November - Panormitis Monastery.

STATISTICS Tel prefix 0241. About 12km long & 10km wide, with a population of 2,500, most of whom live in or around the main town (Chora) & the port (Gialos).

TRANSPORT LINKS

Ferry There are daily ferries to Rhodes, three ferry links a week with Tilos, Nisiros, Kos and Kalimnos, as well as one a week, respectively to Leros, Lipsos, Patmos, Arki, Angathonisi, Samos and Piraeus(M). Additionally there are daily excursion boats to and from Rhodes and Kos.

Hydrofoils During the summer season, weather conditions permitting, there is a daily service to and from Rhodes, as well as a two/three times a week link with Kos, Leros and Patmos.

Much of Simi's history has revolved around their ability as builders of sea-going vessels. The islanders were purported to have supplied battleships as long ago as the Trojan wars, when they built and crewed three of the legendary triremes. The Knights of St John and the Turks, during their respective occupations, used the skill of the Symiot boatbuilders who, incidentally, were one of the first of the Dodecanese islanders to rise up against their Turkish overlords, during the War of Independence.

The official surrender of the Dodecanese to the Allies was signed, on the 8th May 1945, in the building half-way along the north side of Gialos harbour. Apart from boatbuilding, another lost island skill is that of sponge diving, which is now almost entirely the preserve of the islanders of Kalimnos.

The deserted, empty and derelict houses, seen on many Greek islands, are a constant source of bewilderment to overseas visitors. The root cause is the Greek inheritance laws, in addition to which, beneficiaries of a will may be a number of children who fail to agree on the best course of action, in respect of a particular property. On Simi, in common with one or two other islands, the legacies pass through the female line, which has resulted in an even greater migration of young males than is usual.

MAIN PORTS & RESORTS

GIALOS/SIMI The port, as opposed to the Chora, the old

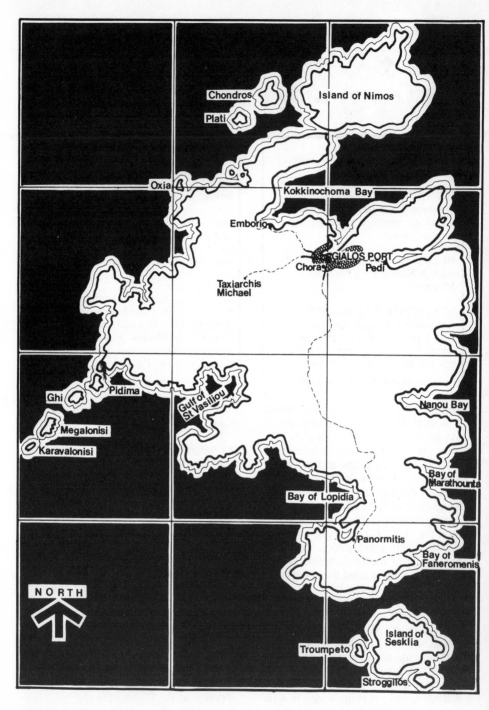

Illustration 44 Simi island

town. Simply, one of the most strikingly attractive Greek island port's, the first visit to which will remain indelibly engraved on any visitor's memory. The lack of the usual Greek social graces should also forcibly strike most tourists.

The inter-island ferries steam into the horseshoe bay, around the steep hillsides of which the buildings rise, amphitheatre-like in the fashion of a Doric set of playing cards. It seems as if each house is piled on the one below.

The chronic shortage of drinking water has been a contributory factor in channelling tourist development of Simi into a day-trip 'paradise'. This results in a daily invasion of up to six or seven excursion boats from Rhodes and Kos - every day, week in, week out, for some seven months.

To get to the beach involves a walk round the north headland of the 'U' shaped harbour quay. The tiny, crowded, fine pebble beach is located in a lovely setting.

Accommodation is comparatively difficult to locate, as well as expensive, and owners often insist on a minimum of two or three days room occupation. The standard varies between 'simple to primitive'. The various eating establishments are also costly.

THE CHORA The old town, high on the hill-side above Gialos Port, to which the bus makes the journey. The Chora may also be reached by scaling the wide, broad flagstone staircase which ascends from the port. This flight of steps decants on to the Chora main square, whereon a hotel to the right of some old windmills.

The Chora and Gialos are as different as a quiet old town and a bustling, frenetic port could be. The Chora is a very large village which has evolved in a maze of garishly coloured houses, lanes and alleys that jig up and down, and round and about.

PEDI (2km from Gialos Port) A narrow sandy shore rings the bay, which is edged by a scattering of spindly trees and a couple of palm trees. The foreshore curves away without even the semblance of a track. The wide, raised concrete patios and steps of the equally spaced houses are connected in a series of small jetties. There are several hotel/restaurants as well as some Rooms.

Panormitis Monastery This lies at the south end of the island and can be reached by an excursion boat or truck trip.

The substantial, if rather palace-like, 18th century Monastery Archangel Michael stretches along the edge of a lovely bay with a small, sandy beach. Entrance to the monastery is free but note the 'clothing rules' are strictly applied, and there is none for hire.

It is possible to stay overnight, for a fee. There are a couple of pricey restaurants and a pleasant waterfront cafe.

The location is the venue for a religious festival, held between the 7-9th November.

Emborio About two kilometres to the west of Gialos Port, Emborio, historically a commercial port, now doubles as a summer holiday beach. There are some Byzantine mosaics still visible.

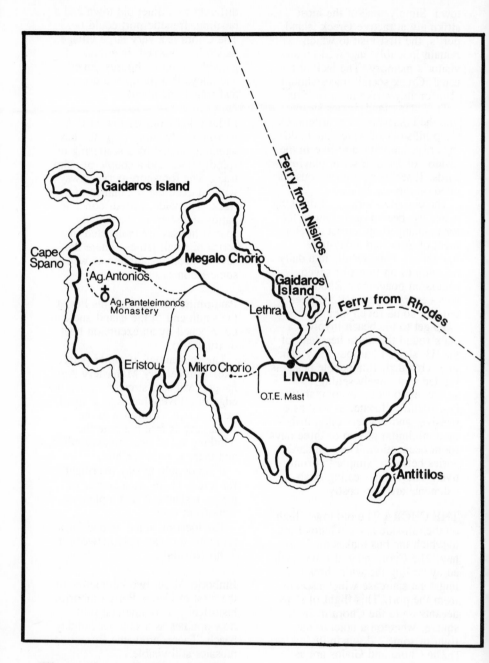

Illustration 45 Tilos island

FACT FILE
ALTERNATIVE NAMES Telos, Episkopi

IMPRESSIONS Quiet; remote; un-developed; clear seas.

RELIGIOUS FESTIVALS include: 15th August - Festival, Panaghia Church, Mikro Chorio; 23rd August - Festival, Panaghia Monastery, Nr Livadia; 27th August - Festival, Ag Panteleimonos Monastery.

STATISTICS Tel prefix 0241. The island is some 17½km, north-west to south-east, & 'waists' down to 3km at the narrowest point, with a population of approximately 300.

TRANSPORT LINKS
Ferry At least three ferries a week proceed to Simi and Rhodes, as well as to Nisiros, Kos, Kalimnos; and once a week to Lipsos, Patmos, Arki, Angathonisi and Samos, as well as Astipalaia, Amorgos, Paros and Piraeus(M).
Room owners sometimes meet the ferries, though they can be missed amid the confusion.

As for the other Dodecanese islands, but one claim to fame is the mastadon skeletons found in hillside caves, some years ago.

Tilos has a pleasant port; plentiful water; an old town, Megalo Chorio; a ruined castle; some very good quality beaches; reasonable ferry-boat connections, and some accommodation. On the other hand there is little or no island transport, and few metalled roads.

MAIN PORTS & RESORTS

LIVADIA (Levadhia). The port is set in a large, broad, hill surrounded inlet. The development is to the west, whilst away to the east sweeps a clean, narrow, almost white, pebble and shingle seashore bordering the bay. From a distance, the whiteness of this sea's edge gives the appearance of waves breaking on a foreshore. The seafront and port is prettily planted with tamarisk and cypress trees, whilst there is a grove of fruit trees to one side of the attractive, 'standard' Italian municipal building, which houses the police and customs offices.

A number of hotels and pensions vie for the business, with a few Rooms scattered throughout the village. For such a small place, the selection of 'diners' is fair enough.

MIKRO CHORIO A quiet, deserted inland village. The pink, red and white church is the only building kept in a good state of repair.

MEGALO CHORIO (9km from Livadia Port) The island's biggest settlement and the only other inhabited village, besides the port, boasting a population of about 200. A pretty, whitewashed village, with narrow streets and steps twisting among the houses. A path leads up to a ruined Venetian fortress, on a rock above the

For greater detail acquire GROC's Candid Guide to Rhodes and the Dodecanese Islands

village. This castle, as is the case of other Dodecanese strongholds, was built on and over much earlier fortifications and incorporates some easily noticeable features from the ancient buildings. These include details of the main gateway as well as the marble flights of steps inside the gates.

There are an almost disproportionate number of churches and a small, single story museum.

Megalo Chorio has Rooms.

Eristou Beach A vast stretch of deserted, golden sand, shaded by tamarisk trees, that grow along a backshore, made up of rough, grainy sand. Near the water's edge, the beach is firm sand and a few fishing boats are pulled up onto the shore, which just goes on and on and on.

Accommodation is available

Ag Antonios The location is peaceful and isolated, with reasonable facilities for bathing, even if the beach is narrow, pebbly and messy. There is an isolated hotel.

PART SIX
CHAPTER 55 EVIA

FACT FILE
ALTERNATIVE NAMES Evvia,
Evoia, Euboea, Eyboia

IMPRESSIONS A number of
ferry-boat ports, gathered together
by a huge length of island.

SPECIALITIES Timber & forests;
agriculture; stock & poultry
raising; fishing; Evia wine.

RELIGIOUS FESTIVALS include:
Lent - Wedding Feast, Ag Anna
(North island); 27th May - St
John, the Russians Feast Day -
Prokopion (North island); 24th
June - 'Klidona' (or folk cele-
brations), St John's Day, at
various Evia locations; 12th
November - Feast of St David
Geronta (East-north-east) & Rovies
(North-east island).

STATISTICS Tel prefix. *See*
individual areas, ports & towns.
Evia is 175km long & between 6
and 50km wide, with an area of
some 3800sq km (compared to the
8200sq km of Crete) & a
population of about 160,000.

TRANSPORT LINKS
Bus The buses from Athens,
either stop at the main Chalkis
terminal, or career on to Kymi
Port, on the east coast, stopping
on the way, at Eretria and
Amarinthos. Travellers, relying
on public transport, can face a
difficult task in getting from one
major resort to another.

Ferry *See* the various coastal
ports including (from top to
bottom, in an anticlockwise
direction):- Agiokampos, Ag
Georgios, Loutra Edipsos,
Eretria, Panaghia, Nea Styra,
Marmari, Karistos and Kimi.

Road The last stretch of the
approach to Chalki, the island
capital, passes through an
industrial area, prior to crossing
over the bridge, spanning the
narrow straights separating the
mainland from Evia.

Train The Athens trains 'pull-up'
on the mainland side of Chalkis
town straits.

Chalkis, Eretria and Kymi were
important City States between the
8-6th century BC, with colonies as
far away as Southern Italy. From
then on, Evia followed the general
course of overall Greek history.
Ownership passed from the Athenians to the Romans (194 BC),
after which it fell under the
Byzantine mantle. The Franks (AD
1207) were followed by the
Venetians (1306-1470), then the

Turks took over for the next 351
years, until the island was incorporated into the new Greek
nation. The Venetian presence is
amply evidenced by the prominent, large, square watchtowers
sprinkled about various hilltops.
As would be expected on such a
large island, Evia has wildly contrasting locations and scenery,
despite which, there are comparatively few large ports or towns.

For greater detail acquire GROC's Candid Guide to the Mainland Islands

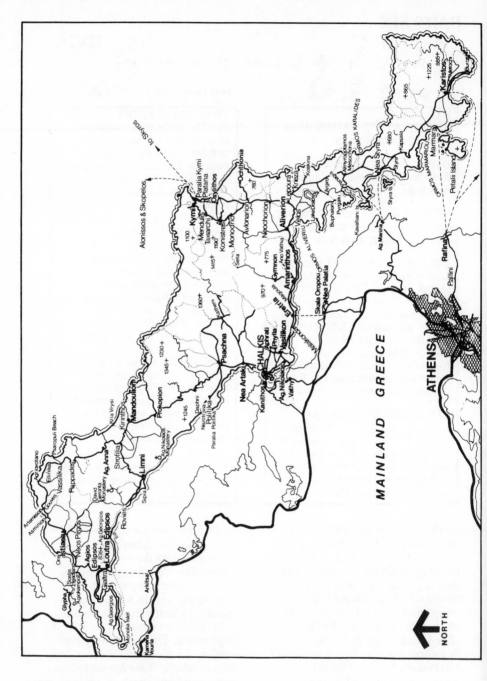

Illustration 46 Evia island

The stretch of coast, due east from Chalkis Town, all the way to Amarinthos, has and is being developed, based on a number of well-established seaside towns. On the other hand, general areas worth investigation include the top northwest (Ag Georgios); the top northeast; without doubt the middle-west coast, around Kymi and Paralia Kymi; and the southern neck, perhaps the most typically island portion of Evia island.

MAIN PORTS & RESORTS
CHALKIS (Chalcis, Chalki, Chalkida, Khalkis, Halkida) Tel prefix 0221. The capital town. Due to the narrow, 37m wide channel between the mainland, bridged as early as 410-411BC, Chalkis is not a ferry-boat port. The straits between Evia island and the mainland are subject to a rare phenomenon in the Mediterranean - a tidal flow.

The modern-day development is adjacent to the Ancient City of Chalcis and straddles the narrows. The town has an air of prosperity and the Esplanade, that borders the north island side of the channel, is amazingly chic, almost Parisian in character. This wide thoroughfare is lined, end to end, with smart cafe-bars and restaurants, on the one side, and their awning covered patios on the other (water) side. To get to a beach it is necessary to proceed to the north-eastern suburbs, or cross the bridge to the mainland, for the Asteria Lido.

There are dozens of hotels but few, if any Rooms, whilst any number of dining establishments border the Esplanade.

ERETRIA (22km east from Chalkis Town) Tel prefix 0221. A spaced out, rather dusty south-west coast development and ferry-boat port, set in treeless, seemingly arid, flat countryside.

Of all the traditional, package holiday Evian resorts, Eretria is possibly the most ideal. It has a combination of one fine beach (and two other not so good); enjoyable swimming; a regular bus service to the capital; a shuttle ferry-boat connection to the mainland port of **Skala Oropou**; and the infrastructure necessary to support holiday-makers' various requirements, including extensive and interesting archaeological remains. Apart from a number of Rooms and tourist hotels, there is a row of smart restaurants.

Places of interest include the **Archaeological Site** north of the main road bypass, and its **Museum.**

In the general area of **Magoula** are various shops, tavernas, restaurants, villas, and holiday-makers.

AMARINTHOS (30km east from Chalkis Town) Tel prefix 0221. The present-day, somewhat old-fashioned town, fully 'stocked' with shops and services, is that of an ancient site. The rubbish littered seafront is a series of tiny beach coves with foreshores of grey, fine sand and shingle, biscuit rock, and pebble.

A couple of hotels are supported by some Rooms.

PARALIA KYMI (Kimi Port) (97km from Chalkis Town) Tel prefix 0221. Despite the name, this location is more the port of Kymi Town than a beach, which is not to decry the splendid, sandy shore to the south of the enormous harbour. The port presents a pleasing combination of typical island charm and commercial activity. The waterfront Esplanade, that runs the length of the village, is pleasantly bordered by mature trees. For those not prepared to subject themselves to the rigours of the climb up to Kymi Town, both buses and taxis ply the route. The port is the main jumping-off point for Skyros island, to which there is a daily ferry-boat. There is a weekly ferry-boat to the islands of Alonissos and Skopelos, as well as Ag Estratios, Limnos and mainland Kavala.

If Paralia Kymi has a drawback, it is the lack of accommodation. But not all is lost as the country town of Kymi, on the mountainside overlooking the port, has hotels and Rooms. In direct contrast to the paucity of beds, Paralia Kymi has an ample supply of kafeneions, restaurants and tavernas.

AGIOKAMPOS (141km from Chalkis Town) This tiny, pleasant, north-west port is set on a large, flat bay. The roadside is tree planted, and gently curves past a shingle waterfront, finishing up on the ferry-boat quay. The 'Esplanade' is lined by low, stone wall houses capped with red roofs, in amongst which are a number of villas, a taverna, a kafeneion.

Daily ferries run a shuttle service to mainland **Glypha**.

LOUTRA EDIPSOS (Lutra Aedipsos, Edipsou) (153km from Chalkis Town anticlockwise) Tel prefix 0226. A classy, north-west coast, health spa, Greek holiday resort and ferry-boat port, that dates back to ancient times. The Esplanade is bordered by swish restaurants, their patios, and shops. Daily ferries link Loutra to mainland **Arkitsa.**

The Rooms are supplemented by dozens and dozens of hotels.

AG NIKOLAOS (3km west from Loutra Edipsos) A small, Greek tourist resort with a very long but narrow beach. The backshore is gritty sand, the middleshore is sandy and the sea's edge is angled biscuit rock.

There are four quality pensions.

AG GEORGIOS (29km west from Loutra Edipsos) This busy, sometimes bustling, small fishing boat village is an absolute find, as long as the lack of a sandy beach is of no concern. The shore is pebbly but there are beach showers. The waterfront road follows the jinks, curves and contours of the backshore. Various, small, short, rickety piers jut into the sea, across from which are a scattering of kafeneions, a couple of tavernas, a periptero and two pensions.

At the height of season a passenger boat connects with Loutra Edipsos, as well as **Kamena Vourla**, on the mainland.

LIMNI (87km from Chalkis Town) Tel prefix 0227. A clean, attractive, red roofed old town and resort. A drawback, in common with other settlements on the north-west coast, is that Limni is set down on the edge of a flat featureless coastline. The shingle, 100m long beach is shadeless.

There are at least three hotels.

PANAGHIA (84km from Chalkis Town) Tel prefix 0223. A splendidly 'doo-hickey', fishing and ferry-boat port on the south-west coast. The pleasantly tree lined sweep of backshore, which edges a narrow, rather scrubbly shore, is bordered by a concreted road. Landing craft style ferries are moored to the foreshore and the ferry-boat link is with mainland

Ag Marina, from whence craft also connect with Nea Styra.
There is a hotel and Rooms.

NEA STYRA (105km from Chalkis Town) A delightfully Greek, resort, with a wealth of accommodation. Between the hotels, and the quay is a nice, wide if not overlong, coarse sand beach. The Esplanade is lined with cafe-bars, shops, tavernas and supermarkets.
Ferry-boats connect with **Ag Marina**, on the mainland.

MARMARI PORT (125km from Chalkis Town) A much larger, more important ferry-boat port than Nea Styra, but not nearly so attractive, with little available accommodation and only a rather distant, narrow, pebble beach.
Ferry-boats daily connect Marmari to mainland **Rafina**.

KARISTOS (Karystos - 133km from Chalkis Town) Tel prefix 0224. A large, busy, well established town and ferry-boat port, at the southern end of the island. The big harbour hosts some sizeable fishing vessels and the quay wall is occupied by smaller fishing craft. Ferry-boats link Karistos to mainland **Rafina**, every day. The beach is a lovely stretch of fine shingle and sandy foreshore.
Apart from the hotels, some of which are large and modern, there are a few Rooms. The Esplanade and main street support a number of restaurants and tavernas.

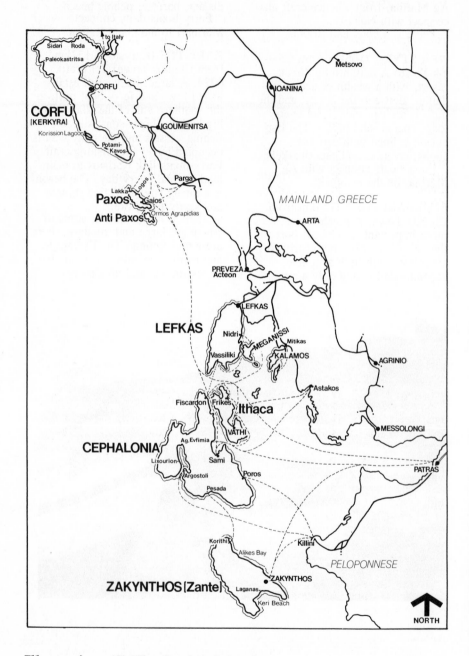

Illustration 47 The Ionian islands

PART SEVEN   THE IONIAN ISLANDS

The Ionian islands are set down off the western coast of the Greek mainland. The group embraces, from north to south, the islands of Corfu, Paxos, Antipaxos, Lefkas, Meganissi, Cephalonia, Ithaca and Zakynthos. I
have included the island of Kithira in the Sporades, as it cannot be reached
directly from any of the other islands in the Ionian group.

Scheduled ferry-boat transport between the islands and the mainland is
reasonably simple, that is with the exception of Zakynthos, for which island
it is necessary to travel to and from the Peloponnese port of Killini. It has
to be admitted, there is a 'height of season' boat plying between Cephalonia
and Zakynthos. Those mainland ports that service the Ionian include Igoumenitsa, Parga, Astakos, Patras and Killini. Inter-island travel has become
dramatically easier in recent years, more especially with the introduction of
a ferry route that incorporates Lefkas, Meganissi, Cephalonia and Ithaca in
its itinerary

Air travel can be utilised to reach Corfu, Cephalonia and Zakynthos from
Athens, and there is an airport at mainland Acteon (Preveza), convenient
for Lefkas. It is also now possible to fly direct from Corfu to Cephalonia,
Preveza(M) and Zakynthos.

Various bus services and the Peloponnese train circuit make connections,
using the ferry-boat links. However, as elsewhere, the frequency of all
forms of travel depends on the time of year.

Owing to their location, on the western side of the mainland, the Ionian
islands do not constantly reflect Turkish historical intrusion. They are more
a reflection of the expansionist nature of the European colonial powers -
France, the United Kingdom and Venice. For example, the *Cantades*, a
Venetian based folk music, is one of the pointers to the different cultural
heritage and certainly is a welcome change to the ubiquitous *Bouzouki*.

As a result of earthquakes that have devastated these islands over the
ages, much of historical note has been damaged or destroyed. Corfu, Paxos
and Lefkas have possibly suffered less, but Cephalonia, Ithaca and Zakynthos lie adjacent to a geographical fault or faults and have experienced a
number of sizeable earthquakes over the last four or five hundred years.
The serious tremors, experienced in 1953, destroyed up to seventy per cent
of the buildings of the latter islands. This explains the lack of old houses
and, conversely, the rather twentieth century, prefabricated look of many
of the present buildings.

Despite much of the present-day prosperity relating to tourism, there is a
very strong agricultural prop to the economy. This is based on grapes,
olives, currants, almonds, vegetables, dairy herds, sheep and goats.
Shipping still plays an important part in balancing various budgets.

Overall the islands are exceptionally green, compared to their Aegean
counterparts - pine, olive and cypress trees are abundant. Vegetation, especially bracken, is thick and lush, even at the height of the hottest summer
months. One of the reasons for the luxurious nature of the flora is the comparatively heavy, winter months rainfall. Even in the summer season it is
not unusual to experience, sometimes prolonged, rainstorms, occasionally
accompanied by the most spectacular lighting and thunder.

Due to the strong association with *Homer's Odyssey*, the islands have received more than their fair share of archaeological attention. Despite all this activity, many key Homeric questions and various island claims, remain unanswered, allowing the islanders to claim that which suits them.

The Corinthians were in occupation during the eighth century BC, but by the sixth century BC, Corfu had decided to go it alone and won a subsequent sea-battle with their overlords. During the fifth to third centuries BC, Athens and the Peloponnese (in the Spartan camp) had a long, drawn-out series of disagreements, with Athens gaining the support of the Ionian islanders. The Romans were invited to take over the administration of Corfu, about 230BC, and during the next hundred years, occupied the rest of the group. All was fine until the Romans were drawn into their own internecine squabbles, but fortunately, the last years of the decline of the Roman Empire were comparatively peaceful, for the Ionian. From AD 300 to 1100, the group were part of the Byzantine domain, suffering bouts of pillaging from various pirate bands.

About 1100, the thrustful Normans were expanding their Western European Kingdom. To help keep them at bay, the Greeks sought an alliance with the City State of Venice, but the Normans slipped in and occupied Corfu, Cephalonia, Ithaca and Zakynthos, and by AD 1200 the Byzantine Empire had totally collapsed. Between AD 1200 and 1500 the Venetians, although nominally in control of the Ionian, left various noble families to run them as their own personal fiefdoms. The increasing threat of the advancing Turks decided the Venetians to formalise their control and administer the islands directly, but they still suffered severe savaging at the hands of raiders, over the next 300 years. After overcoming the Venetians, elsewhere in Europe, in 1797, Napoleon Bonaparte decided to take the Ionian islands under his wing. As soon as this feat was achieved, a Russo-Turkish coalition overthrew the French, leaving the Russians in control. In the meantime (1803) Britain and France declared war on each other and Napoleon repossessed the Ionian islands, an act that pulled the British into this part of the world. By 1807 the latter had taken Cephalonia, Ithaca and Zakynthos, followed by Lefkas, in 1811. Corfu was extremely strongly garrisoned by the French and, to save unnecessary bloodshed, the British haphazardly blockaded the island for the next six years. Following the final defeat of the French, the administration of the Ionian islands was formally granted to Britain, who ruled until 1864. Lasting relics of British rule must include the introduction of then revolutionary advances in agriculture, coupled with land drainage, extensive road building, some administrative buildings of note, and British cemeteries. Corfu also benefited from the added 'delights' of cricket and ginger beer. In 1864 the Ionian islands were handed back to the Greeks.

The Second World War brought in its train, further dramatic upheavals. The Germans give the Italians administrative control in 1941, but seized it back in 1943, after some fairly bloodthirsty events, when the Italians sided with the Greek freedom fighters.

There are very few Byzantine churches, due to the centuries of earthquakes, but the later, Ionian version is better represented. The separately constructed bell towers, or more correctly walls pierced by bell arches, with small, overhanging, tiled roofs are named *Campaniles*.

Panoramically Cephalonia is extremely dramatic, with the majority of the land taken up by mountain ranges. Despite the majestic beauty of the scenery, visitors may well have to persevere with Cephalonia. Admittedly there are a number of drawbacks: the main city of Argostoli was unsympathetically rebuilt after the devastating earthquake of 1953 and the roads that hug the edges of the hills are very mountainous. Despite a widespread bus system, due to the distances involved, it is often difficult to get back to a departure point, on the same day. Additionally, Cephalonia is unusual in that the capital is not the main port, the inter-island ferry-boats docking at Poros or Sami.

Corfu island may come as a pleasant surprise, despite the years of exposure to tourism. Naturally, much of the coastline holiday development has intruded on areas of natural loveliness, previously only visited by the more adventurous travellers. Furthermore, where building growth has not been possible, coach and boat trip exploitation has ensured spoilation of certain beauty spots. Without doubt the island presents an amazing kaleidoscope of the best, and worst, of nearly all Greek countryside, a blend that includes:- mountains, verdant valleys, precipitous cliffs, sandy shores, picturesque inland and coastal villages, as well as highly developed (and ravaged) tourist areas, some squalor, and urban sprawl. Even nowadays, in the country areas, the friendly and hospitable peasant's traditional dependence on the donkey, as a beast of burden, is still in evidence. Ithaca, one of the smallest of the Ionian chain, has a 'village' ambience, with fewer concessions to the holiday-maker. Prior to the blasting of the road system into a coherent, if limited, layout, much travel was by caique. Some vestiges remain in the occasional boat trips between various fishing villages and Vathi, the capital.

The outstandingly beautiful island of Lefkas has, in the main, avoided the worst tourist excesses. The outbreaks of exploitation have been contained to a number of specific centres, 'villa country' stretches of coast.

The Paxos countryside is very different from any of the other Ionian islands and there is an 'enchanted forest' milieu. The olive-blackened roads and tracks wind up and down through extensive, boulder strewn, rambling, cool, shady olive groves, many of which are extremely old. Deep, summer-dry, rocky river-beds, interweave with the roads and are criss-crossed by stone built bridges, an unusual sight on a Greek island.

Zakynthos island is unequally divided by a mountain range which runs from the north-west to the south-east. The narrow, diagonal west coast strip parallels the spine of the hills, descending very steeply into the sea. Almost the rest of the island is a large fertile plain. The countryside remains lovely and rather reminiscent of England, with hedgerowed fields, orchards of trees (even if they are olives, cypresses, orange and pines), tree-topped hills, green-clad slopes and winding lanes.

FACT FILE
ALTERNATIVE NAMES
(Antipaxoi, Andipaxi)

The island, close to the southern tip of Paxos, is three square kilometres in area with a population of about 150. A speciality is the island wine.

TRANSPORT LINKS
During the summer season, there are high speed dory style craft that run a daily 10-15 minute service from Gaios Port (Paxos) to the various eastern coast beaches, and the island's small harbour of **Ormos Agrapidias.**

The rocky coastline of the island is cleft by narrow strips of rocky, pebbly or sandy shores. The gentle hillsides of the east coast encircle a series of bays, some with glorious, sandy beaches, whilst the west coastline is much more dramatic, with towering cliff-faces plunging into the deeps of the Ionian sea.

There are a few smart villas let to the package holiday companies.

To avoid the crowds, arrive early, leave late or keep moving as far south as is necessary.

CHAPTER 57   CEPHALONIA

FACT FILE
ALTERNATIVE NAMES
(Cefalonia, Kefalonia, Kefallinia, Kephallenia)

IMPRESSIONS Dramatic, forest clad, mountainous scenery; pre-fabricated buildings; cypresses.

SPECIALITIES Lemonda; *Robola* wine (white & light); *Monte Nero* wine (red & dry); thyme-scented honey; bacaliaropitta (codfish pies); tserepes (spiced meat in a casserole); mandolato nougat.

RELIGIOUS FESTIVALS include: 17th July - Feast Day, Ag Marina, Vlachata; 15th August - Our Lady Day, Lixourion; 15th August - Assumption of the Virgin, Markopoulou; 22nd August - Our Lady of Loutra, Sami; 8th September - Feast Day of Theotokos Poros.

STATISTICS Tel prefix *See* individual towns & villages. The island, with an area of 782sq km, is up to 35km long & 33km wide. The population numbers about 30,000, of which some 6,000 reside in, or around, Argostoli Town.

TRANSPORT LINKS
Air The airport is about 14km south of Argostoli Town. Only the

Kourkoumeleta bus (also signed *Irina Hotel*) passes the side turning to the airport but there is a rank for taxis. At least one flight a day connects to Athens, and two a week to Corfu and Zakynthos.

Bus There are at least two daily connections between Athens and Cephalonia. Some proceed via Sami Port to Patras(M), whilst others route through Poros to Killini(M).

Ferry Apart from the main ports of Poros and Sami, Argostoli is linked to mainland Killini, in addition to the landing craft style ferries which shuttle back and forth every day to Lixourion. Furthermore there are ferry-boats connecting Ag Evfimia to Astakos(M), Nidri(Lefkas), as well as a connection between Pesada and Korithi Port (Zakynthos). There are daily services between:- Sami port and mainland Patras, as well as Ithaca, Paxos, Igoumenitsa(M) and Corfu; Poros port and Killini; Argostoli Town to Killini; Ag Evfima to Ithaca and Astakos (M); Fiscardon port to Frikes (Ithaca), Nidri (Lefkas) and Meganissi; and a height of season only twice weekly connection from Pesada to Korithi (Cephalonia).

The east coast port of Sami perpetuates the Homeric island name, *Same*, subsequent to which it was named after a local tribe. Archaeologically noteworthy are the Mycenaean 'bee hive' tombs. Subseuent to a period of supreme wealth

and power (circa 1200 BC), there were four city states. Once the Romans seized Sami Port, in about 190 BC, the island followed the historical route of much of the rest of the Ionian.

One of Cephalonia's most

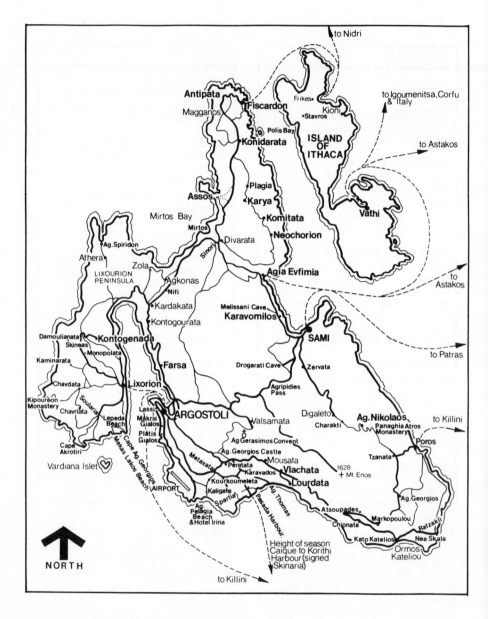

Illustration 48 Cephalonia island

famous citizens was General Metaxas. His eminence was firmly established, on 28th October 1940 when he is supposed to have advised Mussolini 'Ochi' (No), after EI Duce demanded the right of passage for his troops. This day is now a public holiday.

MAIN PORTS & RESORTS
POROS (Porros) (44km from Argostoli Town) Tel prefix 0674. At the southern end of this east coast port is the ferry-boat quay and harbour, across from which are some holiday apartments. The main development is round the hillside. The High Street leads to a shadeless, shingle and pebble beach, with a sandy sea's edge.

There are hotels and pensions, but few Rooms, and plenty of eating places.

KATO KATELIOS (32km from Argostoli Town) Once an isolated fishing boat hamlet, which has now become a rather hillbilly, seaside holiday resort.

NEA SKALA (38km from Argostoli Town) A quiet, low-level, seaside village situated above a long, wide, pebble and shingle beach. A number of houses offer accommodation.

Lourdata Beach (18½km from Argostoli Town) The long beach, with a pebble middle shore and a sandy foreshore, is contained by a substantial concrete sea wall.

ARGOSTOLI (Argostolion) Tel prefix 0671. The capital and minor port is built on a thick finger of land that projects into the Gulf of Argostoli. The town is not overly attractive, due to being reconstructed on a sterile, gridiron layout after the 1953 earthquake.

The extensive paved main square is rather barren in appearance, although the palm trees have now matured. Cafes and restaurants edge its perimeter. The hotel accommodation is comparatively expensive, the majority being taken over by holiday companies.

Despite the lack of any adjacent beaches, (it being necessary to travel some 3km), the proximity of the airport has allowed the town to become a package tourist resort.

Places of interest include the:-
British Cemetery, the **Archaeological Museum** and the **Cultural & Historical Museum.**
Ruins of Ancient Walls of Krani South from Argostoli Town. The remains relate to the fourth century BC, and were part of a large defensive system for the ancient Kingdom of Krani.
Sea Mills The reconstructed, rather unique Sea Mills are two kilometres distant, at the north end of the Lassi Peninsula. They were built in the nineteenth century to exploit the phenomenon of an underground river of sea-water, coursing inland. Scientists recently established that the water reappears the other side of Cephalonia. The 1953 earthquake probably altered the levels, as the flood has slowed to a trickle.

Makris Gialos Beach (circa 5km from Argostoli Town) A lovely sweep of clean, if crowded, sand.

Platis Gialos Beach (circa 6km from Argostoli Town) An equally sandy, clean, crowded but superior location to Makris Beach.

Ag Thomas Beach (circa 20km from Argostoli Town) There are some changing huts, a taverna and beach showers. A tiny, sandy cove is to the left, with a bigger sweep of kelpy beach round to the right.

Kaligata Beach (circa 12km from Argostoli Town) A narrow, sandy, but shadeless shore, serpentines along the foot of low cliffs.

Spartia Beach (circa 17km from Argostoli Town) There is a parking spot above the small cove. Offshore is a chapel topped islet. The narrow sea entrance is almost blocked off by rock.

Pesada Port (circa 19km from Argostoli Town) Pesada is more a small fishing boat harbour than a full-blown port. A height of season ferry links with Korithi on Zakynthos island.

LIXOURION (Lixouri) Tel prefix 0671. A large, sleepy location with a massive but under-used port, which is a pleasant alternative to the clamour of Argostoli.

There aren't any beaches in the town, but 2km distant is :-
Lepada Beach An excellent, broad length of orange sand. There are few if any Rooms, and the hotels and pensions are booked by holiday firms. Several cafes and tavernas are spaced out around the main square.

Megas Lakos Beach (5km from Lixourion Town) A long, beautiful stretch of shadeless, reddy-orange sand. It is edged by a low, 3m cliff of soft, butter-like clay.

Ag Spiridon Beach (16km from Lixourion Town) Sadly, this shore is badly polluted with kelp.

SAMI Tel prefix 0674. The rather oversized, north-east coast main port is set in a lovely bay. The general aspect of the Esplanade is greatly enhanced by the awning covered terraces of the cafe-bars and tavernas bordering the quay wall. There are a number of hotels, as well as a campsite.

AG EVFIMIA (10km from Sami Port) A lovely, north-east coast fishing port, complete with a small harbour, prettily folded around the waters edge. A year-round ferry-boat links Ag Evfimia to Ithaca Island and Astakos(M).

There are a few shops, some Rooms and a hotel.

Mirtos Bay & Beach (34km from Argostoli Town) A wide, dazzling white crescent of shingle, flanked by towering cliffs and edged by a sea of the deepest blue.

ASSOS (38km from Argostoli Town) Tel prefix 0674. Views from the roadway, high above, reveal a dramatically beautiful panorama. Alongside the semi-ruined fishing settlement is a Venetian fortress capped, tear shaped peninsula. There are a couple of tavernas, a few Rooms and a pension or two.

FISCARDON (50km from Argostoli Town) Tel prefix 0674. A captivating but busy, northern, fishing-boat village, set at the end of a very pretty, angled inlet. The port is extensively used by flotilla yachts and is experiencing ever-increasing pressure from ferry-boats and tour coaches.

There is a surprising quantity of accommodation. The quayside is attractively edged by kafeneions, tavernas and restaurants.

FACT FILE

ALTERNATIVE NAMES Kerkira, Kerkyra, Korfu, Corfou

IMPRESSIONS Traffic congestion; tall, once gracious, crumbling buildings; green countryside, olive-tree & fern covered.

SPECIALITIES Mandolato nougat; the liqueur *Coum Cout*; Koumm-kuat candy; pastitsada (spiced, braised veal & macaroni); sofrito (spiced, fried & baked meats).

RELIGIOUS FESTIVALS include: 21st May - Ionian islands union with Greece; 6th August - Pana-ghia, Mouse island; 14th August - Assumption of the Holy Virgin, Mandouki; Palm Sunday, the following Saturday, the 11th August and the first Sunday in November - Services and processions.

STATISTICS Tel prefix 0661. The island is 56km long, has a maximum width of some 27km & an area of 593sq km. The population numbers about 99,000, of which some 32,000 live in Corfu Town.

TRANSPORT LINKS

Air The airport is close to Corfu Town. Buses run by the airport access road. Hotel and Olympic coaches, as well as taxis, are present. At least three flights a day connect with Athens, whilst two a week fly to Cephalonia, Preveza and Zakynthos.

Bus London and the other major European capitals spawn a number of coach operators, who journey to Corfu island, trans-hipping from Italy or Igoumenit-tsa (Greek mainland).

There is a scheduled service from Athens, via Rio-Antirio and Igoumenitsa, then a boat.

Ferry There are two ports, the Old and the New. The Igoumen-itsa(M) and Paxos island ferries dock at the Old Port, the inter-island ferry-boats, international craft and cruise liners tie up at the New Port. part from the procession of international craft, there are daily connections to Igoumenitsa(M), Paxos, Ithaca, Cephalonia and Patras(M).

The British administered Corfu be-tween 1815-1864, a regime that resulted in some lasting peculiarities. These include a number of fine buil-dings; brass bands; the Esplanade cricket pitch (albeit of sandstone); the large British cemetery, as well as the availability of ginger beer. The island is also remarkable for the presence of a thriving Roman Catholic population.

MAIN PORTS & RESORTS

CORFU The capital town, main port and airport, which varies from 'modern squalid' to old-fashioned beautiful, with an interesting blend of Venetian, French and British architecture. The Old Quarter, built on a headland hill with all round, lovely seascapes, is a maze of narrow streets, lanes and alley-

For greater detail acquire GROC's Candid Guide to Corfu and the Ionian Islands

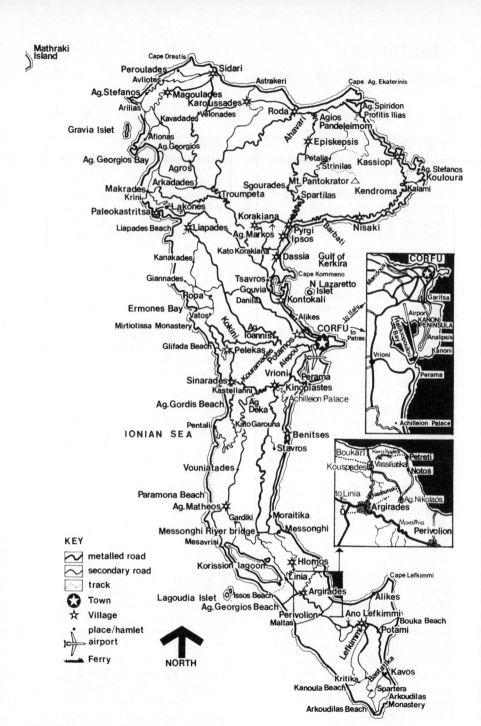

Illustration 49 Corfu island

ways piercing the tall, eighteenth century buildings.

Corfu Town does not have any 'proper' beaches, just three lidos.

There is a plethora of accommo-dation, including many Rooms. Corfu is well serviced by some reasonably priced tavernas with imaginative menus, even if the options are rather spaced out.

Places of interest include the:-
Esplanade Divided into two: the sandy, gravelly Plateia, whereon are played occasional cricket matches, and the grassy Spianada.
Old Fort or Citadel Truly a magni-ficent sight from the sea. The overall impression is of over-grown, neglected ruins.

There is a *Son et Lumiere* show, preceded by Folk Dances.
The Liston Building French de-signed and constructed (1807-1814), with large colonnades and arcades. Fashionable cafe-bars line the Esplanade-facing ground floor.
Palace of St Michael & St George A very impressive pile, complete with triumphal arches. The re-stored building now contains a museum and public library.
The Greek Orthodox Cathedral The Cathedral, built in 1577, is the repository for the headless remains of St Theodora.
The Church of St Spiridon Con-struction of this lovely church be-gan in 1589. It houses the remains of the much revered St Spiridon. These are paraded around the town four times a year, as he is credited with saving the Corfiots from death and destruction, on numer-ous occasions.
The Catholic Cathedral Construc-ted in 1632, but severely damaged by aerial bombing, in 1943.
New Fort Built about 1580 and the subject of late improvements by the British. It fell into disuse until taken over by the Greek Navy.
Archaeological Museum Close to the Garitsa Bay Esplanade, it con-tains several unique exhibits.
The Solomos Museum The muse-um is in an Old Quarter lane. Dionysios Solomos (1795-1857), a famous poet, was a native of Zakynthos, but settled on Corfu.
British Cemetery The grounds contain many interesting head-stones of British sailors, soldiers members of the Armed Forces and a few civilians.
Mon Repos Built, in 1831, as the summer residence of the British High Commissioners. It became the property of the Greek Royal Family and the Duke of Edinburgh was born here. Archaeological digs have established that the gardens probably overlay part of the site of Ancient Corcyra.
Vido island Prettily set in the sea to the north of Corfu Town and a fifteen minute 'voyage'.

To the north of Corfu Town are:-
KONTOKALI (7km from Corfu Town) Possibly once a village but long ago 'Kosta'd'. There are a number of hotels.

GOUVIA (8km from Corfu Town) A better class of tat borders the main street, as do numerous hotels and restaurants.

DASSIA (12km from Corfu Town) Almost wholesome, with a seem-ingly endless, thin ribbon of gritty, shingle beach. Apart from a camp-site, there are plenty of hotels.

IPSOS & PYRGI (14.5 & 16km from Corfu Town) Originally a couple of small hamlets, tucked away at either end of a long, bay, bordered by a narrow, undulating, fine shingle foreshore. The inland side of the main road is almost entirely infilled with holiday developments and hotels.

Mt Pantokrator A serpentine scramble, seemingly for the roof of the world, passes through the mountain hugging villages of **Spartilas, Petalia** and **Strinilas** (circa 28km from Corfu Town) The latter is an extremely pretty, tree shaded, tidy mountain village.

The much modified monastery, topping a bare mountain summit, is not only ugly, but dominated by the spread-eagled feet of an 'Eiffel tower', communications mast. The views over Corfu, and supposedly as far as Italy, are phenomenal.

BARBATI (18km from Corfu Town) This new hamlet, some 100m above sea-level, possesses a taverna, Rooms and holiday villas. The beach is pebble.

GLYFA (20km from Corfu Town) A path descends to another pebble beach and a taverna, prior to the outskirts of the tree lined, southern approaches to:

NISAKI (22km from Corfu Town) The villas, furnished apartments and Rooms of this rather polite location are a long walk from the shingle beach.

KENDROMA (25km from Corfu Town) Although it is a prodigiously long way down, one or two small hotels allow access to their private beach, even if it is on foot. There are Rooms to let.

GIMARI (Guimari), (26km from Corfu Town) Signs indicate Rooms and the pebble beach is kelpy.

KALAMI (30km from Corfu Town) Once an extremely pleasant, caique fishing village, wherein a dozen old houses, a couple of reasonably priced restaurant bars and a taverna, situated on the edge of a shingly beach. The threatened development has occurred and there is holiday accommodation, as well as Rooms.

KOULOURA (30km from Corfu Town) A tiny hamlet, with a harbour, located on the northern side of the headland that separates it from Kalami - unlike which it remains an enchanting spot.

AG STEFANOS (circa 35km from Corfu Town) A well-established, well-heeled, well-groomed tourist resort spread around the informal waterfront at the bottom of the bay. There are a few hotels.

KASSIOPI (36km from Corfu Town) Perhaps the extensive history of the location is the most interesting feature of this once quiet backwater, which has become a 'typical' fishing village holiday resort. Apart from apartments, there is at least one hotel.

Ag Spiridon (50km from Corfu Town) A sweep of sandy beach.

RODA (37km from Corfu Town) A very English resort with a sandy beach and a number of hotels.

ASTRAKERI (36km from Corfu Town) A rather scruffy, busy little place with two hotels. The settlement is at the east end of a large, flat bay bordered by a huge sweep of shore.

Ag Andreas Beach (36km from Corfu Town) A glorious length of wide, sand beach, bordered by low cliffs of varying heights.

SIDARI (37km from Corfu Town) A low-rise, but vigorous, crowded seaside development, complete with furnished apartments, hotels and Rooms. The resort possesses a splendid, wide, sandy beach with a shallow shelving, sandy sea-bed.

Sidari tour offices offer day-trips to the offshore, westernmost Greek islands of:-

Mathraki; Othoni, the largest and most attractive of the group, with a couple of tavernas and a store; and **Erikoussa,** with a small taverna.

PEROULADES (40km from Corfu Town) Beautifully sandy, if narrow beaches lie to either side of towering cliff faces close to this village.

AG STEFANOS (44km from Corfu Town) Sited on the northwest coast, Ag Stefanos possesses a magnificent length of sandy beach. The hamlet has been overtaken by the steady encroachment of development. There are Rooms, but most of the accommodation is holiday villas.

Arilias Beach (circa 41km from Corfu Town) Not nearly so attractive as nearby Ag Stefanos, the beach is narrow.

Ag Georgios & Afionas Beach (circa 35km from Corfu Town) A once deserted, grand stretch of sand, now bordered by the worst type of haphazard, partial tourist development, which includes hotels, pensions, Rooms and restaurant/tavernas.

PALEOKASTRITSA (25km from Corfu Town) Tel prefix 0663. The

view is sensational. The Monastery appears to hang out over the sea's edge, being built on a 100m high promontory. Of the five or six coves, some form a clover leaf-like shape. Unfortunately, the general development associated with the holiday industry has detracted from the overall beauty. Apart from hotels there are some Rooms, and many restaurants.

Paleokastritsa Monastery Originally constructed in the 13th century, it is splendidly sited.

Liapades Beach (23km from Corfu Town) A beautiful cove edged by a small, stony shore of pebbles and grit. Little of the beach is visible as most is obscured by pedaloes, sun-beds and sun umbrellas. There are pensions, Rooms and tavernas.

Ermones Beach (17km from Corfu Town) The gritty sand beach has a wide band of small pebbles and a strip of sandy foreshore. The hotel and beach-bar are smart, the ambience dignified and expensive.

Glifada Beach (circa 14½km from Corfu Town) The magnificent sandy beach is extremely crowded, the accommodation and eating establishments are luxurious.

Pelekas Beach (15km from Corfu Town) A bay filled by a lovely stretch of sandy beach, with one taverna. The comparative isolation is threatened by development.

Ag Gordis Beach (17km from Corfu Town) A wide, sandy beach. Apart from the magnificence of the surrounding scenery, Ag Gordis is not pretty.

Korission Lagoon (circa 29km from Corfu Town) Great sand dunes divide the sea from the lake. The shoreline is a staggering stretch of sand and beach.

Issos Beach (29½km from Corfu Town) A majestic sweep of beach at the southern end of the Lagoon.

AG GEORGIOS (31½km from Corfu Town) A soulless Esplanade set back some 50m the narrow beach. The rather shanty village is entirely forgettable.

Maltas Beach (37½km from Corfu Town) This small settlement must be rated as the best of the Corfu package holiday resorts. Apart from being neat and clean, the beach is superb, there are sufficient pensions and tavernas to make life interesting, whilst exploitation remains at an acceptable level.

POTAMI (Potamos) (41km from Corfu Town) Tel prefix 0661. An inland village with a Bailey bridge spanning a prettily tree lined river. There are apartments for rent and a number of houses with Rooms. The river banks 'host' some kafeneions and tavernas.

A river-quay edging street becomes an unsurfaced, wide track all the way to:-

Bouka Beach (42½km from Corfu Town) To the right of a long breakwater protecting the river mouth, is a small, sandy beach.

KAVOS (47km from Corfu Town) The long, tree shaded main street winds through a 'mess' of low-rise buildings. The lovely shore, with a slowly shelving, sandy sea-bed, is covered with people, sun-beds and umbrellas.

MESSONGHI & MIRANGI BAY (23km from Corfu Town) Rather more 'serene' than Benitses. The wide, 200m long strip of sandy beach, has pebbles at the sea's edge. In addition to the hotels and villas, there are some Rooms.

MORAITIKA (20km from Corfu Town) A 'Kosta'd' seaside resort with the usual package holiday facilities of hotels, villas, bars and mock tavernas. There is a 300m long beach, with a pebbly sea's edge and a sandy sea-bed.

BENITSES (12½km from Corfu Town) 'United Kingdom' popular Benitses epitomises all that is worst in the Greek holiday industry. This hotch-potch of cocktail bars, tavernas, guest houses, hotels and Rooms straggles along a few pitiful bits and pieces of shore, most of the waterfront being rocky.

PERAMA (7km from Corfu Town) A pretty location with plenty of tree cover. There are excellent views of the much photographed, twin islets of **Kanoni**.

FACT FILE
ALTERNATIVE NAME Ithaki.

IMPRESSIONS Mellifluous sheep bells; Martello towers; fjord-like indents; drinking-water short.

SPECIALITIES Homer; ravani; baklava; wine.

RELIGIOUS FESTIVALS include: 1st May - Festival Taxiarchon, Perachori; 24th June - Festival of Ag Yiannis, Kioni; 20th July - Panaghia, Ag Elias Church, Kioni; August - Wine Festival, Perachori; 5-6th August - Festival, Sotiros Church, Stavros; Midsummer - Theatre Festival, Vathi; 8th September - Feast day, Monastery of Kathara; 14th September - Folk Festival, Anoghi.

STATISTICS Tel prefix 0674. The island is 29km long, up to 6½km wide, with a total area of 92½sq km. The population is some 3650, of which the capital, Vathi, houses some 2,000.

TRANSPORT LINKS
Ferry The island is well serviced, not only by the larger, inter-island ferries, but by a craft that docks at Astakos(M) and Ag Evfimia(Cephalonia), as well as a Frikes link to Fiscardon (Cephalonia), Nidri(Lefkas) and Meganissi. Daily boats connect with:- Paxos, Igoumenitsa(M), Corfu, Cephalonia and Patras(M); the Cephalonian ports of Ag Evfimia and Sami, as well as Astakos.
    Ferry arrivals are often met by owners of accommodation.

The island's past is dominated by the 'Homer connection', despite some archaeologists dashing about the Ionian. The association has resulted in the prolification of locations associated with this or that reference in *Homer's Odyssey*. Otherwise the relatively recent history has followed that of the other Ionian islands.

    Despite the 'drawbacks', or more accurately the lack of concessions to the twentieth century traveller, visitors will invariably be left with fond memories of their visit, more especially the warmth of the islanders. To the north, the few villages have a surprising number of English speaking natives who are only too pleased to engage in long and detailed conversation.

MAIN PORTS & RESORTS
VATHI (Ithaki) The capital and main port is built along the bottom end of a beautiful, deeply indented, horseshoe bay, on a narrow coastal plain, hemmed in by a low range of hills.

    In appearance the town is not unlike Dartmouth in Devon, the houses clinging to the hillside and linked by shallow steps.

    What accommodation is available, is quickly taken as Vathi lacks an abundance of hotels, pensions or Rooms, but there are any number of establishments at which to eat.

Places of interest include the:-
Archaeological Museum, and the
The Cathedral Ag Georgios The

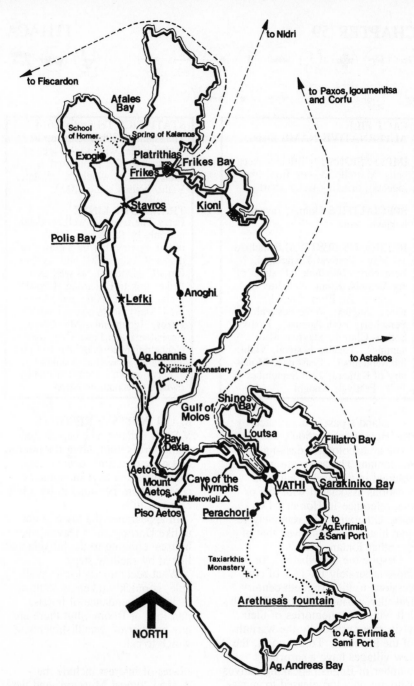

Illustration 50 Ithaca island

latter possessing an icon, possibly executed by El Greco.

N Lazareto Island A rather incongruous, tiny harbour islet, once a prison and quarantine stop and floodlit at night. Byron is reputed to have taken a daily constitutional swim to the islet and back, whilst residing on Ithaca.

To the east are:-
Sarakiniko Bay (circa 2km from Vathi Town) Made up of two coves, one of which has been occupied by a self-supporting community of Germans. It would be nice to report the site was a model of 'Green' aspirations, but the place is a rather squalid shambles.

Filiatro Bay (3km from Vathi Town) A once very lovely location now blighted by the presence of a free-wheeling commune.

Shinos Bay (2km) A large pebble, small beach, hardly worth the trip.

Piso Aetos (5km from Vathi Town) This western shoreline is very pretty with olive trees edging the road, about 6m above sea-level. A small sweep of stony beach is part covered in kelp and polluted by some tar and rubbish.

STAVROS (17km from Vathi Town) The pleasant, northern island, mountainside village has a wide main street with a tree shaded main square, as well as a number of restaurant/tavernas and Rooms.

Polis Bay (18½km from Vathi Town) The quay is used by a small fleet of fishing caiques. There is a smidgin of sand and a summer months Cantina.

FRIKES (19½km from Vathi Town) The outskirts of the pretty village port are marked by a number of old houses, which spread up the valley. The backshore of the cove, which plays host to a number of benzinas and caiques, curls round to the left, as does most of the settlement. A few private houses offer accommodation as can a small hotel, and there are a couple of cafe-bar tavernas. The pretty harbour is an attractive port of call for flotilla yachts, as well as an important ferry-boat link for the independent traveller, with a daily connection to Lefkas and Meganissi islands.

KIONI (24km from Vathi Town) The oldest part of the village is on the hilltop, overlooking the 'U' shaped harbour set in the bay below. The harbour beach of this still pretty holiday resort is nothing more than a pebble foreshore at the end of the bay. Beach loving holiday-makers have to travel further afield, along the cliff-top lane to the right of Kioni.

Apart from package tourists, Rooms allow independent travellers to stay.

From the mainland port of **Mitikas**, a caique departs every day for the half-hour trip, returning the next morning.

KALAMOS The capital is on the south-east side of the island. The village displays a number of earthquake-shattered facades of once substantial stone buildings. Some of the houses of this rugged and beautiful island appear very prosperous - and one village owner is reputed to have a tap to water each and every tree in his garden, despite the shortage of water.

If there is no accommodation on arriving, then visitors have a bit of a problem - and there is little or no accommodation! In the height of season months one house opens up, close to the harbour, with four rooms. The local people seem apologetic about this general omission and a taverna owner is helpful, but it is best to enquire prior to leaving Mitikas, and try to get some-thing arranged, before setting out. There is an acceptable beach close by the settlement.

EPISCOPI This is the other island hamlet, on the north-east side of the elongated island, which has to be reached by donkey track.

FACT FILE	TRANSPORT LINKS
ALTERNATIVE NAMES Lefkada, Levkas	**Air** There are flights from Athens to Preveza airport. The cheapest method of reaching Lefkas from the airport is to take a taxi for the 2km drive to Acteon, from whence there are buses to Lefkas. There are at least five flights a week to Athens, and two a week to Corfu.
IMPRESSIONS Tin reinforced, wooden buildings in the towns; mountainous but beautiful countryside; wonderful beaches; womens' brown dresses.	
SPECIALITIES Honey; mandolato, an almond sweetbread; pastelli, a sesame seed & honey pastry; island brandy & retsina.	**Bus** There is a regular daily service from Athens, as well as Acteon. The latter connects by ferry to Preveza, from whence buses link with the mainland ports of Parga and Igoumenitsa.
RELIGIOUS FESTIVALS include: Fifty days after Easter - Panaghia, followed by dancing and feasting, Faneromeni Monastery (Fryni); 11th August - Festival in honour of St Spiridon, Karia; the last two weeks of August - Music and folk dance festival.	**Ferry** There aren't any large, scheduled inter-island ferry-boats. On the other hand there are a couple of smaller, landing-craft style ferries, as well as a number of passenger boats, that run daily scheduled services to the islands of Meganissi, Cephalonia and Ithaca, from Nidri resort, and to Cephalonia from Vassiliki port.
STATISTICS Tel prefix 0645. The island is 38km long, up to 16km wide, with an approximate area of 300sq km. The population numbers some 22,000, of which about 7,000 live in Lefkas Town.	

The old cutting, separating the island from the mainland, was excavated in the fifth century BC, and deepened in the nineteenth century AD. The German archaeologist, Mr Dorpfeld, proclaimed that Lefkas was, in fact, the ancient Ithaca of Homeric connections. On the road between Lefkas Town and Nidri there is the site of one of his 'digs'.

At the southernmost tip of the island is Cape Lefkatas. The myth-ological poetess Sappho, having been spurned in love, is reputed to have thrown herself over those particular cliffs.

MAIN PORTS & RESORTS
LEFKAS (Lefkadas) The capital and main port has a long, active waterfront which hosts commercial boats, as well as private and flotilla craft. It certainly possesses immense charm and generates infinite interest. The very long,

---

For greater detail acquire GROC's Candid Guide to Corfu and the Ionian Islands

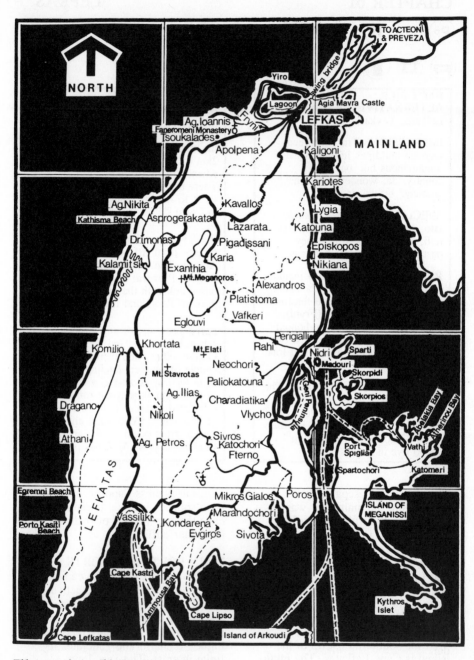

Illustration 51 Lefkas island

gently meandering High Street threads past a number of the old, single storey buildings displaying an intriguing range of architectural styles and materials. Other oddities include the church clocks being mounted on skeletal iron frameworks, the open gully drains and the traditional dress of the women. These latter costumes consist of a brown bodice and shawl, and similarly coloured, pleated skirt.

To enjoy a beach it is necessary to proceed along the Lagoon perimeter road for about 2km. The sea facing, shadeless, unattractive expanse of tar and rubbish polluted, fine pebble shore stretches all the way around the inland sea. The south-west corner becomes a magnificent sweep of beach, which continues west along the north facing coast, edged by sporadic, rather doo-hickey development.

There are a number of hotels and pensions. The flotilla yachts have tended to sky-rocket prices in tavernas and restaurants within walking distance of the waterfront.

Places of interest include:-
Pantokrator Cathedral Built in 1684 but subject to constant reconstruction, due to earthquake damage over the years.
Church of Eisodion Theotokou Cream and white, with railings fencing off the front.
Church of Ag Minas Prior to earthquake damage, a very fine church, built in 1707, but now most noticeable for the angle-iron, meccano-like clock tower.
Festival, Annual Once a year, during the last two weeks of August, the island hosts an international festival of drama, folk dance, singing and speech.
Archaeological Museum The exhibits in the small and unimpressive building are only labelled in German and Greek.
Other **Museums** include the **Folklore** and **Phonographic**.
Philarmonic Orchestra An active, enthusiastic, amateur band which holds a parade, once a month.

At the outset, the south-east route edges a mainly rocky coastline. The overall setting is pretty with the mainland looming up across the sound, imparting a Norwegian fjord milieu. After a short distance the thoroughfare hugs the shoreline. Along this are various small outcrops of villa resorts, close to little shingly beach coves, and bordered by Rooms and apartments, to left and right, almost all the way to Nidri.

KARIOTES (5km from Lefkas Town) A spaced out straggle, with a campsite and Rooms.

LYGIA (6km from Lefkas Town) A very small, fine shingle beach and sizeable quay are followed by a circular cove, with a shingly shore bordered by tall gum trees. There are a number of Rooms.

NIKIANA (9km from Lefkas Town) Contains a mini-market with a metered telephone, restaurants, an Express Market, over which are Rooms, a restaurant, more accommodation in private houses, a taverna, more Rooms and another restaurant/taverna.

PERIGIALI (14km from Lefkas Town) The small beach hosts a burgeoning windsurfing 'industry', hotels and Rooms.

NIDRI (Nydri) (17km from Lefkas Town) The beautiful situation of this attractive, one time fishing port would have ensured its popularity, without the rapid increase in villa holiday tourism.

To seawards, the various inshore islets are delightfully speckled about the sound with the bulk of the mainland forming a backdrop. Onassis family trusts still own the adjacent islet of **Skorpidi**. On the Nidri facing shore of the tree-covered **Madouri** is an imposing Palladian fronted building set in apparently close-cut, green lawns.

To the south, the beautiful, fjord-like bay of Vlycho cuts into the island, the eroded land forming a thick, crooked, mountain finger. The waters are awash with wind surfers, motorboats and yachts. The number of boats is not surprising as the port hosts at least two flotilla fleets.

The long 'High Street' has somehow retained a village 'innocence', even retaining one or two older, Lefkian style buildings. Parallel to the High Street is a very pleasant, long waterfront from which a large quay juts into the bay. Restaurants, tavernas and cafe-bars, line this 'Esplanade', with the tree and bamboo bordered Mithos beach to one side. Not only is it small, but it is narrow, the main body of which is shingle, whilst the fairly steeply shelving foreshore is sand and tiny pebble. Considering the crowds of people, the beach is kept quite clean.

Nidri is a port of call for the year round, small, car ferry link between Nidri and the islands of Meganissi, Cephalonia and Ithaca.

There are plenty of Rooms, and villas, a few pensions and a hotel. Prices reflect the popularity of the resort. Drinks and meals are comparatively expensive.

Mikros Gialos Beach (31km from Lefkas Town) A clean, 150m stretch of broad but shadeless, pebble beach supporting a campsite, a taverna and one private house with accommodation.

SIVOTA (Syvota) (31km from Lefkas Town) A previously beautiful, rather deserted inlet which is becoming a full-blown, 'undiscovered', get-way-from-it-all, villa brochure find', with several smart tavernas and some Rooms.

VASSILIKI (36km from Lefkas Town) Once a small fishing boat port, it is now a world renowned, windsurfing centre, based along the magnificent sweep of beach.

Much of the accommodation has been appropriated by the travel companies, but there are hotels and houses with Rooms. The windsurfing bias to the package tourist trade has resulted in an outbreak of 'chromium plated', fast food joints.

Porto Katsiki Beach (circa 41km from Lefkas Town) The scenery, views and wilderness that surround this glorious beach, bounded by sea cliffs, are most impressive.

Kithisma Beach (14km from Lefkas Town) Yet another splendid length of sandy beach, at the foot of gradual mountain slopes.

AG NIKITA (12km from Lefkas Town) A pretty, small, rather 'chi-chi', Greek look-alike for a Cornish fishing village, with only one road in, and the same road out. This 'High St' is bordered by Rooms, cafe-bars and restaurants, terminating on the backshore of a 80m long, fine pebble beach.

FACT FILE
ALTERNATIVE NAMES
Meganisi

STATISTICS An area of some 20
sq km supports a population of
about 1300.

TRANSPORT LINKS

Ferry Almost surprisingly there is
an excellent, landing craft style
ferry-boat, year round link with
Nidri(Lefkas), as well as Fiscardon
(Cephalonia) and Frikes(Ithaca).

80m long, fine pebble beach.
Certainly, of all the Ionian islands,
this has remained one of the most
delightfully Greek. Most of the
women still dress in the Lefkiot
habit, but with black trimmings,
and it is a common sight to see the
ladies portering loads balanced on
their heads. Weaving looms are
almost plentiful and the washing of
clothes involves a washboard...
and or the rocks.

There isn't any public transport, so visitors might consider
bringing a scooter, but not a car -
the Chora roads are too narrow.

There are sufficient Rooms and
tavernas for those who visit and
want to stay for a few days.

MAIN PORTS & RESORTS
PORT SPIGLIA The port for
Spartochori is a quiet, sleepy hamlet, set on the extreme side of a
very large, deep, irregular shaped
bay, overlooked by the Chora
dwellings. There are a couple of
tavernas spaced out close to the

fine pebble, steeply shelving
beach, one of which also offers
accommodation.

SPARTOCHORI (The Chora)
This must rank with some of the
other, magical, bygone age, island
capitals, too few of which are now
left unspoilt. This village is a
labyrinth of dwellings, lanes and
alleys, in amongst which are some
Rooms and a taverna or two.

KATOMERI (3km from the
Chora) A large, interesting hill
village, which is also a maze, but
not so photogenic as Spartochori.
Apart from kafeneions and a taverna, there is a large, community
owned and run hotel.

VATHI (Vathe, Vathy) (4km from
the Chora) The other island ferry-
boat port, Vathi is a quite large,
dusty fishing boat harbour set at
the bottom of a 'U' shaped bay. A
bigger settlement than Port Spiglia, with a village, a few cafe-bar
tavernas and accommodation.

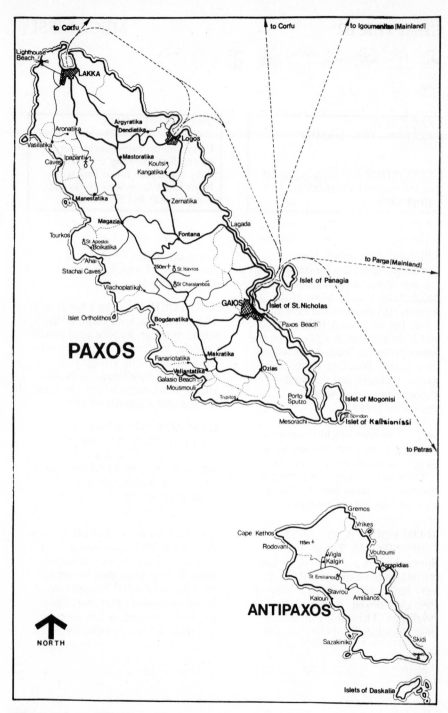

Illustration 52 Paxos island

FACT FILE

IMPRESSIONS Boulder strewn hillsides & dry river beds; olive groves; narrow, olive-blackened roads; old, ruined buildings; saline drinking water; few sandy beaches.

SPECIALITIES Olives & olive oil.

RELIGIOUS FESTIVALS include: 15th August - Assumption (Dormition) Day, Gaios Port.

STATISTICS Tel prefix 0662. The island is approximately 10½km long, 4½km wide, with an area of about 19sq km. Paxos has about 2500 inhabitants, of which some 500 live in Gaios port.

TRANSPORT LINKS

Ferry The larger, inter-island ferries dock at the New Port (or quay) of Gaios port. The smaller, Corfu ferries call in at all three island ports - Gaios, Logos and Lakka, as well as mainland Igoumenitsa. High speed passenger craft shuttle back and forth to Antipaxos, daily in the summer months. Every day a ferry-boats link with Corfu, Ithaca, Cephalonia and Patras, whilst local craft link the three island ports, Corfu Town and Igoumenittsa(M) least once a day. Once a week the local ferry goes to Antipaxos, as well as Parga(M).

Mythology advises us that the Greek god of the sea, Posidon (the Roman Neptune), tiring whilst travelling between Corfu and Lefkas, struck the sea with his trident and the island of Paxos bubbled up out of the watery depths.

The island's oldest recorded churches date back to the 6th century AD and are located in the Ozias region, reputably the earliest settled area of Paxos.

Naturally, the history of Paxos closely mirrored that of Corfu. The Venetians constructed the castle on the Gaios harbour islet of St Nicholas. The islanders were a plucky lot and, in 1810, rose up against their then French masters.

The island's agriculture is almost entirely based on the olive. Apparently derelict buildings and long abandoned olive presses

are littered about amongst the forests of olive trees.

A number of factors combine to make Paxos a difficult island on which to find accommodation, and an independent traveller's nightmare, at the height of season. For instance, the few Gaios hotels are, respectively, block booked by a sailing school and a tour operator. To make matters more difficult for short-term stopovers, the three port/villages are fully occupied by family holiday-villas, the various specialist tour companies having staked out nearly all the houses and flats. These drawbacks do not interfere with the waves of day-trippers from the Corfu resorts of Kavos, Ipsos and even Kassiopi, as well as the adjacent mainland ports who, in the height of season months, mainly swarm over Gaios.

For greater detail acquire GROC's Candid Guide to Corfu and the Ionian Islands

MAIN PORTS & RESORTS

(Porto) GAIOS (Paxi) The capital and main port borders a small bay into which the large islet of St Nicholas fits, leaving a wide channel running all the way round the quay. The New Port is at the far, north end of the harbour and is separated from the main port and waterfront by a curving road.

Gaios spreads along the quayside and radiates out from the attractive town square over the narrow, sea-level valley. The settlement is rather beguiling and many a traveller stays on and on.

There isn't a port beach, it being necessary to take to the Mogonisi Islet road. Beyond and south of the town statue, is a tiny, pebbly beach and a few hundred metres further on, another pebble cove.Mind you, apart from Mogonisi beach and those of Antipaxos, the island's pebble edged bays and coves are a disappointment. The track that continues on north beyond the New Port Quay, towards Fontana village, passes by two or three attractive, but pebble beaches.

The lopsidedness of the tourist development, concentrating as it does on villa-lets, has distorted the more usual island mix of accommodation and there aren't any welcoming house owners. In the busy summer months, the lack of sufficient habitation has occasioned the authorities to insist that independent travellers must have guaranteed accommodation, prior to purchasing a ferry ticket to Paxos. To ease the difficulties, there are 'Rooms For Sale' desks, close to the Corfu ferry-boat departure point. There are numerous restaurants/tavernas and the main square is adequately endowed with cafe-bars and their patios.

Along the north-east coast are:-
Lagada Beach A quite large cove of white pebble, backed by a pleasant olive grove.

LOGOS (Loggos) (circa 10km from Gaios Town) Despite almost every other house appearing to be a holiday let, Logos remains an extremely pleasant, pretty, if rather gushy, one-time fishing boat port. The attractively situated, but distant and pebble beach is edged by a large olive grove.

LAKKA (about 11km from Gaios Port) The very pleasant, northern harbour bay is almost totally enclosed by the horns of the encircling headlands. Dusty Lakka, criss-crossed by a network of poorly surfaced streets, has a 'recently erected' ambiance and the drains smell.

English is well spoken and understood, not only because of the high level of British tourists, but due to the presence of a scattering of English expatriates here. As elsewhere on the island, the high percentage of 'villa lets' has reduced the available accommodation to a trickle. The couple of establishments that used to be conventional hotels/pensions have, in part, allowed their rooms to be block booked by the holiday companies. There are a number of quality tavernas, a few 'basement sleazys' and an excellent 'local', but the holiday-maker pressure tends to ensure that prices are on the high side of reasonable.
Mogonisi islet & beach (3km) At the southern end of Paxos island, the beach is narrow but sandy, even if there are some pebbles. A beach-bar taverna conveniently edges the backshore.

FACT FILE **ALTERNATIVE NAMES** Zante, Zakinthos **IMPRESSIONS** English county lanes & fertile plains; primitive agriculture; motorbikes; friendly people; dramatic views; beautiful beaches; tourist with excursions. **SPECIALITIES** Mandolato nougat; pastelli - a sesame & honey biscuit; perfumes; sea turtles; raisins. **RELIGIOUS FESTIVALS** include: (The whole) Easter weekend, Zakynthos Town; 24th August & 17th December - Feast of St Dionysios, Zakynthos Town. **STATISTICS** Tel prefix 0695. The island is about 36km wide & 28km	long, with an area of 435sq km. Of the 30,000 residents, about 10,000 live in Zakynthos Town. **TRANSPORT LINKS** **Air** The airport is some 7km from Zakynthos Town. There is one flight a day to Athens, and two a week to Cephalonia and Corfu. **Bus** The daily Athens bus arrives via the mainland port of Killini. **Ferry** The island is not the easiest to reach by ferry-boat. The only scheduled links are daily with the mainland ports of Killini(M) and Patras(M). Between the middle of May and the end of August, a small car ferry operates, at least twice a week, between Korithi port and Pasada (Cephalonia).

The island's name dates back to Homer, the Venetians coining the alternative Zante. The island's great artistic traditions were reinforced by Cretans fleeing the Turkish invasion of their island.

In the short space of some ten years, tourism has galvanised this previously quiet, green and pleasant land. Now package tourists rule and their support facilities prosper. The once deserted country lanes, remote beaches and laid back hamlets buzz with tourists, hauled from here to there in air conditioned tour coaches or under their own steam, on a stream of hired scooters, motorbikes and cars. No unturned stone or quiet niche is left undisturbed. Even the turtle nesting site of **Gerakas Beach**

is exploited, by sun loving hedonists and locals money-mad enough to capitalise on the demand for sun umbrellas and beds.

MAIN PORTS & RESORTS
ZAKYNTHOS (Zante) The capital and main port was extensively damaged by the 1953 earthquake. Fortunately the citizens preferred reconstruction to take place along the lines of the previous layout, rather than have a grid imposed on them. Certainly the town has an air of vigorous commerce and prosperity. Much of the old back street ambience has been maintained by the retention of attractive, colonnaded walkways and first floor covered pavements. In

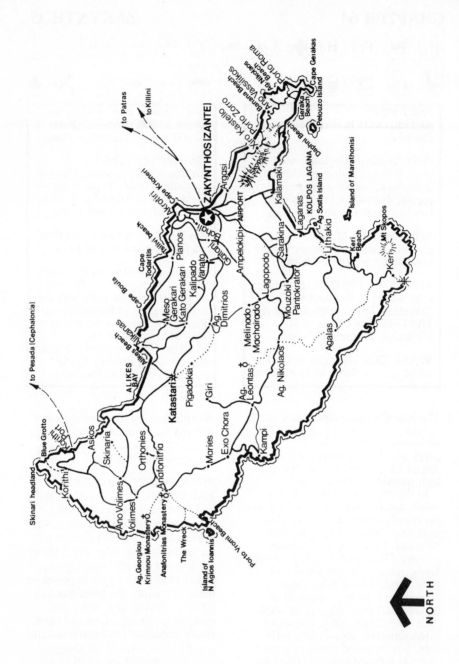

Illustration 53 Zakynthos island

contrast the harbour Esplanade and the large main squares have benefited from a spacious and imaginative redevelopment.

The town's drab, stony foreshore stretches away to the north and south. Beside the northern Esplanade is a Lido, a very pleasant, orderly, clean, well run facility, with changing rooms and showers.

Apart from Rooms, there are plenty of hotels. The paved square at the outset of the town's High St, is attractively lined with cafes and restaurants.

Places of interest include the:-
The British Cemetery and the:
The Castle The remains of the old Venetian fortress allows magnificent views of the town, much of the island, the Zante channel and the Peloponnese.

A number of the town's churches are noteworthy, including:
Ag Dionysios Easily identified by its distinctive tower and dedicated to the patron saint of the island.

Nearby, and to the west are the:-
Church of Phaneromeni This was the island's finest religious building and has been very sympathetically rebuilt.
Krias ton Angelon (Lady of Angels) A very pretty church.
Museums One displays Ionian art, as well as some splendid icons. The other Museum is close to the High St Main Square and is dedicated to and named after a famous Zakynthos poet.

Tsilivi Beach (5km from Zakynthos Town) Tsilivi is a delightfully sandy beach to the north of Zakynthos Town. At a distance are some holiday resort facilities set in rather scrubby countryside.

ARGASI (4km from Zakynthos Town) South of Zakynthos Town, this is a 60s style, 'Sunset Strip' of a High Street, with the pebble foreshore edged by a seemingly endless row of massive hotels.

A side turning advances to the small beach which is a 50m long by 10m wide strip of hard-packed, dark sand.There is another very small, triangular beach at the far, east end of the waterfront.

Daphni Beach (circa 10½km from Zakynthos Town) Travellers must bear in mind this is an extremely hazardous detour. To add to the fun there is an unposted tri-way choice of routes. The left one curves back round to the **Monastery Skoptissas**, centre descends to Daphni Beach and the right one to an unnamed beach. The very rocky centre track plunges towards the coastline where a number of shacks, in various states of disrepair, are scattered about, as are piles of rubbish. The long beach has a pebbly shore, and a very sandy, few metres strip of foreshore. The right-hand choice is an appallingly steep, rough and, in sections, sandy auto-cross route, edging a deep ravine. The rather wild, not over-pretty, but certainly isolated, small bay is encircled by two horns of low rock which enclose the sandy beach. This is a turtle nesting site.

Offshore is **Pelouzon** islet, which possesses some small, sandy coves also hosting the turtles.

PORTO ZORRO (11km from Zakynthos Town) The bay is hemmed in by hillside cliffs clad with fairly substantial bushes. The right-hand horn of the bay is very prettily edged by a cluster of rocks, beyond which is a tiny cove. The extremely pleasant, sandy beach is about 100m from side to side and 50m deep. The sea's edge is fine pebble and the sea-bed gritty sand. A pension and restaurant border the backshore.

Vassilikos or Banana Beach (13km from Zakynthos Town) An almost unbelievably enormous sweep of exposed, hard, golden sand backed by wide sand dunes.

St Nikolaos Beach (16km from Zakynthos Town) The access road passes by some holiday development and a rock music beach bar. The beach of the small bay is divided by a small outcrop of rock.

PORTO ROMA (18km from Zakynthos Town) A very Greek harbour hamlet. To the right is an enclosed harbour and prominent headland. The not very wide, sandy beach, with some pebble and a distinct belt of kelp, sweeps round to the left.

Gerakas Beach (18km from Zakynthos Town) A beautiful stretch of broad, gently shelving, sandy beach. This is bounded by the long, curving headland of Cape Gerakas, to the left, and a higher, less prominent bluff, to the right. If the natural attractions of the site were not enough, the beach is one of the last remaining Mediterranean locations at which sea-turtles lay their eggs.

LAGANAS (10km from Zakynthos Town) This south coast resort has been wantonly 'Kosta'd', with wave upon wave of hotels, restaurants and bars. The hard sand, gently shelving beach unfolds to the ease for some kilometres.

ALAMAKI (7½km from Zakynthos Town) An inexorable build-up is filling in the surrounding farmland. A low cliff top overlooks a short length of sandy beach. To the west is a crumbly headland, the other side of which is the outset of the shore, all the way back to aforementioned Laganas.

Keri Beach & Bay (circa 20km from Zakynthos Town) A scattering of dwellings precedes the bay. To the left is an extended, not over-wide pebble beach which has a firm, sandy sea's edge and sea-bed. Trees have been planted along the backshore, but they are rather too small to give any shade.

Back on the north-east coast:-
PLANOS (6km from Zakynthos Town) A widespread holiday development, at the far west end of Tsilivi Beach. The beach is narrow and almost entirely covered with sun-beds. Apart from numerous hotels, there are some Rooms.

ALIKES (18km from Zakynthos Town) A low-rise, busy seaside resort stretching out along the long curve of Alikes Bay, which is bordered by a 15m wide sweep of sandy beach. The mouth of a fairly large river flows across the beach and effectively divides the shoreline. The west end of the bay is a wide, shadeless, unattractively coloured grey sand.

Korithi Port (39½km from Zakynthos Town) This northern sprinkling of buildings is hemmed in by parched, mountain foothills. There are several, low-key hotels as well as a couple of tavernas. The small harbour 'hosts' the summer months ferry-boat connection with Pesada, on Cephalonia.

PART EIGHT   NORTH EAST AEGEAN ISLANDS
(Eastern Sporades)

Some of the islands that make up this group are rather less well-known than many other Greek islands, with perhaps the notable exceptions of Samos and Thassos. They are geographically amongst the furthest from mainland Athens, hugging the west Turkish coastline. Partly as a result of this comparative insularity, the ferry-boat connections up and down the N.E. Aegean are rather fragmentary and disjointed.

Ag Estratios, administratively linked with Limnos, is the least winsome of the smaller, more isolated islands in the group, due to an earthquake devastating the old port in comparatively recent times. The shattered buildings and homes were replaced by ugly, concrete 'prefabs', during the erection of which the once sandy beach was all but destroyed. Even fewer tourists 'chance' the vagaries of the journey to this island, as it is necessary to transfer from the ferry to a small pass-boat, in mid-sea, for the last portion of the sea voyage. Similarly to Fournoi and Psara, there isn't much of a road system and thus there are very few vehicles.

It is said that the rich ship masters of Chios once opposed tourism. Problematically the loveliness of the countryside and the inland villages, some of which are unique, is offset by the almost total lack of sandy beaches. Additionally Chios Town, the capital and main port, is unattractive. Grey, precast concrete high-rise buildings dominate the seemingly never-ending, treeless, and thus shadeless, harbour quay. Incidentally this facade conceals an intriguing, old market area.

The N.E. Aegean chain is well sprinkled with those 'off the beaten track', small islands which the true Grecophile aspire to visit. Fournoi, close by Ikaria, more than repays a traveller's efforts to make the journey. Admittedly there is only one settlement of any consequence, that is the bustling, agreeable fishing boat port, but there are a number of delightful beach walks, and the people are exceptionally friendly.

Ikaria, which appears to be almost vertically mountainous, lies to the west of Samos. Despite this the island does not enjoy particularly frequent ferry-boat connections, and must be a nightmare to anyone who suffers from vertigo. Ag Kirikos, the main port, is rather dank and the inhabitants are not particularly welcoming; the northern port, Efdilos, is scrubbly, and the only worthwhile, sandy beach resort, Armenistis, is reached by a rather frightening bus journey.

Lesbos is massive, the third largest of all the Greek islands. Mitilini, the main town and port, might initially, appear unappealing, but has an engaging, almost circular inner harbour, a number of 'stately' buildings, as well as amply tree planted parks. Furthermore the island is more than fortunate in possessing four most attractive seaside resorts, of which only Molivos does not possess a very sandy beach. To atone for this 'deficiency', Molivos boasts a 'film set' port and very pleasing, hill-hugging Chora.

Limnos is blessed by being the only island in the group to have not just one, but three sandy beaches, all adjacent to the captivating port and town of Mirina. The countryside is extensively farmed but the downside is that the inland villages and other seaside settlements are unattractive.

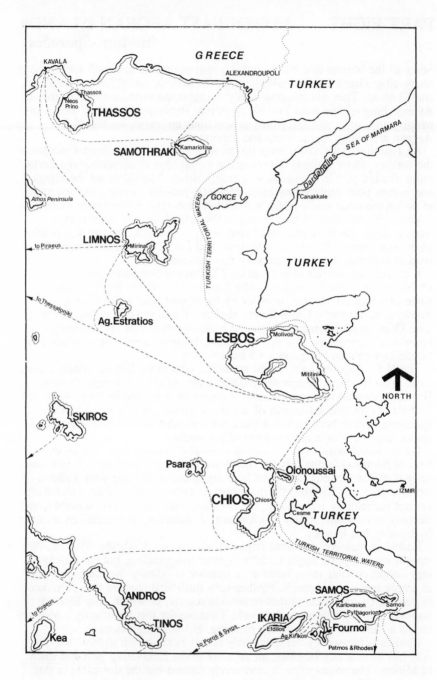

Illustration 54 The North Aegean islands

Oinoussai is the largest of a little scattering of oft forgotten islets to the east of Chios, but the daily boat's schedules are so structured as to require visitors to stay overnight.

Psara is one of the 'undiscovered' islands in the group, a point reinforced by the necessity to make a four hour, small ferry voyage from Chios. The port, the only settlement, is not wildly engaging, and the inhabitants are rather reserved. However there are two good beaches, and, as few other tourists bother to make the journey, Psara well repays the effort required in arranging a visit.

Samos has welcomed package tourism, which the sheer size of this lovely, verdant island has, to date, been well able to contain. Certainly the airport, coupled with an excellent ferry-boat service from Piraeus, has helped to encourage this growth, with the result that Samos can no longer now be regarded as other than a resort island.

Least attractive of the group must be Samothraki, and the ferry-boat connection is awkward, not linking in with any other islands. It must be stated that Samothraki is quite large, with lovely countryside, an interesting Chora and a few, pretty inland villages. Unfortunately these advantages do little to overcome the lack of any but a large pebble shoreline (that completely encircles the island) and the dusty, dirty, charmless port of Kamariotisa, the inhabitants of which are noticeably disinterested in visitors.

Beautiful Thassos, close by the north-eastern mainland of Greece, has long been a favourite with Greek and Germans alike. They both take advantage of the short sea crossing on the well serviced ferry-boat route, even if Thassos is not directly linked by ferry with other islands. The Germans, who find the island particularly beguiling, motor down through Europe in large numbers to camp or reside in the plenteous accommodation.

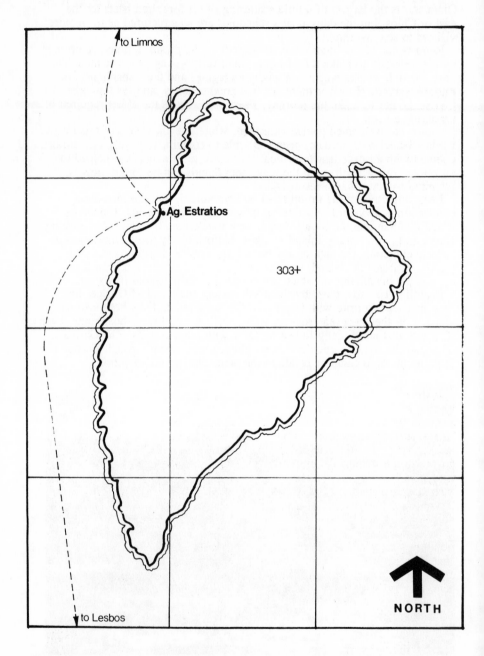

Illustration 55 Ag Estratios island

FACT FILE
ALTERNATIVE NAMES Evstratios, Aistrates, Efstratios **IMPRESSIONS** Ruined, old port; 'Soweto' style prefabs; oak trees. **STATISTICS** The almost triangular island has an area of 44sq km & a population of about 270.

TRANSPORT LINKS
Ferry There are three ferries a week, two connecting with Limnos and Kavala(M), and one a week with Evia island. They stop in the bay, setting down and taking off passengers from local boats. Visitors are met by an inquisitive crowd of villagers, but there is only one pension.

Ag Estratios island is the least visited of the group, which is not entirely surprising due to the ferry-boat arrangements.

The port is the only settlement and the islanders are slow to warm to visitors, although a day or two makes a difference. The island was a place of exile and, as recently as 1954, 1250 policemen oversaw 5000 prisoners.

If the difficulties of actually getting to the island were not enough, the port had the misfortune to suffer a calamitous earthquake, as late as 1968. This destroyed nine-tenths of the original, attractive buildings which used to stretch up the northern hillsides. To mitigate the disaster, in which forty-eight people died, a new village was hastily erected in the adjacent river valley. The resultant, soulless, stereotyped concrete buildings, the sterile grid road system, coupled with the remnants of the old village strewn about the hillside, and the massive concrete lining of the river-bed, does not make a pretty sight.

To see how attractive the location was, prior to the disaster, it is only necessary to pop into the kafeneion, across from the boat quay, and have a good look at the sepia photographs on the wall. One of these details, not only the old village, but six windmills, either side of the hill-top chapels. Alternatively walk a couple of hundred metres up the river-bed, past the concrete streets, to the valley - a fertile maze of smallholdings, orchards and agricultural plots. Another of the photographs shows the, once magnificent, sweep of beach which was, unhappily, ruined during the rebuilding works.

Despite the various shortcomings, the island is an ideal spot for travellers who simply wish to immerse themselves in a very Greek island way of life, who have a well stocked store of paperbacks, and who do not easily get bored. Furthermore the immediate countryside is rewarding, and on the east coast, some two hours walk away, is a long, volcanic, black sand beach.

Even Ag Estratios is touched by the current Turkish situation and hosts a miniscule army camp in the hills, manned by three soldiers.

MAIN PORTS & RESORTS

AG ESTRATIOS The only village and port for which the introductory remarks set the scene. The villagers become friendly after a day or two, but some Greek is a distinct advantage, if not a necessity. Despite the partial ruination of the original, sandy port beach, of which some still remains, there is still a rather wild, sandy and pebble shoreline.

There is only one pension at which a double room might be available, but there is one taverna and several snackbars, even if the menus are very restricted.

Places of interest include the two chapels (requisitioned as a donkey stable) which overlook the port from a small, wall enclosed, oblong plot. They top the northern hill up which the village used to spread. Inside one of the chapels are the 'graves' - labelled tin boxes piled one on top of the other.

The old school, shattered by the earthquake but still standing, is on the way up to the chapels. It is well worth a look over, as the erstwhile magnificence and size seems totally out of proportion to the modern-day, small, depopulated island. It only goes to show what a thriving place Ag Estratios must have been, in the past.

CHAPTER 66   CHIOS

FACT FILE
ALTERNATIVE NAMES Xios, Khios, Hios

IMPRESSIONS Comparative lack of tourists; the Army; motorbikes & traffic; friendliness; mobile banks; donkey agriculture, in the south.

SPECIALITIES Mastic acquired from lentisk trees.

RELIGIOUS FESTIVALS include: 23rd April - Festival of Ag Georgios, Vrondatos; Easter Monday - Festival of old traditions, Mesta; 14th May - Festival of Ag Isidoros, Chios Town; 1st July - Festival Ag Anargyri, Thymiana; 22nd July - Festival Ag Markella, Volissos; 27th July - Festival Ag Panteleimon, Volissos; 6th August - Festival of Metamorphosi, Kardamila & Volissos; 4th September - Festival Ag Ermioni, Thymiana; 8th November - Festival of Taxiarches, Mesta; 11th November - Festival of Ag Minas, Chios Town; 21st November - Festival of the Monastery of Mersinidiou, Vrondatos.

STATISTICS Tel prefix 0271. The population of about 50,000 live on an island which is up to 50km from top to bottom & 28km from side to side, with a land mass of 841sq km. Half the islanders reside in the capital, Chios Town.

TRANSPORT LINKS
Air The airport is conveniently close to the town, on the plain of Kambos (Kampos). There are at least two flights a day to Athens, as well as a once a week connection with the islands of Lesbos, Mykonos and Samos.

Ferry The inter-island ferries moor to the north of the harbour, while the local ferries and Samos island boats tie up at the south end. Scheduled ferries connect to Lesbos and Piraeus daily, Limnos and Samos twice a week, the Dodecanese islands and Thessaloniki(M) once a week, whilst local craft link with nearby Oinoussai daily and Psara three days a week. There is a Turkish connection to Cesme.
   Owners of accommodation generally do not meet the ferries, perhaps because the police discourage the habit.

The island has a long recorded history dating back beyond the 10th century BC, when the Ionian culture settled on Chios. The island also claims (together with some seven other islands) to be the birthplace of Homer (8th century BC), at either Kardamila or Volissos. The golden age, both commercially and artistically, was the 7/6th century BC. The Persians ruled, for a short time, circa 500 BC, but after their overthrow the inhabitants swayed between allegiance to the Athenian Confederancy and the Spartans. Chios declared independence in the 350s BC, was taken over, about 330 BC, by Alexander the Great, who was followed by the Romans, only to suffer destruction by Mithridates in the 80s BC. The Romans reasserted their

For greater detail acquire GROC's Candid Guide to Samos and the N.E. Agean Islands

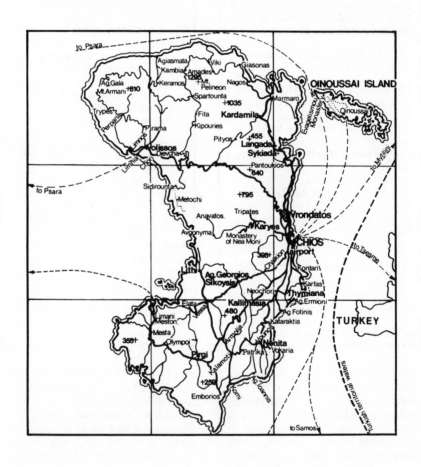

Illustration 56 Chios, Psara & Oinoussai islands

suzerainty, but, after their decline, the island experienced the ravages of pirates and 'barbarians' for the first ten centuries AD.

During the 11th century the island's prosperity recovered, causing the Venetians and Genoese to show a great deal of interest. The prize was mastic. The Genoese triumphed, in 1261, remaining as rulers until 1566, after which, they lost out to the Turks

The islanders joined in the 1822 Independence uprising, but the Turks recaptured the island and spent five months exacting a terrible revenge, slaughtering a large number of the natives. It took until 1912 for the island to be united with Greece.

The cataclysmic earthquake of 1881 destroyed most of the Genoese mansions and buildings that the Turks had left standing. It also cut a swathe through the population, that the Turks had left living.

The countryside presents an amazing variety, incorporating almost every known feature and facet of island topography. Added to this there are half a dozen medieval, inland villages, each one of which, on any other tourist oriented island, would be subjected to endless coach trips. Despite these advantages Chios has not been over exploited.

MAIN PORTS & RESORTS

CHIOS (Xios, Khios, Hios) The massive, uninviting, capital town and main port is, unfortunately, more often than not a visitor's first sight of the island. This initially unattractive appearance, combined with an overwhelming number of high powered motorbikes and cars, persuades many travellers to seek fresh pastures, quickly. As it happens, the ugly facade of Chios

Town conceals a fabric and lifestyle in many ways almost more Greek than Greece. The shambling lanes and alleys of the market area simply should not be missed.

The only town beach is an NTOG, man-made lido, but there are other island possibilities.

There is a satisfactory mix of hotels, pensions and Rooms. Strangely, with one or two noticeable exceptions, tavernas are substandard, but the splendid souvlaki bars and galaktozacharoplasteions more than compensate.

Places of interest include the:- Market Bazaar; the remains of the Genoese Fort; the Museum of Byzantine and Post Byzantine Art, housed in the Old Mosque; and the Archaeological Museum.
Turkish Cemetery This is within the walls of the old Kastro. The small cemetery has some of the distinctive, carved headstones.
Kastro The original structure was Byzantine but the present castle is the result of various reconstructions, between 1330 and 1748.
Municipal Gardens, Park & Main Square The well laid out gardens and paved areas form an attractive 'lung' for the city.

VRONDATOS (5km north of Chios Town) Almost the Greek equivalent of a 'Garden City'. The spread out town covers a large area, the seafront of which is a series of narrow, dirty, shallow, curving coves. To the north of a sea-water swimming pool, a headland, and the fishing boat harbour, is the only shore suitable for swimming, even if the beach is large pebbles, as is the sea-bed.

LANGADA (18km from Chios Town) An attractive fishing village. The bay forms a natural harbour edged, on the south side, by thickly planted, pine tree clad slopes. To the side of the pretty, quayside waterfront, bestrewn with kafeneions and tavernas, is a river inlet and a smidgin of shingle foreshore. There are Rooms.

MARMARO (28km from Chios Town) An unattractive seaport, and large waterfront, set in a big bay. There is at least one house with accommodation in the development, which spreads up the valley. At the, bottom of the bay is a shingle, kelpy, dirty foreshore.

NAGOS (31km from Chios Town) This pleasant hamlet is situated on a deeply inset cove with a clean, grey pebble beach. Beyond a church and an Army topped bluff, is a fairly long, pebble beach.

LIMNOS (50km from Chios Town) A tiny, one-eyed fishing hamlet, with a scattering of houses, and two 'dead' tavernas, edging the pleasant, brown sand and pebble beach of the small bay.

LIMNIA (49km from Chios Town) Simply a north-west coast harbour, with a splendid, brown sand and pebble beach on both sides.

KARFAS (7km from Chios Town) This large, clean, fine sand beach, is the nearest, presentable option to (the south of) Chios Town.

AG ERMIONI (9km from Chios Town) The original, old fishing port is being expanded.

KATARAKTIS (16km from Chios Town) An attractive, unspoilt,

working fishing boat port. The long sea frontage, dotted with kafeneions and tavernas, follows the undulating backshore, with a large pebble, kelpy foreshore in the shelter of the harbour wall.

EMBORIOS (33km from Chios Town) A 'U' shaped, narrow bay hosting a fishing boat port, with hills to left and right. In the lee of the left-hand hillside is a meagre, dark sand and pebble cove. The rest of the slender shore is pebbly. The fame of Emborios is due to the nearby splendid, volcanic black pebble and sand beach.

PIRGI (26km from Chios Town) A truly amazing, inland medieval village. Apart from a hotel, there are Rooms as well as sufficient eating places.

OLYMPOI (33km from Chios Town) Anywhere else this fortified inland village would rate as an island jewel, but it has to be compared to, amongst others, nearby Pirgi and:-

MESTA (36km from Chios Town) Totally different from the exuberant atmosphere of Pirgi, possessing a more cloistered, 'museum calm', with most of the lanes covered in by arched and vaulted stonework. There is a pretty, medieval hotel, Rooms, as well as one or two tavernas and kafeneions centred around the main square.

Limani Meston (40km from Chios Town) A large, almost circular, west coast bay. The foreshore is narrow, pebbly and rather dirty. Apart from Rooms, there is a taverna with a large terrace.

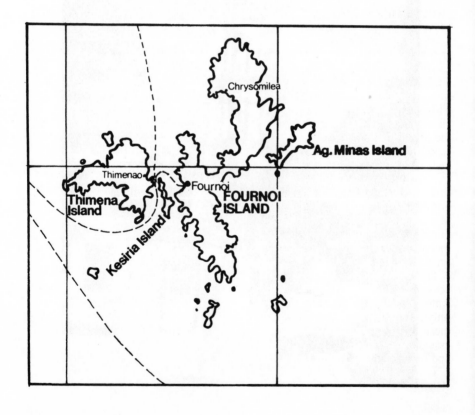

Illustration 57 Fournoi island

CHAPTER 67   FOURNOI & Thimena

FACT FILE
ALTERNATIVE NAMES Fourni, Furni, Phournoi

IMPRESSIONS Friendly, 'smiley' people; fishing boats.

RELIGIOUS FESTIVALS include: 23rd April - Festival Ag Georgios; 6th December - Festival Ag Nikolaos.

STATISTICS Tel prefix 0275. The Fournoi group comprises a collection of some twelve islands, & islets, two of which have settlements of any size. Only Fournoi island encourages visitors.

TRANSPORT LINKS
Ferry At least one scheduled ferry-boat a week drops anchor in the bay. A daily caique links with Ikaria island and a large caique connects twice a week with Karlovasion (Samos). The planned timetables of the latter two are subject to a certain amount of uncertainty as inclement weather can play havoc with the schedules.

FOURNOI The main village and port with an extensive fishing fleet. This varies from small to medium sized caiques and guarantees that the life of the port carries on, regardless of outsiders. The lack of a sizeable ferry-boat quay ensures that the visitors who do land are dedicated island hoppers. They will not be disappointed, as many of the fast disappearing, traditional island human qualities are present. These include welcoming, candid curiosity, as well as a wish to be friendly.

The lack of roads means that the normal method of travel is by water. At the last count there were only a few trucks on the island and these were only used to move essential supplies about the port, and its immediate environs.

The paved High Street climbs steadily to the upper part of the village and is lined with carefully pollarded plane trees. Parallelling the High St is another street, lined with lovely oleanders.

The scrubbly port shore is supplemented by two beaches, within easy walking distance.

Apart from a number of Rooms, there are two pensions and several good tavernas, as well as an excellent kafeneion.

THIMENA The other large island in the group has one village, Thimenao. The dwellings steeply climb up the hillside, almost like a flight of steps from the small quay, on the edge of the medium sized bay. The inhabitants actively discourage visitors, so it is best to resist the temptation to get off the inter-island caique, as there are no facilities whatsoever.

For greater detail acquire GROC's Candid Guide to Samos and the N.E. Agean Islands

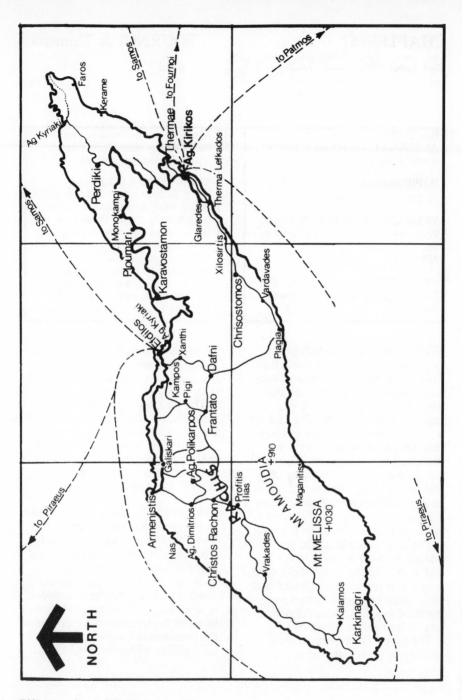

Illustration 58 Ikaria island

FACT FILE
IMPRESSIONS The mountain range; unfriendly islanders; sleazy kafeneions; goatskins; thermal baths; (only) Greek spoken; indented coastline.

RELIGIOUS FESTIVALS include: 17th July - Festival to celebrate defeat of the Turks, Ag Kirikos; 26th July - Festival at Ag Paraskevi, Xilosirtis; 27th July - Festival at Ag Panteleimon; 6th August - Festival at Christos Rachon; 8th September - Festival at Maganitis.

STATISTICS Tel prefix 0275. The island is 40km in overall length, up to 9km in width, an area of 270sq km, & a population of 8,000.

TRANSPORT LINKS
Ferry Most ferries dock at the south coast port of Ag Kirikos, but some call in at the northern port of Efdilos, and timetables must be scrutinised to ensure the correct landfall is made. Three ferries a day call in, except Sunday when that number drops to two. There are daily links to Samos and Fournoi; four ferries a week to Paros; two a week to Syros; and one a week to Chios, Lesbos, Limnos, Kavala(M), the Dodecanese islands and Piraeus(M).

Ikaria had little notable history, although mythology assured the island's place in the legends of the world. Daedalus and Icarus, father and son, chose to flee from King Minos of Crete by fashioning giant wings, in the style of birds, in order to fly away to safety. But Icarus, delirious at the delights of airborne travel, flew too close to the sun, melting the wax fixing the feathers. The wings disintegrated, causing him to plunge to his death (supposedly off Xilosirtis) to the south of the island, which then adopted his name.

Venetian overlords were followed by Chios based Genoese nobility, and then the Turks who were booted out by the islanders, in July 1912. The Ikarians set up an independent state, issuing their own money and stamps.

This gesture of UDI only lasted until the October of the same year, when they were 'encouraged' to join the Greek nation.

The mountains range the length and fill out the middle of the elongated island, sloping steeply to the sea on both north and south coasts. The flanks of the towering terrain are remarkably well vegetated with plenty of trees.

Even during the summer onslaught, only Armenistis really welcomes the holiday-maker, the inhabitants of the two ports of Ag Kirikos and Efdilos tolerating them with a lack of grace.

The mountainous countryside does not lend itself to walking so the unreliable bus service, with its incomprehensible journey schedules, and the not inexpensive taxis are the only methods of medium

---

For greater detail acquire GROC's Candid Guide to Samos and the N.E. Aegean Islands

distance travel. The renowned thermal baths dotted about the island ensure that visitors must compete with the Greeks for accommodation, eating out and the haphazard services.

MAIN PORTS & RESORTS
AG KIRIKOS (Ag Kirykos) The capital and main port has a languid air of disrepair and ennui. There are a reasonable number of hotels but few eating places.

The town does not have a beach, the nearest being some 15 minutes walk to the south-west or at 4km distant Thermae!

Excursions of interest include the local boats, which daily run to **Faros** and **Kerame**, on the northeast coast. Both have beaches and Faros is the site of a 3rd century BC tower. Weekly caique connections also run to **Maganitis** and **Karkinagri**, isolated fishing boat hamlets, built on steep hillsides, on the south-west coast, and inaccessible to road traffic.

THERMAE (Therma) (4km from Ag Kirikos) A thermal spa, seaside resort known to the Romans. The higgledy-piggledy buildings of the village, quite a number of which are modern, are jammed into the available space between the steep, constricting hillsides.

A clean beach of fine pebble edges the rather short waterfront of the 'U' shaped cove and the backshore, to left and right, is edged by pleasant bars and tavernas. The sea-bed quickly becomes large pebble and distant Fournoi island seems to be framed in the mouth of the bay.

XILOSIRTIS (10kms from Ag Kirikos) This is a very pretty, green, profusely tree planted, stream- running village with a small port balanced on and around a headland bluff.

EFDILOS (Evdilos, Evdhilos) (41km from Ag Kirikos) The island's second, north coast port.

Efdilos is rather derelict but, despite being a mere "way station' between Ag Kirikos and Armenistis, does possess a fair beach. Visitors are catered for by one hotel, a pension, some Rooms, and a few tavernas.

ARMENISTIS (57km from Kirikos) This seaside resort village is very quiet out of season, but incurs an invasion of up to some 1000 Western European summer visitors. They camp on the backshore of the extensive, golden, coarse grained sand beach, which is divided into two by a headland. Naturally some debris results and the Plaz Messachitis, the far beach from the village, is edged by a rather swampy, tufted grass backshore. The two beaches lie to the east of Armenistis, which spreads over a bluff at the west end.

Rooms and tavernas are plentiful and the residents are friendly.

CHAPTER 69   LESBOS

FACT FILE

ALTERNATIVE NAMES Lesvos, Mitilini, Mytiline

IMPRESSIONS Olive groves as far as the eye can see; verdant country-side; men in headress; goat skins.

SPECIALITIES Olive oil; ouzo.

RELIGIOUS FESTIVALS include: 8th May - Festival of Theologos, Antissa; 26th July - Festival, Ag Paraskevi; 26th August - Festival of St Ermolaou, Palaiokipos.

STATISTICS Tel prefix - See individual areas. Lesbos is the third largest Aegean island after Crete and Evia (Euboea), is up to 68km from side to side & 50km from top to bottom, with an area of 1625sqkm. Population estimates vary between 100,000 & 120,000.

TRANSPORT LINKS

Air The airport is some 9km south of Mitilini. There are at least three flights a day to Athens; one a day to Thessaloniki(M); four flights a week to Limnos; two a week to Mykonos and Rhodes; and one a week to Chios and Samos.

Ferry Ferry-boats link Chios and Piraeus(M) six days a week; Limnos twice a week; Ag Estratios, Kavala(M), Thessaloniki(M) and the Dodecanese islands once a week. Some owners of accommodation meet the ferries.

British excavations, between 1930-1933, revealed the existence of a civilisation based on Thermi dating back to circa 3000 BC, a culture closely tied to that of Troy and invaded by incoming Aeolians in 1000 BC. Homer refers to the island in the Iliad and Odyssey.

The peak of the island's cultural and intellectual achievements was between the 7th and 6th century BC, more especially under the rule of the dictator Pittakos, one of the Seven Sages of Ancient Greece. Sappho, the poestess, was his contemporary and achieved immortal fame, not so much for her poetry but because of her school for females. Her notoriety was such that the island's name has been hijacked to describe lesbianism.

Overall control of Lesbos, never in the hands of the islanders, swapped sovereignty often between the 5th century and 88 BC, after which the Romans took over. Under their rule the island was put to such disparate uses as a holiday resort and a place of exile.

After the division of the Roman Empire, Lesbos experienced a number of plunderings and invasions until a comparative period of peace and prosperity under the Genoese. The latter ruled between 1355 and 1462, when they were ousted by the Turks who held on until 1912, after which a couple more years passed, prior to formal recognition of the union with mainland Greece.

The countryside of Lesbos is

For greater detail acquire GROC's Candid Guide to Samos and the N.E.Aegean Islands

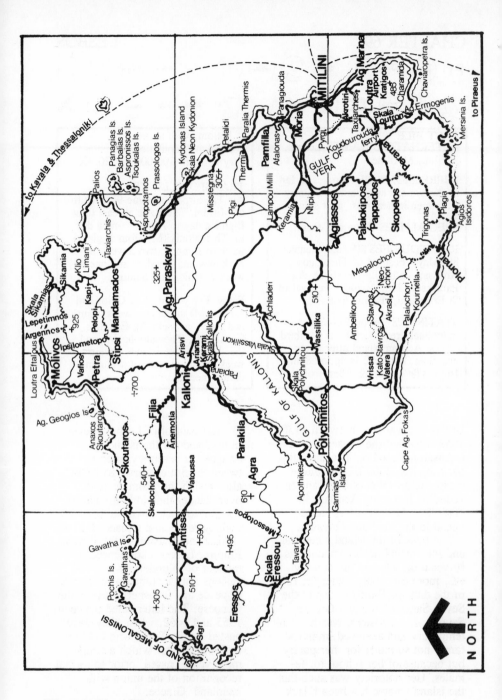

Illustration 59 Lesbos island

most attractive, if not beautiful.
Almost the whole landscape
appears to be covered with olive
trees and that which is not, in the
more mountainous areas, supports
forests of pine trees. Even the
moorland tracts of the north-west
are well covered and green. The
various roads lead through marvellous scenery, with many wonderful vistas. The inland villages
are unexceptional, and first class
beaches are few and far between,
despite which the island is host to a
number of well exploited package
holiday centres, fortunately very
spaced out. These are as diverse as
Molivos in the north; Plomari, still
essentially a Greek resort, with a
bustling, provincial Chora; and
Skala Eressou set in lovely surroundings and possessing a magnificent beach with a small development, almost entirely the result of
tourism. Mind you, the sheer size
of Lesbos easily absorbs all the
manifestations of the holiday industry, still leaving a number of
wholly unexplored seaside ports
and villages.

MAIN PORTS & RESORTS
S.E. LESBOS

MITILINI (Mytilini, Mytiline) Tel
prefix 0251. The capital and main
port, despite its large size and industrial nature, has retained an
attractive character.

Despite the almost permanent
roar of traffic along the Esplanade,
thankfully there is not the preponderance of 'mega motorbikes' that
infest Chios Town. The inner harbour hosts some large fishing
boats, a number of purposeful
looking Navy patrol craft, as well
as a few excursion boats.

The town only has an NTOG
man-made lido, but the rest of the

island more than compensates.

Accommodation is extensive but
the general standard of eateries is
not very appetising.

Places of interest include the:-
Archaeological Museum An interesting collection housed in a
once private mansion. Many of the
larger items are littered about the
front lawns.
Teriad Museum & Library Situated in the village of Akrotiri, four
kilometres south of Mitilini. Teriad, born locally, became a noted
Parisian art critic/collector, in the
1920s, and the patron of a local
artist, Theophilus. Teriad also
founded the adjacent:-
Theophilus Museum Theophilus
was a colourful primitive who the
art critic met only six years before the end of the painter's life.
Teriad managed to put on an exhibition of the artist's work, in the
Louvre, but this patronage occurred too late to save Theophilus
from dying in poverty.
Castle A very large fortress capp-
ing the northern city headland, the
walls of which are in a relatively
good condition. Probably Byzantine in origin, the Genoese made
additions and the Turks erected a
number of buildings, considerably
strengthening the structure.
Traditional House The ground
floor is a family home arranged to
represent a 19th century interior.
Theatre, Ancient Overlooking the
northern part of modern day
Mitilini, dating from the 3rd
century BC.
Trip Boats There are a number of
inner harbour-based craft that ply
to and from various seaside
destinations.

LOUTRA (7½km from Mitilini)
A pleasant, large village with a

beach alongside an olive factory.

KOUDOUROUDA (8½km from Mitilini) A fishing hamlet set round a very small quay with a taverna to each side and a rather large hotel. There is no sea-shore, only rocks.

PARALIA THERMIS/(Lower Thermi) (11km from Mitilini) A pretty fishing port to the north of Mitilini. To the right of the harbour is a small cove with a gritty sand, kelp strewn, narrow foreshore and large pebble, slimy sea-bed. This is a Greek holiday village set in green, pleasant, flower and tree planted surroundings. It There are innumerable Rooms.

SKALA NEON KYDONION (19km from Mitilini) A very nice spot with several tavernas and a small fishing boat harbour. The large bay is divided by a taverna topped bluff. To the right of this is a stony foreshore and a narrow strip of beach.

SKALA SIKAMIAS (48km from Mitilini) The final approach to this most attractive, northern fishing boat port is bordered by one or two modern buildings. The dusty, irregular main square, ringed by cafe-bars and taverna/restaurants, edges the small, almost enclosed harbour around which the buildings crowd. To the left is a narrow, stony foreshore and to the right, beyond the harbour entrance, a small cove rimmed by a narrow, grey sand, gravel beach. Apart from a couple of Rooms, there are several pensions, as well as a few eating places.

AG ISIDOROS (38km from Mitilini) A pleasant, south coast

seaside resort with a long, clean beach, mainly composed of small pebbles, but with some sand. Rooms and tavernas supplement the settlement's facilities.

PLOMARI (42km from Mitilini) Tel prefix 0252. The comparatively large fishing port and commercial town doubles as a summer holiday resort, with an increasing percentage of package holidaymakers. A hotel is supplemented by many Rooms, numerous restaurants and tavernas.

VATERA (54km from Mitilini) A grey sand, shingle and pebble beach, in excess of four kilometres long. The backshore is tree lined in the centre of this straggling hamlet, from whence the beach, spreading to the west, is dirty. There are a number of pensions, Rooms and tavernas.

SKALA POLYCHNITOS (49km from Mitilini) The port is to the left and a long, narrow, grey, sharp sand beach stretches away to the right. The backshore is lined with young, scrawny tamarisk trees. The foreshore is kelpy, the shallow sea-bed weedy and muddy. The straggling village is dusty and has a pension, as well as tavernas and restaurants.

N.E. LESBOS

PETRA (55km from Mitilini) The holiday development spreads along the Esplanade bordering Petra's splendid beach. The foreshore is sandy, the middle and backshore a fine gritty gravel, but it is a pity that there are so few trees.

Apart from a couple of hotel/ restaurants and some Rooms, The Womens Co-operative, on the main square, is probably the best bet for locating accommodation.

MOLIVOS (Mithimnia, Mythimna) Tel prefix 0253. A holiday village and port.

The main cobbled lanes of Molivos zig-zag up and down the very steep sides of the castle-topped, cone-shaped hill. The lanes may not be whitewashed, they are prettily shaded by a thick mat of trellis supported vines and wisteria. The cobbles are uneven, and the by-ways and alleys very steep.

Visitors arriving by bus are beseiged and harried by 'land ladies'. An excellent Municipal Tourist office looks after all and any visitors' needs. Considering the number of tourists, it is not surprising that there are a large number of eating places, but sadly few that are memorable.

The long, large pebble beach is narrow, with a grey shingle foreshore. The first metre or so of the sea-bed is shingly but, happily, becomes sandy.

Places of interest include the:-
The Castle Constructed by the Genoese, in the 14th century, on the top of the hill, and around the western flanks of which the present-day village is draped.

Loutra Eftalous (6km from Molivos) An unmade track stretches along the coast past three coves, around the first two of which are some smart hotels. Only the last two coves are suitable for swimming but the beaches are definitely substandard, being narrow and made up of grey, gritty sand on which is scattered some rubbish. The third or last cove is hemmed in by the walls of old buildings, two of which are thermal establishments. More hotels would appear to be in the planning stage.

SKALA ERESSOU (74km from Molivos) Tel prefix 0253. The 2½ km long, magnificent, south-west coast, wide sandy beach, edging the clear blue sea, ensures that Skala Eressou is popular with the tour operators. A number of hotels are supplemented by Rooms.

SIGRI (66km from Molivos) Tel prefix 0251. This west coast port is a super spot, with not a package hotel in sight.

The High Street runs through the centre of the village, over to a neat, tree lined, semi-circular cove, rimmed by a grey sand beach. Although the beach is rather dank in the middle, it is very pleasant at both ends, where it broadens out to become banked, sandy sections.

Accommodation is available at a hotel, or in Rooms, and there are one or two good tavernas.

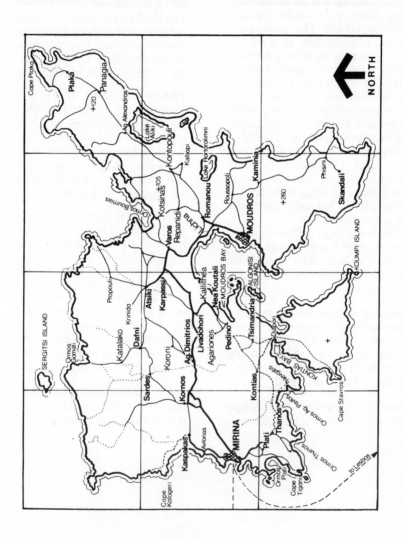

Illustration 60 Limnos island

FACT FILE

ALTERNATIVE NAMES Lemnos

IMPRESSIONS Golden wheat; prairies; poor roads; the Armed Forces; water short.

SPECIALITIES Red & white wine.

RELIGIOUS FESIVALS include: 21st April - Horse races, Kalliopi; 21st May - Pig fair, Pamanou; 20th July - Festival of Profitis Helias, Kornos; 26th July - Festival of Ag Paraskevi, Thanos; 6th August - Festival of Sotiras, Plaka; 23rd August - Festival of Panaghia, Kornos; 23rd August - Festival of Panaghia, Repanidi; 30th November - Festival of Ag Andreas, Kornos.

STATISTICS Tel prefix 0254. The island is approximately 60km from side to side, 46km from north to south, with an area of 475sq km & a population of some 26,000.

TRANSPORT LINKS

Air The airport, which is dominated by the Armed Forces, is set in a large, agricultural plain, some nineteen kilometres distant from Mirina. There is at least one flight a day to Athens; four a week to Lesbos; and one a day to Thessaloniki(M).

Ferry Ferries link with Kavala(M) four days a week; with Ag Estratios three days a week, Lesbos at least twice a week; Chios, Skopelos, Evia, Samos, Ikaria, and the Dodecanese islands once a week.

Incoming ferry-boat travellers are not 'overwhelmed' by the owners of accommodation.

The island's culture and development was closely tied in with that of Troy, after which the Athenians held sway over the island, off and on, for some five or six hundred years, with Rome interfering every so often. After the lawlessness of the 4th-6th centuries AD, the Byzantine empire ruled, a suzerainity interrupted by Venetian dominance, for 70 to 80 years. The Venetians were followed by the Genoese, who spent a few years in occupation, only to be supplanted by, successively, Venetian, Turkish and Venetian forces. In 1478 the Turks settled the matter and did not yield until Limnos was united with Greece, in 1912. The island was used during the First World War as a staging post for the Allied Expeditionary Forces assault on the Dardenelles.

It is a lowland island, hardly possessing a decent hill, let alone a mountain, with an abundance of farm animals and wheat fields. This is despite Limnos being drier than its lush, southern neighbours in the N.E. Aegean chain. The lack of water causes the yellowy-brown colour of the summer countryside. Whatever minor disruptions might be caused by the water shortage, nothing can detract from the excellence of the beaches, more especially those adjacent to the port and capital of Mirina. Added to this, the town has the advantage of being rather intimate

For greater detail acquire GROC's Candid Guide to Samos and the N.E.Aegean Islands

and Cycladean in layout.

The dearth of good roads and the lack of attractive villages throughout the island is matched by a public transport system that hardly inspires travel. But why bother voyaging to far-flung locations, that is as long as the nearby villages and beaches of Plati and Thanos, as well as the large expanse of beach at Nevgatis, are visited The expedition north of the port, through and beyond Kaspakas and round some five or six bays and coves, will not disappoint walkers.

MAIN PORTS & RESORTS

MIRINA (Myrina, Kastron) The town and main port is the most picturesque and intimate of all the N.E. Aegean islands, especially to visitors who arrive by ferry-boat. First impressions take in the picturesque inner caique harbour and the medieval fort. These are followed by a pleasant mix of old and new dwellings edging the High Street that snakes the length of the town.

A pleasant spectable is to watch the fishermen rowing out to sea in their benzinas (small boats). Over their stern are suspended very large, multi-lamps, which once lit, attract the fish.

The town has not one, but three sandy beaches, two of them being superb sweeps of shoreline with tree shaded backshores. Top of the class is the furthest but that is only a fifteen minute walk. This gently curving beach and sea-bed is lovely sand slowly shelving beneath the sea. The backshore is edged by a band of olive trees.

For such a large island, it is difficult to get used to the fact that there are comparatively few tourists. This lack of visitors is not a bad thing, as there are very few

Rooms available, and the hotels are rather expensive. There aren't any souvlaki pita bars, but there are some 'fast food' shops, as well as a number of galaktopoleio and zacharoplasteions. Mirina also has a quantity of recommended tavernas and restaurants.

Places of interest include the:-
The Castle The Venetian fort is draped over the volcanic rock outcrop that dominates the port and town. The Castle is now in ruins, so much so that the walls are quite difficult to discern, from sea-level. **Museum** Contains many exhibits from archaeological sites.

Ag Giannis (7½km from Mirina) To the north of Mirina Town, the pebbly foreshore is dominated by a large, rather strange volcanic rock outcrop that rises out of the sea, dividing the bay, and is most unexpectedly topped off by a tiny chapel. On the far side is a cove with a pleasant, sandy beach, backed by pebbles.

PLATI (2½km from Mirina) This pretty village, to the south-east of Mirina Town, is draped over a hill, below which is a lovely sandy beach that fills the bay.

THANOS & Thanos Beach (5km from Mirina) To locate the beach from the village it is necessary to negotiate a maze of contradictory, uneven tracks. The first, almost circular cove is rimmed by a truly amazing golden sand beach, perhaps one of the finest, most beautiful, small beaches in the Aegean. There are two tavernas, the one closest to the beach backshore, being excellent.

CHAPTER 71 OINOUSSA

FACT FILE
ALTERNATIVE NAMES
Oinousses, Oinousa, Oenoussae,
Oinousa, Inousses

STATISTICS Tel prefix 0272. A
group of islets, the largest of which,
Oinoussai, is inhabited.

TRANSPORT LINKS

Ferry A boat departs from Chios
Town every afternoon, returning
the next day.

Fortunately there are two hotels,
so an overnight stay is possible

Initially, Oinoussa (Mandraki)
port and village appears to be a
prosperous location, but many of
the once elegant mansions are no
more than shells. The pleasant,
cosy village ambiance is pervaded
by obvious wealth. This affluence
was based on seafarers who made
their fortunes. In gratitude they
constructed a nautical school, the
Navtiko Gymnasio. No wonder
Oinoussai is titled *The Ship
Owners Island.*
  To the west of the port is a
medieval castle.
  There are two hotels, as well as
a number of kafeneions and
tavernas, with fish a predominant
dish of the day.
  The beaches are magnificent.

FACT FILE	TRANSPORT LINKS
IMPRESSIONS Haphazard streets; churches with unusual roofs; wind; a scattering of red fire hydrants. **STATISTICS** Tel prefix 0272. The island is 41sq km in area, with a population of about 400/500.	**Ferry** The local ferry-boat is scheduled for three visits a week, from Chios. Craft are met by most of the islands' inhabitants, with the to-be-expected quayside melee. The few owners of accommodation do not meet the boats.

The island is the birthplace of Admiral Kanaris, the Greek Naval officer who used fire ships to such good effect, against the Turkish Navy and merchant shipping, during the Wars of Independence. The islanders joined forces with Admiral Kanaris to such effect that the Sultan decreed the island was to be laid to waste. After the assault only a few, a very few, of the population survived the annihilation. One story goes that rather than submit to capture, and the inevitable torture, many of the islanders blew themselves up. Those left living, and who escaped, established a settlement at Nea Psara, on Evia island, but Psara never recovered from the cataclysm.

The inhabitants are unquestionably reserved, if not totally disinterested in visitors. Despite the Greek Tourist Board converting a prison into a hotel, and a quarantine station into a restaurant, these excellent facilities remain closed outside the height of the season months.

Generally speaking, the scenery is unlovely, arid and unimpress-ive, and the layout of the village port dusty and disorganised. But for those travellers not over-concerned about surroundings, and requiring peaceful solitude, Psara may well be ideal. There is one fine, easily attainable beach and the citizens do warm, if slowly, to those who reside for more than a day or two.

Some Greek is essential, although there are quite a number of islanders who, speak more than adequate 'American'. But unlike Chios, and in line with the islanders underlying characteristic of diffidence, they are rather slow to come forward.

MAIN PORTS & RESORTS

PSARA The only village and port. It is worth noting that the islanders do not consider the holiday season starts until the 15th June.

There are four sandy beaches, two alongside the port, one a ten minute walk and one about 30 minutes distant, the furthest being a majestic sweep of shore.

There is the aforementioned hotel, as well as a pension and quite a few eating places.

FACT FILE

IMPRESSIONS Flowers; yellow broom; beauty of the landscape.

SPECIALITIES Wines & brandy.

RELIGIOUS FESTIVALS include: Pentecost (Whit Sunday) - Festival of Ag Triada, Marathokambos; 20th July - Festivals of Profitis (Prophitis) Ilias, Karlovasion & Marathokambos; 6th August - Festivals of Metamorphosis, Pythagorion & Karlovasion; 8th September - Festival of Panaghia Vrondiani, Vourliotes; 14th September - Festival, Monastery Timiou Stavriou, Mavratzei; 21st November - Festival Eisodia tis Theotokou, Pythagorion; 6th December - Festival of Ag Nikolaos, Pythangorion & Samos Town; 12th December - Festival of Ag Spiridon, Samos Town.

STATISTICS Tel prefix 0273. The island is some 48km from east to west, 20km in depth, with an area of 475sq km. Estimates for the population vary between 31,000 & 42,000, about a quarter of which are split between Samos Town & Karlovasion.

TRANSPORT LINKS

Air The airport is some 15km from Samos Town and the usual airport bus connects the two. There at least two flights a day to and from Athens, as well as one or two flights a week to Chios, Kos, Lesbos, Mykonos and Thessalonniki(M).

Ferry The island of Samos acts as a pivotal point for north-south ferry-boat travel, up and down the islands skirting the western Turkish coastline. The Piraeus ferries dock at Samos Town, as do the comparatively small craft that connect with Chios island. The ferries that link with the Dodecanese islands berth at the southern port of Pythagorion. On average, ferries proceed to Ikaria and Piraeus(M) daily, Paros four times a week; Patmos twice a week; Chios and Syros twice a week; Lesbos, Limnos and Kavala(M) as well as the Dodecanese islands once a week. There is a daily excursion craft to Kusadasi, Turkey.

Samos town owners of accommodation meet the ferries, but rarely those of Pythagorion.

Despite a Homeric mention, the history becomes interesting only after a period of overseas expansion, which included the establishment of colonies on Samothraki (7th century BC) and the mainland. Sylosontas was the first of a family dynasty of famous Samos Tyrants, during which period the island reached a pinnacle of religious, artistic, philosophical and mathematical achievement. It was Sylosontas' grandson, Polykrates, who raised the island to the heights of accomplishment but the world renowned Pythagoras could not live under the regime, joining other island exiles on the Italian mainland. The Persians tricked Polykrates into a meeting and

For greater detail acquire GROC's Candid Guide to Samos and the N.E. Aegean Islands

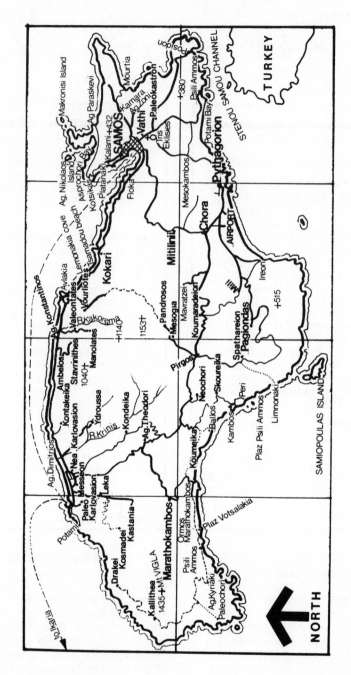

Illustration 61 Samos island

then crucified him, after which the influence of the island declined. The Romans made the place popular as a holiday resort.

In the Middle Ages the Genoese, Venetians and Turks were followed by the Russians, who then lost the island to the Turks. During the War of Independence, Samos ejected the Turks, in 1821, and kept them out until 1830, when the European Great Powers ruled that the island should become an autonomous state, under the overall care of the Turkish Sultan. In 1912, Samos was integrated with the Greek nation.

A wonderfully verdant and lush island with a varied range of scenery to suit most tastes - sandy beaches; agricultural plains; hillsides thick with a wide variety of trees and pierced by running streams; terraced vineyards; majestic mountains; colourful ports and attractive seaside locations.

The delightful mountain villages remain largely unaltered and there are one or two still relatively undiscovered beaches.

MAIN PORTS & RESORTS

SAMOS (Vathy) The capital town and main port (also listed as Vathy, which is in reality the old town, Samos) are situated to the left of the deeply indented Vathy Bay. The main development ascends the steep hill, a few streets back from the Esplanade that encircles half the 'U' of the bay. Despite the demands of package holiday-makers and a formidable military presence, the waterfront has retained a dignified appearance, with many of the large, 19th century buildings remaining intact.

The town is not blessed with much of a beach, there only being a small cove at adjacent **Gangou**

Beach Pensions, if not Rooms, are plentiful but the owners tend not to advertise, and many of the hotels are fully booked by package holiday firms. There are an inordinate quantity of cafes and cocktail bars, but only a few out of the ordinary places at which to eat.

Places of Interest include the:-
Archaeological and **Byzantine Museums**
Public Gardens A pleasant municipal feature with an aviary and one or two caged animals.
Turkey Samos Town excursions boats sail to Turkey, landing at Kusadasi, for Ephesus.

VATHI (2km from Samos Town) The old island capital is an attractive, small town built on a steeply sloping hillside. Spaced out throughout the alleyways are bakers, old-fashioned shops and stores, as well as a few tavernas, but no Rooms.

AG PARASKEVI A scattering of dwellings set on a lovely, small, circular bay, 8km to the north-east of Samos Town.

PSILI AMMOS (8km from Samos Town) The approach road to this south coast site loops along a big pebble shoreline. The inland side is marshy, low-lying and swampy. The road circles around a small headland, and curves down to the right-hand side of a fine sand, gently sloping beach, backed by spindly arethemusa trees and dunes, self-planted with low vegetation. A two kilometre wide sea channel separates Samos from the dramatically mountain backed shores of Turkey.

There are two beach tavernas, to the right of the bay.

For greater detail acquire GROC's Candid Guide to Samos and the N.E. Aegean Islands

KOKARI (Kokkarion) (10km from Samos Town) The original north coast headland village and port has been swamped and enlarged by the holiday industry, but still remains picturesque. A promontory divides the long sweep of pebble beach to the left and the shorter, curved, almost enclosed cove to the right. There are a number of hotels, pensions and Rooms, in addition to the extremely pleasantly located waterside tavernas and their patios.

Tsamadou Beach (11km from Samos Town) A lovely, crescent shaped cove reached down a path. The rather overrated pebble beach is backed by agriculture holdings.

AVLAKIA (16km from Samos Town) Once a moribund fishing port, clinging to a bluff, but now being developed. The rather small beach is pebbly.

AG KONSTANTINOS (20km from Samos Town) A somewhat narrow, dusty village of red tiled roofs, squeezed between the sea and the main road. The waterfront is backed by an 'Esplanade' along which are spaced a few tavernas. A couple of hotels edge the main road.

KARLOVASION (Karlovassi) (33/36km from Samos Town) The second town and port of the island. It is a great pity Karlovasion is such an uninviting place. The three centres that make up the settlement are very spread out, being up to some 4km apart. Once a well-to-do industrial centre, with a preponderance of tanneries, it has suffered a serious decline. The degeneration is such that the originally grand, four-square buildings spaced out besides the long water-

front now resemble some run-down, inner city dockland area.

For a location as large as this, there are surprisingly few hotels or Rooms, but the centre has plenty of taverna/restaurants.

PYTHAGORION (Pithagorion, Tigani) (10km from Samos Town) A south coast port and holiday resort, which is a most picturesque location, popular with yachtsman, package holiday-makers and backpackers alike.

Pythagorion was the ancient capital of Samos island. Most of the hotels are tour operator booked and harbour waterfront is awash with restaurants.

Places of interest include the:-
Archaeological Museum Apart from the exhibits inside, there are many humps of ancient stonework scattered about the square.
Castle of Logothetis Occupies a 'low rise' hillock, on the west shore of Pythagorion. The present remains, built on the walls of a Venetian Castle, achieved fame due to the exploits of Lykourgos Logothetis, and his men, who fought off the Turks in 1824.
Church of Transfiguration Next door to the Castle. On the 6th August, annually, the 1824 victory is celebrated.
Ancient Wall The ramparts enclosed the ancient city, had a length of some 5,500m, with 35 towers and 12 gates. The fortification not only encompassed the town and port, but the hills of Spilianis and Kastri, as well as other sites. These included the:
Ancient Theatre and the **Monastery of Panaghia Spiliani.**
Eupalinus Tunnel More an aquaduct, built to carry water to the city, from the north of the moun-

tain. The 1100/1200m long tunnel was dug from both ends at once. It was hacked out of rock with a height of 1¾m, a width of 2¼m, and a conduit duct in the floor. Only about 700m is now accessible, due to a rock fall.

Sanctuary of Heraion (18km from Samos Town). Also known as *Kolonna*, due to the single column left standing on the site. This was once a major support of the Temple of Hera, which measured some 105m by 54m, and was 23m in height. The original building, constructed in the 8th century BC, was rebuilt on a number of different occasions, over the next 500 or 600 years. One particular shrine revered a sacred tree. Apart from the Sanctuary, which included temples, porticos and an altar, there was also a town. This was first laid waste in AD 270, subsequently rebuilt with a Christian basilica, but destroyed again, leaving the whole area to become arable. The Sanctuary was connected to the Ancient City of Samos by a Sacred Road, some 5000m in length. On either side of this were statues, temples and tombs.

IREON (19km from Samos Town) South coast Ireon is now a dusty, incomplete sprawl of picturesque squalor spread along the seafront. Some out-of-place, smart hotels jostle with waste plots, cafe-bars, restaurants, lesser hotels and pensions. The beach of varying size pebbles and fine shingle is broken up by a scattering of tavernas.

ORMOS MARATHOKAMBOS

(49km from Samos Town) A small, truly delightful, attractively native, fishing and boat building port. The foreshore of small pebble and shale stretches away to the east,beyond a tiny section of sand, set in the angle of a large quay.
  For those beguiled by the ethnic, homely ambience, there are several hotels, a few Rooms, tavernas and one or two cafe-bars.

PLAZ VOTSALAKIA (52½km from Samos Town) An unexpected, spaced out ribbon development, scattered along the long, sand and pebble beach edging the coastal plain. At the outset of this rather Greek resort is a very small, pleasant, sandy cove.

Psili Ammos (of Marathokambos) (54km from Samos Town) A stuning, white shingle and sand expanse, edging the turquoise coloured, 'Caribbean' sea. Closer examination reveals that the sandy portions of the beach are large areas, set in amongst fine shingle.

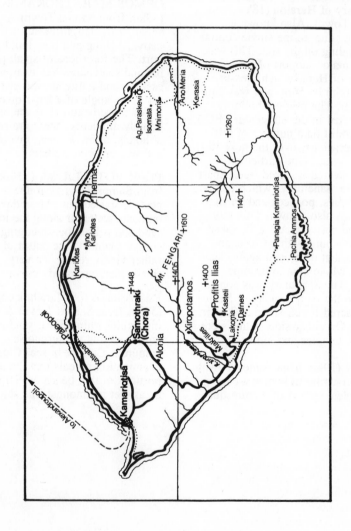

Illustration 62 Samothraki island

FACT FILE
ALTERNATIVE NAMES
Samothrace

IMPRESSIONS Dust; lack of beaches; pebbles; prairie fields; commercial fishing; large trees.

RELIGIOUS FESTIVALS include: 20th July - Festival of Ag Profitis Ilias, Profitis Ilias; 26th July - Festival of Ag Paraskevi, Perashata; 9th August - Festival, Therma.

STATISTICS Tel prefix 0551. The island is oval in shape, about 23km from east to west, & 14km top to bottom, with an area of 178sq km.

The population is some 2,800.

TRANSPORT LINKS
Ferry There is a minimum of a once-a-week service to and from mainland Kavala, which is a most convenient port as it allows travellers to link up with a ferry-boat service to the island of Thassos and separately to the islands of Limnos, Ag Estratios and Lesbos. The main Samothraki ferry-boat link is to mainland Alexandroupoli, almost at the eastern end of Greece and the second to last major station on the railway line.

The tall mountain peaks of Mt Fengari (161m) are most impressive, especially from a distance, and the God Poseidon is reputed to have watched the seige of Troy from these heights. The island was so named because, in historical times, the citizens of Samos colonized the island, naming it Son of Samos.

It is difficult to imagine, viewing the Samothraki of today, that in the 6th century BC, the island was powerful and rich enough to have territory on the mainland, an independent Naval fleet and a Mint. These past glories are manifested by the truly magnificent site of the Sanctuary of the Gods, exposed by the remarkable archaeological excavations at Paleopoli. Despite becoming a satellite of various overlords, the religious importance of the island

did not diminish until the 4th century AD, when the Romans imposed Christianity as the official religion. The decline was hastened by an earthquake, in the 6th century AD, which destroyed the various buildings at the Sanctuary.

The usual train of Genoese and Venetian overlords were followed by the Turks (1457-1912).

The general countryside is very attractive; the landscapes are some of the most appealing in the group; the interesting Chora and few outlying villages are quite acceptable. It is a great pity that almost the whole of the island's foreshore is made up of large, grey pebbles; the port and main village, Kamariotisa, is dusty, gritty, flyblown and unattractive; and the proximity to the mainland warrants that the island is a Greek resort. The surprising number of tourists ensures that Samothraki is not even an isolationist's dream.

MAIN PORTS & RESORTS

KAMARIOTISA This capital village and port is one of the most wildly contrasting of Greek island ports. Nowhere else can there be such a long, dusty, messy, unmade Esplanade/High Street for such a small population, nor can there be so many 'smarty' cafe-bars scattered along a waterfront's length. There appear to be ambitious plans for the Esplanade and beach area, but once one project has been completed, it has usually taken so long that other pieces of the development are falling apart.

There are no old buildings and some of the development is ugly, very ugly. The harbour is extremely large and the local fishing fleet is probably one of the most numerous in all of the N.E. Aegean. Not only are there big, middle distance boats but any number of sardine caiques, with their large stern hung lamps.

The number of Rooms are very restricted, there are two good hotels, and a quantity of souvlaki snackbars, a couple of which are excellent. Some of the cafe-bars masquerade as 'rock-bars', and are frequented by faintly menacing youngsters, whilst others are unfriendly, somewhat piratical and very ethnic.

THE CHORA (Samothraki, Samothrace) The village is the old capital where islanders retreated from marauding pirates. The main port road spills on to an unlovely square, on the edge of which is a monument and a kafeneion, dominated by a ruined castle topping off a pillar outcrop of rock.

The rest of the not unattractive village is layered up the hillside, in the style of a Greek Odeion. On the left, where the High Street climbs out of the square, is a modern 'block of flats' and Rooms. The street then curves into the 'Chora proper', which bubbles away with busy activity.

The village is the base for any assault on the heights of Mt Fengari (1611m). As the paths are poorly marked, it is sensible to ask around for a local 'sherpa', for the five hour trek.

PALEOPOLI (5km from Kamariotisa) The site of an ancient city, still with the ruins of some medieval defensive towers and an abandoned quay.

Sanctuary of the Great Gods (6km from Kamariotisa) This magnificent site is set in a pretty hillside cleft and dates back to the 6th century BC. The original Kabeiroi cult, of which little is known, were absorbed by the Greeks and the Romans, only for the Sanctuary to be destroyed by an earthquake in the 6th century AD. A museum displays many of the finds, including a copy of the headless, winged statue of the Victory of Samothrace - the French having snaffled the original.

THERMA (Loutra) (13km from Kamariotisa) The present spa village is a comparatively messy and ugly development, straggling up the extensively tree shaded river valley. The restaurants are crammed with Greeks, here for the curative waters. Those seeking accommodation can find Rooms and there is one hotel.

For greater detail acquire GROC's Candid Guide to Samos and the N.E. Aegean Islands

---

FACT FILE
ALTERNATIVE NAMES Thasos

IMPRESSIONS Pine trees; marble; beaches; asphalted roads; brightness; crickets; turquoise seas; few churches, chapels, soldiers or wild flowers; unusually shaped house roofs of slate; German spoken.

SPECIALITIES Loukoumades; olives; honey.

RELIGIOUS FESTIVALS include: 18th January - Festival of Ag Athanasios, Limenaria; 23rd April - Festival of Ag Georgios, Limenaria & Prinos; 29th June - Festival of the Marriage of Thassos,

Theologos; 30th June - Festival of Ag Apostoli, Prinos; 27th July -Festival of Ag Panteleimon, Prinos; 26th October - Festival of Ag Demetrios, Theologos.

STATISTICS Tel prefix 0593. The island is almost circular in shape, being 26km from north to south & 22km from east to west, with an area of 379sq km & a population of between 13,000 & 16,000.

TRANSPORT LINKS
Ferry There is a ferry-boat shuttle from mainland Keramoti and one ferry-boat a day makes the journey between Thassos port and Kavala, on the mainland, via Skala Prinos.

The island had an unexceptional history. There was the overall wealth attributable to mining activities in general, and gold in particular. In the 18th century the Turks bequeathed the island to the then Turkish governor of Egypt. He was a local lad born at Kavala, on the adjacent mainland, and brought up on the island. Due to these connections, Thassos became almost a self-governing outpost of Egypt with many advantages. This state of affairs deteriorated, after the benefactor's death, to such an extent that the islanders eventually implored the Turks to re-establish their authority. The Germans organised a major mining company and the island gained independence from their Turkish overlords, in 1912. During the Second World War,

German occupation was taken over by the Bulgarians who, in their turn, were 'relieved' of control by the Allied forces, in 1944.

In recent years, prospecting discovered Greece's only offshore oil, in the waters close by Thassos, the oil well platforms of which are brilliantly lit at night.

This was an island of massed pine forests and olive grove covered, marble hills and mountains. The extent of the forestry and mining was such that timber and marble were shipped throughout Greece. Unfortunately, in 1988, a serious fire destroyed great swathes of the forests.

The other growth industry is tourism. Years ago the Germans discovered the ease with which they could motor down through Europe to gain the delights of

---

For greater detail acquire GROC's Candid Guide to Samos and the N.E. Aegean Islands

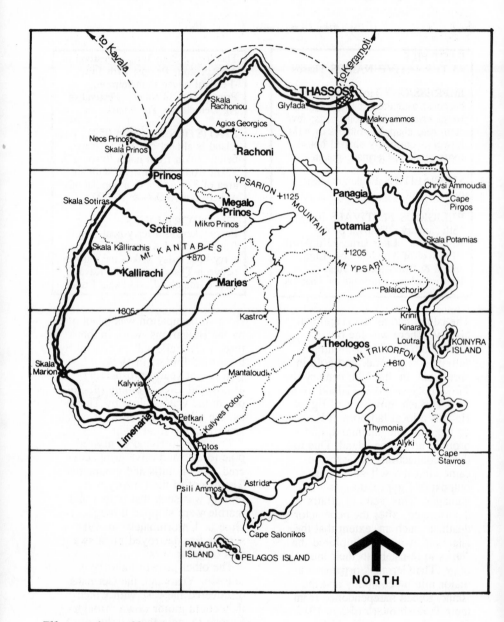

Illustration 63 Thassos island

Thassos. These original forays are slowly but surely being extended to package holidays. A welcome by-product is that there are probably more Rooms, camp-sites and restaurants than elsewhere on the Greek islands.

The beauty of the landscape is matched and possible excelled, if that is possible, by the majesty of one or two of the truly golden, almost white sand beaches. Admittedly those staying at the capital and second port of Thassos have to travel to reach these beaches.

MAIN PORTS & RESORTS

THASSOS (Limenas) The capital town and second port is large, agreeable, pleasing and interesting, with a pretty, old harbour. Despite being a port, rather than a distant mountain topping Chora, this function is subsidiary to unattractive Skala Prinos, some eighteen kilometres to the west.

There is a very small beach, at the Old Harbour.

There are many Rooms, a large number of pensions, and a lot of hotels. Those who enjoy cafe-bar society are well indulged and a couple of the tavernas are in the main acceptable.

Places of interest include the:-
The Agora Sited on the north side of the town, but the excavations are overgrown.
The Old Harbour A number of very large, tall plane trees are ranged around the nearside.
Museum South of the Agora, in a pleasant park.
Theatre, Ancient The smallish, 3rd century BC amphitheatre is extensively tree shaded.
Trip Boats A number of craft moor up stern to the Old Harbour quay. Destination, itineraries and prices are chalked on boards.

Wall, Ancient Vestiges of the wall and gates that encircled the ancient city are visible in places.

Makryammos Beach (2km from Thassos Town) A splendid, sandy beach set in lovely, tree covered hillsides, on which have been built discreet, luxurious holiday villas.

CHRYSI AMMOUDIA (Avlakia) (14km from Thassos Town) There are some three kilometres of sweeping, golden sand, with a gently shelving sea-bed, set in a backdrop of pine clad mountains. There are a few, acceptably priced, backshore restaurant/tavernas, shaded by very tall plane trees, and a small quay to which tie up the trip boats. Almost the entire sweep of the gently curving bay is devoid of any buildings, apart from a number of Rooms.

SKALA POTAMIAS (Chrysi Akti) (14½km from Thassos Town) A busy little fishing boat harbour/holiday resort with a small golden sand beach.

KINIRA (22km from Thassos Town) An old, headland hamlet, with a modest pebble beach. Accommodation is available in the two hotels and a few Rooms.

ALYKI (33km from Thassos Town) A very attractive, small, stony cove tucked into the nearside or east of the headland. This was once the site of an ancient 7th century BC shrine and there are still remains of a terrace and collonades. The picturesque, tiny hamlet of square, stone clad, white slate roofed cottages circles the edge of the little 'U' shaped inlet, snuggled in hillside jaws of marble to the right and rock to the left, both pine tree clad. The sandy

For greater detail acquire GROC's Candid Guide to Samos and the N.E. Aegean Islands

254 COMPANION GUIDE TO THE GREEK ISLANDS

beach has a stone backshore and a narrow band of pebbles about a metre into the sea. A simple taverna serves good quality but basic fare, and at the nearside is a house with Rooms.

POTOS (54km from Thassos Town) Now a modernish, unpicturesque resort, rather reminiscent of the Spanish Costas in the 1960/70s. There are hotels and Rooms. The beach is sand and pebble, with more pebble, in addition to a couple of other beaches, to the right of a rocky mole.

PEFKARI (44km, now in an anticlockwise direction from Thassos Town) More pleasant than Potos, despite a number of two storey hotels and restaurants. The nice cove is hemmed in by pine trees but the sandy beach has a swathe of pebbles at the sea's edge. The sea bottom is mainly rock and weed, though there is a wide spur of sand out to sea.

LIMENARIA (42km from Thassos Town) The curious ambience about this bustling, provincial resort must be entirely due to the once, all pervading presence of the

German mining community. Limenaria certainly does not evoke the usual Greek atmosphere.

Many hotels and restaurants, interspersed by large Victorian seaside houses, line the town's Esplanade, hotels to the right and restaurants to the left.

The long, large pebble beach improves in quality towards the far west end of Limenarion Bay.

SKALA MARION (31km from Thassos Town) A sleepy, colourful and charming fishing village. The sandy beach of the foreshore is lined with old-fashioned, vertical post windlasses and littered with boat beaching frames.

SKALA PRINOS (Ormos Prinos): (19km from Thassos Town) The main port. Skala is an unattractive, ferry-boat 'way-station', which makes it even more extraordinary that the place should appeal to so many package holiday-makers.

The narrow strip of development that stretches along the waterfront is a loose mix of the occasional hotel, some Rooms, a few restaurant/tavernas and cafe-bars. There is more accommodation spaced throughout the settlement.

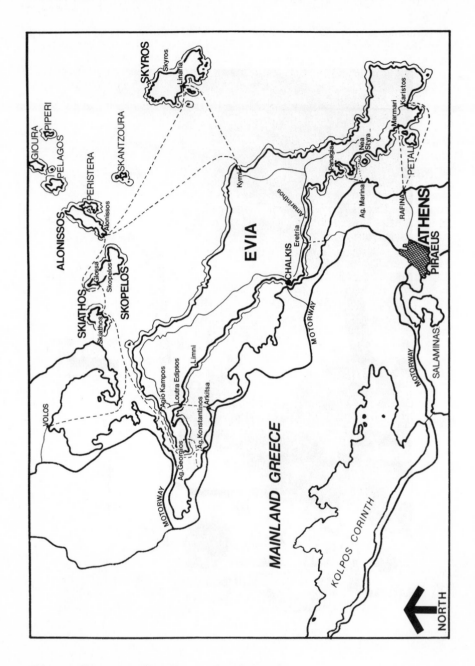

Illustration 64 The Sporades islands

PART NINE   THE SPORADES

Some islanders still refer to the Sporades as 'The Balkans', a name used over the centuries. In order to achieve the greatest satisfaction, I can only advise travellers to the Sporades to visit the islands in the order of Skiathos, Skopelos, Alonissos and lastly Skyros.

The citizens of Alonissos island would be happy with all and any visitors that manage to avoid the siren calls of Skiathos and Skopelos. An earthquake destroyed much of the old town, high upon the hill. The hastily erected port and the two adjacent bay settlements make up the sole development of any size and are joined together by the only swathe of metalled road on the island. The wooded interior is most attractive but none of the numerous and pretty beaches are anything but pebbly.

Skiathos has, depending on your viewpoint, the 'advantage' of an airport, which is probably why it is the most tourist ravaged of the Sporades. It is occasionally difficult to assess why this or that island has achieved the pinnacle of packaged holiday desirability, and Skiathos must rate as one of the imponderables. The port and main town, which on first impression appears attractive, is really rather messy, and the overall countryside may be pretty but is not outstanding.

Skopelos is, administratively, the number one island, but resents the popularity of Skiathos. Why they should worry, I don't know. Skopelos port and town has a stunning Chora, the countryside and scattered beaches are mainly very pretty and there is the added attraction of Glossa, the northern port and old town.

Skyros is the furthest of the group from the mainland, from which it is separated by the bulk of Evia island. It's greatest appeal is that the island has managed to retain much of the old world attractions of yester-year.

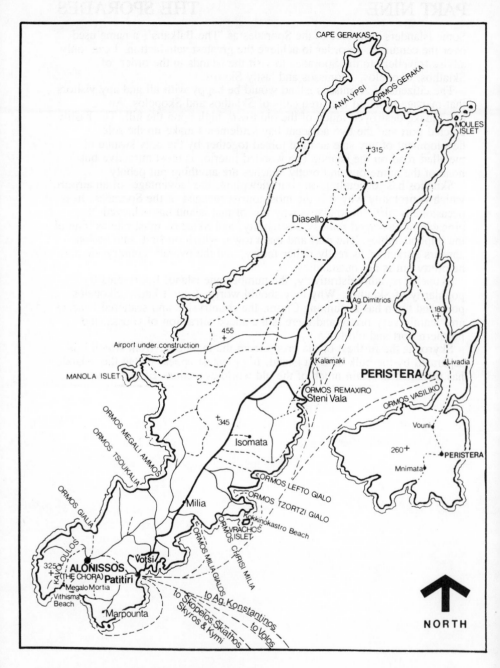

Illustration 65 Alonissos island

FACT FILE

ALTERNATIVE NAMES
Alonnissos, Alonnisos

IMPRESSIONS Pretty country-side; untidy port; lack of villages; multiplicity of pebble bays; beautifully clean sea; unmade roads; green & profusely vegetated countryside; women's head-dress; rustic squalor; trip boats & flotilla yachts; absence of church bells on Sunday; 'suspect' drinking water.

RELIGIOUS FESTIVALS include: 8th September - Panaghia, at the Monastery, on the nearby island of Kyra Panaya (Pelagonissi).

STATISTICS Tel prefix 0424. Alonissos is 20km from top to bottom, is up to 5½km wide & has an area of 64sq km. The population totals about 1400.

TRANSPORT LINKS
Ferry The island is connected into the various Sporades timetables.

Ferry-boats dock and go on to Skopelos and Skiathos six days a week; Ag Konstantinos(M) and Volos(M) four days a week; Trikeri(M) three days a week; and once a week to Kymi Port (Evia), which then proceeds to the N.E. Aegean islands of Ag Estratios and Limnos, and on to Kavala(M). Arrivals are met by owners of accommodation.

Hydrofoil Craft proceed to Skopelos, Skiathos, Volos(M) and Ag Konstantinos(M) seven days a week, and Moundania(M) and Skyros two days a week.

The island's history was undis-tinguished. Even the name or, more correctly, to which island the ancient name Alonissos re-ferred, is in some doubt. The island was probably called Ikos, whilst Alonissos may have been the name of the adjacent, small island of **Kyra Panaya** (Pela-gonissi), or even **Psathouria** islet.

In recent years the island has suffered two catastrophies: in the 1950s the vines were devastated; and, if this were not enough, in 1965, an earthquake struck. The latter was sufficiently powerful to devastate the old Chora (Aloni-ssos Town) prettily perched high on the side of the Kalovoulos mountain range. The Greek government, faced with the enormity of this disaster, had to instantly create a new settlement and chose the then small port based around *Paralia ton Linon*, or 'The Beach of the Wine Press'. Not surprisingly, the hastily con-structed, jerry-built township is a bit of a hotchpotch.

In order to lengthen the pitifully short summer season, the inhabi-tants of Alonissos were promised an airfield. The construction commenced in 1984 but, to date, only 1000m of the incredibly unyielding rock has been roughly flattened. Many locals are convinced that only completion of this facility will solve all the islands ills, imagined and actual. This, despite the fact that the supply of drinking water is extremely uncertain, even for the level of tourism now in existence. Visitors are strongly recommended, as elsewhere in the Sporades, apart from Skyros, to purchase bottled mineral water.

The island is a one-settlement location. There are no other centres of population than Patitiri Port, that is, apart from the still largely deserted Chora and the very small, fishing boat hamlet of Steni Vala. All the island roads are unmade except those which encompass the port and the two adjacent, 'suburban' bays of Rsoum Gialo and Votsi. The main, but unsurfaced island road heads off for the far, northern Bay of Geraka with sidetracks off to the lovely but pebbly beaches that crop up with startling regularity along the length of the eastern coastline. To service these an efficient system of water taxis, based at Patitiri Port, has developed over the years.

The women wear a distinctive shawl head-dress as an everyday item of apparel, maybe to keep the all-pervading dust out of their hair. Despite all the signs beseeching visitors to keep the island tidy, Alonissos remains rather scrubbly - and the Greeks ensure it stays that way!

PATITIRI PORT The capital town and port is a result of the original, small settlement being rapidly expanded, at the instigation of Central Government. The development, that now stretches up the slopes surrounding the port, is a rather ugly rash of concrete boxes. The wide splash of concrete surfaced main road circles Patitiri port to incorporate the hamlets on Ormos Votsi Bay and Rsoum Gialo, the latter being a small bay between Patitiri and Votsi.

There is the small, not very wide, town beach at the left-hand side of the Esplanade, but it is made up of small pebbles and rather dirty. An alternative within walking distance, apart from nearby Rsoum Gialo & Votsi Bays is the **Rope Beach**. The water taxis and trip boats have an agreement not to stop here, so it is necessary to 'scale' the Marpounta road and turn off to the left, after about ten minutes. A certain amount of nudism here, despite the shore being pebbly. The final descent is by abseiling down with the aid of a rope, thus the name.

Arrivals are met by Room owners on the quayside, but those offered accommodation at Votsi Bay must bear in mind it is a good twenty minutes walk. This inconvenience is well compensated by the additional quietness. The Port restaurants and tavernas, especially those lining the 'Beach Esplanade', are inundated by crews of the fleet of flotilla yachts moored in the harbour.

RSOUM GIALO BAY (1km from Patitiri Port) A concrete, waterfront road edges the rather dirty, large pebble beach on which are drawn up the occasional benzina and caique.

The advantage of this spot is that few, if any, publications mention its existence. In addition the bay is rather too exposed and small to take many of the flotilla yachts, thus remaining just that little quieter and secluded. There are some Rooms and tavernas.

VOTSI BAY (2km from Patitiri Port) An attractive, quietly popular location, set in deep hillsides, which hosts a number of Rooms and pensions, as well as restaurants and tavernas.

Vithisma Beach (circa 1 ½km south from Patitiri Port) It is necessary to clamber the last 20-30m down to the nearside of this large, pebbly beach, which edges a beautifully clean sea. The pebbles of the shore continue into the water for a little way, after which the shelving sea-bed is clean sand, making for a lovely swim.

Marpounta Hotel & Coves (2km south from Patitiri Port) A rather shabby, tawdry hotel set in unkempt surrounds, bordered by a rocky coastline, offshore of which is a tiny islet.

Milia Gialos Beach (Some 4km north-east from Patitiri Port) The big pebble, quite pretty beach is set in a very large, 'U' shaped bay that has every appearance of being chiselled out of the coastline. The surrounds are rather scrubbly.

Chrisi Milia Beach (Some 6km from Patitiri Port) A narrow, large pebble beach, from which stretches a sandy sea's edge, all the way along to a far headland bluff.

Kokkinokastro Beach (Some 8km from Patitiri Port) The left-hand end of the clean, fine pebble beach is dramatically bounded by a sandstone headland that angles down into the water. There are a few

boulders in the sea and the middle and backshore are made up of large pebbles, as is the seashore to the right.

Tzortzi Gialo Bay (Some 8km from Patitiri Port) The bay is pebbly with a fine pebble sea's edge, as is the first 6-10m of sea-bed.

Lefto Gialo Bay (some 9km from Patitiri Port) Another 'U' shaped inlet, bordered by an almost white pebble beach, edging a crystal clear, turquoise sea, the only track to this location is one of the roughest on the island.

STENI VALA (12km from Patitiri Port) This small hamlet, which spreads over the slope backing the waterfront, has a surprisingly large fishing boat quayside. The traditional fishing boat caiques and benzinas, that once had the place to themselves, are now interspersed with and outnumbered by flotilla yachts.

There is accommodation, as well as a couple of tavernas and a shop.

KALAMAKIA (14km from Patitiri Port) A comparatively large settlement with a taverna, a small concrete fishing boat quay and absolutely no concessions to tourism.

Geraka Bay (some 23km from Patitiri Port) At the north end of the island. The large building, in the lee of the headland, is, for a change, not a hotel but the Institute of Marine Biology, with especial responsibility for the protection of the Mediterranean Monk seal. The scooter ride from top to bottom of the island takes approximately one hour.

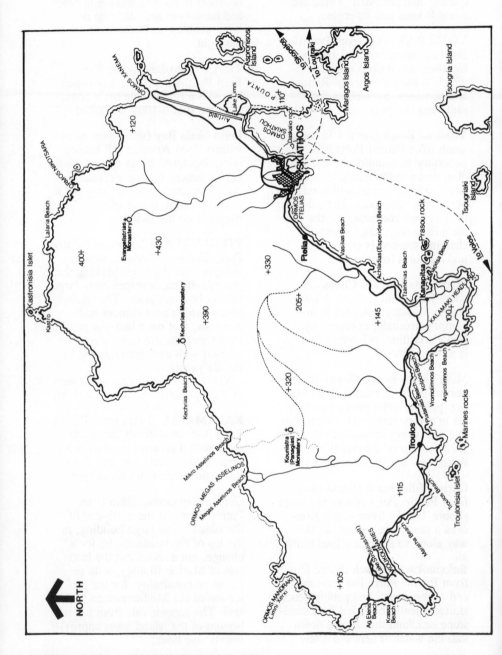

Illustration 66 Skiathos island

FACT FILE

IMPRESSIONS A picturesque harbour; uninteresting town; appalling s†ate of the town's streets; mass tourism; expensive; credit cards acceptable, almost everywhere; sandy beaches; green, attractive countryside & forests; mule rides.

RELIGIOUS FESTIVALS include: 20th November - Religious festival, Kounistra Monastery.

STATISTICS Tel prefix 0427. The island is some 12km from side to side, 9km from top to bottom, with an area of approximately 77sq km & a resident population of 4,000.

TRANSPORT LINKS
Air The runway is close to the town. There are at least three flights a day to Athens and three a week to Thessaloniki.

Ferry & Hydrofoil There is an extensive daily service to the various mainland ports and the other Sporades islands. (See Skopelos island for the details). The ferry and hydrofoil berths are conveniently located. Accommodation owners meet arrivals.

It is perhaps strange that nearby Skopelos was historically much wealthier than Skiathos.

During the Persian Naval incursion of 480 BC, under the leadership of the legendary King Xerxes, battle was engaged with the Greek fleet off Cape Artemisium (Evia island). Legend has it that the Persian deployment was interrupted by foul weather, forcing King Xerxes to seek refuge in a Skiathos bay, still named after him (Limni Xerxi or Ormos Mandraki). During his forced stay, the King is supposed to have caused the construction of the first lighthouse in the world, on a reef between Skiathos and the mainland.

Constant harrying by pirates, despite the sporadic presence of the Venetians, encouraged the islanders to construct a Kastro, on the northernmost tip of the island, and to fortify the tiny inshore islet of **Kastronisia**. It was to this remote citadel that the islanders fled when threatened but the Castle was besieged and overrun by the Turks, in 1538.

Considering its natural attributes, it seems inconceivable that the new town and port were only constructed as late as 1829/ 30, to coincide with Greek Independence. The inexorable growth of this development finally sealed the fate of the old Kastro, which disintegrated due to lack of use.

During the Second World War, occupying German forces destroyed a number of houses in an act of retaliatory punishment. Needless to say estimates of the damage vary from about thirty houses, to the whole town being razed to the ground!

To 'appreciate and savour'

Skiathos it is probably best to call there first and follow up with visits to Skopelos, Alonissos and lastly Skyros - in that order! Only then will the next island be compared more favourably with the last, for Skiathos holds the (dubious) honour of being one of the most tourist 'polluted' islands in the Aegean. Now indefatigable hordes of Greeks and foreigners, swamp this once idyllic and previously sophisticated island. Prices are at an almost unacceptable level; accommodation, except at the beginning and end of the season, is almost impossible to obtain; diners may have to queue at the popular restaurants; and it is 'standing room only' on most of the easily accessible beaches. Package tourism and its inevitable demands predominate On the other hand, Skiathos has one or two undeniable attractions. There are a number of sandy beaches, including a long, if narrow one, adjacent to the town; there are superb countryside forest tracks and walks; the Kalamaki headland is attractive; and Koukounaries beach is a lovely, if overcrowded, location.

MAIN PORTS & RESORTS

SKIATHOS The capital town and port. Seaborne arrivals can only be impressed by the initially attractive appearance of Skiathos. The Bourtzi promontory pleasantly intrudes to divide the waterfront into two unequal lengths. Round to the left is a smallish, almost circular, natural harbour, wherein berth the fishermen and trip boats, with a backdrop of the Chora houses, rising steeply up behind the Esplanade. To the right stretches the large commercial quay, whereat dock the ferry-boats and

merchant ships. This latter length is overlooked by the Old Quarter's steepling lanes and alleys, edged by a 'tumble' of housing. Skiathos Bay runs out in the shallows, away to the right.

The twin hillocks, over which the town is draped, are separated by a flattish section up which the High St drives, parting a mishmash of dwellings divided by thoroughfares, lanes and alleys.

It is necessary to walk to **Megali Ammos Beach**, which is narrow, edging a long, gentle crescent of a bay. The inland side is bordered by vine covered, trellis shaded terraces of single storey buildings. The beach extends for some 400m and, at the outset, is very sandy, gently sloping beneath the sea. Even out of the height of the season, the shore becomes quite crowded at the town end.

Arrivals by sea are met at the gates of the Esplanade quayside. The hotels are expensive, with very few exceptions, and there are Rooms scattered throughout the town. Similarly to accommodation, comestibles and beverages are comparatively costly.

Places of interest include the:-
Bourtzi promontory Hardly a peninsula, this pleasantly wooded outcrop was once an islet.

It is necessary to walk, catch a donkey or hire transport for:-
Monastery Evangelistrias (circa 5km from Skiathos Town) The immediate surrounds, of this now unoccupied monastery, are not very attractive but the overall setting is stunning. The buildings, partially screened by cypress trees, were erected in the 18th century and are set to one side of a summer trickling, rocky gorge.

Kastro Beach There is a recently bulldozed track to the north-west coast. It is a twenty minute hike to the pile of rubble and couple of churches - all that is left of the once majestic fortifications. The views are magnificent.

Lalaria Beach As this famed, north coast beach is pebbly, it is doubtful if the journey is worthwhile.

Achladias Beach (4km from Skiathos Town) A once pleasant, if still pretty spot, is dominated by a monstrous hotel. A track leads along to a lovely, sandy if not very wide beach.

Tzanerias Bay (5½km from Skiathos Town) The bay is divided into two small, pebbly coves.

Kanapitsa Beach (6km from Skiathos Town) From the nearside, steps descend to a neat, sandy beach backed by a field and set in a small curved bay. Unfortunately, across the road from where the track branches down to the beach is a brand new hotel.

Vromolimnos Beach (9 ½km from Skiathos Town) An attractive, sandy, sweep of wide beach with a small pebble foreshore.

Platanias Beach (8km from Skiathos Town) The approach is via a rough track. The lack of any tree cover tends to detract from the allure of the splendid sweep of broad, sandy shore.

Megas Asselinos Beach (14km from Skiathos Town) The track spills out on to the reverse side of the backshore of a clean, wide, steeply sloping, 200m long, fine grit beach. There isn't any tree cover, but the hill-sides of the shallow, wide, 'U' shaped bay are clad with olive trees and scrub.

Troulos Beach (10km from Skiathos Town) The smallish, very sandy, if somewhat messy and not overly attractive beach is set in a shallow bay.

Maratha Beach (12km from Skiathos Town) The backshore is hemmed in by conifer trees. The seabed has a patch of pebble, about a few metres from the foreshore, and there is a tiny beach bar.

Koukounaries Beach (13km from Skiathos Town) The wide, beautifully sandy 1000m or so sweep of shore stretches away, edging a wide bay. The attractiveness of the spot is enhanced by a band of thick-set, tall pine trees that border the backshore. The serried ranks of deck chairs, sun-beds, beach umbrellas and holiday-makers, makes it difficult to see the sand!

Krassa (or Banana) Beach (13km from Skiathos Town) A 120m long, broad, sandy beach, on which are 'plonked' lots of beach umbrellas and deck-chairs. The backshore is pleasantly shaded by mature pine trees.

Ag Elenis Beach (13km from Skiathos Town) Apart from a shingle foreshore, the beach is very sandy and pleasantly set in pine clad, low hillsides.

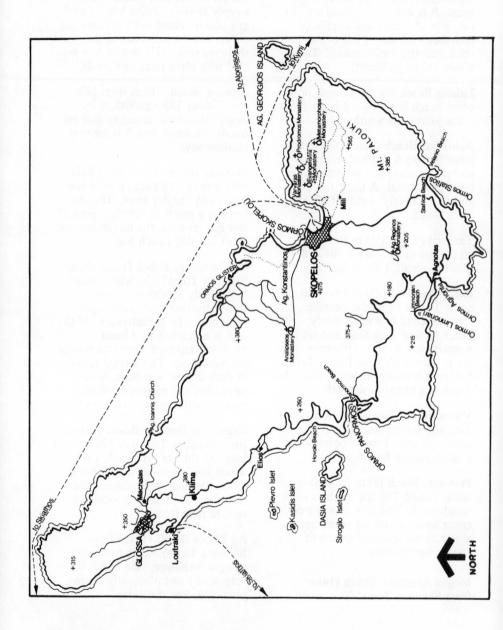

Illustration 67 Skopelos island

FACT FILE	TRANSPORT LINKS
ALTERNATIVE NAME Scopelos	Well situated, there is an excellent daily network of ferry-boat and hydrofoil connections between the island ports of Skopelos and Loutraki, other islands in the Sporades, as well as a number of mainland ports.
IMPRESSIONS Picture postcard prettiness; grey slate roofs; distinctive churches; a Chora maze of streets, lanes & alleys; blocked drains & harbour pong; lovely countryside; pine trees.	
RELIGIOUS FESTIVALS include: 25th February - Festival of St Reginos, Monastery Ag Reginos; 6th August - Festival of Transfiguration of the Saviour, Monastery of Metamorphosis.	Ferry Boats connect seven days a week to Skiathos, Volos(M) and Alonissos; four days a week to Piraeus(M); and two days a week to Ag Konstantinos(M), Skyros and Thessaloniki(M).
STATISTICS Tel prefix 0424. Skopelos is 20km from north-west to south-east, 12km across, at the widest point, with an area of 95sq km, & a population of 5,000.	Hydrofoil Craft link seven days a week to Skiathos, Volos(M), Ag Konstantinos(M) and Alonissos; two days a week to Moundania (M) and Skyros. Craft are met by owners of accommodation.

Named Peparethus by the ancient Greeks, the island was a colony of Minoan Crete. Legend has it that one Staphylus was both the founder and ruler of the island, an association recognised in the name of Stafilos Bay, on the south coast. This affiliation was brought vividly to life by the archaeological finds of a Minoan settlement discovered at Stafilos, in 1936. The dig revealed an enriched grave, the artifacts of which included a gold handled sword worthy of a king. Naturally the popularists assumed this was the property of Staphylus.

The island was terrorised by pirates for thousands of years. This wayward tyranny was interrupted by various periods of more legitimate overrule by, for instance, the Athenians and Romans. There was also a spell as a Byzantine internment camp. This unhappy coalition climaxed, in 1538, with the sacking of the island by Babarossa, the fearsome Turkish Admiral and pirate, a devastation coupled with the wholesale slaughter of all the inhabitants. The eventual repopulation coincided with the War of Independence, in which the islanders took an active part.

It has to be admitted that the level of tourism may prove unattractive but be that as it may, the dazzling attractions of the Port

For greater detail acquire GROC's Candid Guide to The Mainland Islands

and Chora are matched by the beauty of the island's countryside and the numerous beaches.

MAIN PORTS & RESORTS

SKOPELOS (Scopelos) The capital town and main port is probably one of the most photogenic of all the island port/towns. The upper Chora is an absolute delight, a wonderful kaleidescope of balconies, cats, a jumble of differing architectural styles, donkeys, people, streets, lanes, alleys, steps and flowers. The multitude of buildings, many with old, grey slate roofs, tumble over and up three distinct hillsides, much in the manner of a Cycladean Chora. The valley in which the town is built is reputedly the most fertile of this comparatively lush island.

The town beach is sandy, broad at the harbour end, pleasantly bordered by a line of pollarded trees and the sea-bed shelves very slowly. The drawback is the adjacent harbour. Apart from the appearance of the grey, murky emulsion that makes up the solution, the odour is unpleasant, often pungent.

There aren't many hotels or pensions in the port or town. Conversely, there are any number of package holiday hotels, in the far, eastern suburbs. The Esplanade is lined with tavernas and restaurants.

Places of interest include:-
Castle A ruined Venetian structure at the top of the Chora. Within the walls is an early church and the views are magnificent.
Churches There are reputably some 125 churches, in the town alone. The archetypal Skopelot church has whitewashed walls and slate roofs topped off with a flattish, conical slate dome. Eyebrow dormers are incorporated in the tiling in order to accommodate small windows.
Museums The Town Hall is the repository for various archaeological finds from island sites.
Monasteries It is necessary to travel to visit the religious houses adjacent to the port.
The Monastery Evangelistria (4km from Skopelos Town) From the far end of the bay a dusty, unsurfaced track ascends the foothills to a fork in the road. The left-hand turning crosses over to the north, rocky valley slopes and winds up to the monastery. This was rebuilt in 1712 and is now a nunnery.

Back at the fork, the track winds round to:-
The Monastery Metamorphosis (5km from Skopelos Town) Rather ordinary and farmhouse in appearance. The building is cypress tree shaded and set down on a small, bare, almost circular plateau that the road loops round. The monastery dates back to the 16th century, and possesses a fine altar screen but is uninhabited.

Once over the brow of the climb the countryside is much softer and more agricultural. On the left is:-
The Monastery Varvaras (6 ½km from Skopelos Town) A pretty looking monastery, surrounded by a high fortified wall, which may have been constructed, as early as the 15th century.

Across a depression in the land, a kilometre or so further to the east, is:-
The Monastery Prodromos (7½km from Skopelos Town) A large, magnificent and well preserved building, now a nunnery. Rebuilt in 1721, it may date back to about the 14th century.

Stafilos & Velanio Beaches (5km from Skopelos Town) Stafilos Beach is attractively located on the edge of a curving crescent of a bay, stopped off by a jumble of rocks on the nearside and, at the far end, by a blob of headland. The fairly narrow, fine grit beach is hemmed in by a cliff-face.

The gritty sand sweep of **Velanio Beach** is reached from the far, east end of Stafilos Beach.

AGNOTAS PORT (8km from Skopelos Town) A narrow but deep, 'U' shaped bay with a disproportionately large concrete ferry-boat quay edging the south side of the inlet. The pebble foreshore stretches all the way round the foot of the bay, widening out into a pebble beach on the north side. A taverna edges the south end of the backshore.

Limonari Beach (9 ½km from Skopelos Town) A lovely location with a pleasant, circular bay enclosed by olive tree and brush covered hills, the latter slightly set back from the shore. The beach is almost white sand with a few large pebbles dotted about. The first metre or so of the sea-bed is sand and pebbles, becoming larger stones, despite which the middle section is mostly sand. There is a pension/taverna set back a few metres from the beach.

Panormos Beach (16km from Skopelos Town) A gentle curve of fine shingle backshore and a small pebble surfaced beach. A number of Rooms, a hotel and a couple of tavernas are spaced about.

GLOSSA (30km from Skopelos Town) This very nice, very Greek, northern village clings to the side of the mountain. It is a fairly large settlement with quite a lot of new buildings being erected and an air of quiet affluence. The very narrow main street winds through the village, past various shops and stores. There are several rather ethnic Rooms, thus the independent traveller might well consider foregoing the 'delights' of Skopelos Town to stay here or Loutraki, the adjacent port.

LOUTRAKI PORT (32½km from Skopelos Town) The widespread settlement hosts a very large harbour at which dock scheduled ferry-boats and hydrofoils.

The accommodation is quite plentiful considering the comparatively small size of the place and includes hotels, pensions and Rooms. Close to the bottom of the ferry-boat quay are at least two side-by-side tavernas, with pleasantly, tree shaded terraces, in addition to which there are a couple of other snackbars.

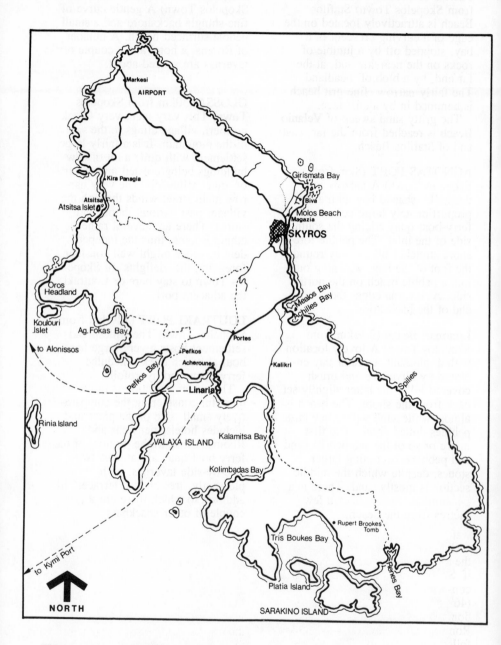

Illustration 68 Skyros island

FACT FILE
ALTERNATIVE NAMES Skiros

IMPRESSIONS Fig trees; the army; friendly people; lovely beaches; older mens distinctive apparel; 'bubbling' Chora; few package tourists; a scarcity of 'proper' hotels.

SPECIALITIES Rupert Brooke; homes decorated with plates.

RELIGIOUS FESTIVALS include: February/March prior to Easter - Carnival/Panaghia, Chora; 23rd April - Festival for island's patron saint; Monastery Ag Georgios, Chora; 2nd September - Festival, Ag Mamas, close by Kalamitsa.

STATISTICS Tel prefix 0222. The island is approximately 40km from the north-west to south-east, up to

19km wide & some 215sq km in area. The population is approximately 2700, most of whom live in the Chora.

TRANSPORT LINKS
Air Despite a flight a day to and from Athens, the island is the least tourist effected of the Sporades group. Nor, yet, has the presence of an airfield resulted in a rash of new hotels.

Ferry Skyros is not connected by ferry with the other Sporades islands, but there is a daily boat to Kymi Port (Evia).

Hydrofoil A hydrofoil makes a twice weekly link to the islands of Alonissos, Skopelos and Skiathos, as well as proceeding on to mainland Volos.

Skyros is famed as the hiding place of mythological Achilles. Odysseus found and persuaded him to join in the Trojan War where the prophesy of his death came true, when he was struck on the heel by an arrow. This was the portion of his body held by his mother when he was immersed in the magical waters of the Styx.

Ownership of the island followed the average historical course, even if Skyros was, for a time, almost considered a suburb of Athens (469-340 BC). Occupying Macedonians were booted out by the Romans, after which the island followed the star of the Byzantine

Empire, interrupted by a brief, fifty year period of Frankish suzerainty. After the demise of Byzantium, the Venetians were in occupation but the Turks pushed them out, in 1538, until they were finally ousted during the War of Independence. A famous, adopted son of Skyros was Rupert Brooke. He tragically fell ill and died on 23rd April 1915, probably due to an infected mosquito bite. He was on board a British ship bound for the First World War campaign at Gallipoli. Ironically, a year previously, he had penned some of the most famous lines of comparatively modern poetry:-

---

If I should die, think only this of me:
That there's some corner of a foreign field
That is forever England
                              The Soldier.

His tomb is situated close by the bay of **Tris Boukes** at the south of the island.

Skyros possesses a rather medieval or old world ambience. These impressions are reinforced by the conspicuous and distinctive peasants' dress. The medieval, even pre-Christian, milieu is manifested by the Chora Carnival held before the Greek Orthodox Easter. During these part religious, part pagan celebrations, groups of at least three men put on fancy dress, two of whom wear a face mask made of a goatskin.

The Chora possesses many old, 16/18th century homes, often of small dimensions, filled with wooden furniture. Some are almost doll's house sized, the walls festooned with brass, ceramic, copper, pottery and wooden bowls, dishes and plates. These plates originated, not only in Rhodes and Europe, but as far away as Korea and China.

The comparative lack of package tourists ensures Skyros is an independent traveller's delight, apart from which, or maybe because of which, prices are comparatively low for eating and drinking out, if not for the actual nights stay.

MAIN PORTS & RESORTS
LINARIA The port is a small, clean, pretty, classic Greek harbour, set in a 'U' shaped inlet. Due to the lack of accommodation it is difficult for visitors to stay here, which is a pity because the port is well 'equipped' with tavernas.

Eight kilometres distance from Linaria is:-
THE CHORA (Skyros Town) The island capital is a most attractive, hill-climbing, Cycladean style Chora. The vehicle-free, cobble and paved High Street climbs the hillside, with lanes and alleyways stepping off to either side and bordered by dwellings.

There are even the remains of a brown, crag topping Castle, below which, and hugging the cliff-face, are the splash of the whitewashed buildings of the Monastery Ag Georgios. Both Castle and Monastery overlook the Chora.

To arrive at nightfall is a magical experience. All the main street lights are switched on and the grocers, ironmongers, cafes, bars, tavernas, restaurants, chemists, and numerous other shops, are lit up in an orgy of neon. The steeply climbing concourse is a constant *ramblas* night and day.

Travellers disembarking from the bus will be mobbed by families offering accommodation and there are a widely varied selection of eating establishments, ranged along the High Street.

Places of interest include the:
Castle The fort was probably built at the end of the 13th century AD, on the site of earlier fortifications. Entrance is not always possible.

The Monastery of Ag Georgios Founded in the 9th Century AD and hangs on to the rock face, to the west of the Castle cliffs. Within the whitewashed walls of the monastery is Ag Georgios Church, built in 1680.
Archaeological Museum The building is overlooked by the Rupert Brooke statue.
Museum Faltaitz To the north of

the Rupert Brooke statue is this most interesting, if rather ethnic establishment, housing an unrivalled cumulation of Skyriot artefacts and memorabilia based on collections of the Faltaitz family. They were one of the island's upper ruling class, or *Megali Strata*. **Rupert Brooke Statue** A bronze nude dominating not so much a square, more a 'threshing circle'. From these heights are dramatic views out over the surrounding countryside and seascape.

Hardly a 'Place of Interest' but worthy of note is the distinctive local dress. A number of the older men wear the traditional Skyriot costume. This consists of a straw hat, or black cap, a check shirt and blue or black baggy pantaloon trousers, tucked into black woollen stockings, the feet shod in (medieval) leather sandals with (modern-day) rubber tyre sections used as the soles.

MAGAZIA (2km from The Chora) Out of the height of season months, the shoreline of the settlement, which is really a continuation of Molos Beach, is almost empty.

Molos Beach (3km from Skyros Town) A wide, beautifully sandy beach, edged by clear seas which stretches away past Magazia hamlet, as far as some low cliffs, on

the eastern flanks of the Chora. The Castle topped rocky outcrop, and the surrounding whitewashed buildings of the Chora Town, which are draped over the hillside, form a magnificent backdrop.

ATSITSA (16km from Skyros Town) A prominent, solid, looking, three storey house dominates and overlooks the lovely indented bay of the hamlet, in which is set a conical, rocky islet. To the right of the the bay, is a very small beach with a sandy shore bordering crystal clear seas covering a stony, weed covered sea-bed.

Pefkos Bay (27km from Skyros Town) Despite the prettiness of the location, the immediate backyard surrounds to the not-so-neat taverna are messy and rural. A path falls down, between a pair of large fig trees, to the sandy backshore of a glorious, wide beach that extends away to the right.

KALAMITSA (8km from Skyros Town) A quite large bay, bordered by a large pebble shore with smidgins of sand here and there, and whereon a pension.

Tris Boukes Bay (15km from Skyros Town) In the mouth of this wide, deserted bay are the large, low islets of **Platia** and **Sarakino**.

INDEX

Artwork: Ted Spittles &
Geoffrey O'Connell
Packaging: Willowbridge Publishing
Plans & maps: Graham Bishop &
Geoffrey O'Connell
Typeset: Disc preparation Viv Hitie
& Willowbridge Publishing